BOOZE BOATS AND BILLIONS

BOOZE BOATS AND BILLIONS

SMUGGLING LIQUID GOLD!

C. W. HUNT

M&S

Canadian Cataloguing in Publication Data

Hunt, C.W. (Claude William), 1931–
Booze, boats and billions

Bibliography: p.
Includes index.
ISBN 0-7710-4265-5

1. Smuggling – Ontario – History – 20th century.
2. Smuggling – United States – History – 20th
century. 3. Prohibition – Ontario. 4. Prohibition –
United States. 5. Distilling industries – Ontario –
History. 6. Hatch family. I. Title.

HV5091.C3H86 1988   364.1'33   C88-094455-2

Printed and bound in Canada

Maps by Kong Tik Njo

McClelland & Stewart Inc.
The Canadian Publishers
481 University Avenue
Toronto, Ontario
M5G 2E9

To Glady and Mildred

CONTENTS

PREFACE

The idea for this book resulted from a chance meeting. I was visiting the Mariner's Museum, situated in the rolling farm land of Prince Edward County and overlooking the peaceful waters of South Bay. It was built to honour the seamen from the county and to preserve its seafaring past. Most of its artifacts are from the days when wooden sailing ships carried barley across Lake Ontario to supply the breweries of northern New York State.

The museum is staffed by volunteers. On the day I was visiting, the volunteer was one James McConnell, former lighthouse keeper and commercial fisherman, itinerant musician, and raconteur. I asked Jim about a wooden sign on the fence outside that advertised "Smugglers Cove Camp Grounds." Why the reference to smugglers? I found that I had unleashed the storyteller in Jim McConnell. He held me transfixed for over an hour with his stories of the rum-running years. When new visitors finally forced Jim to turn his attention elsewhere, I left, intent on learning more about the men and women who had braved the hazards of Lake Ontario in small boats, smuggling Canadian liquor and beer into the United States.

Rum-running flourished from 1920 until the end of 1933, when the United States finally ended the great social experiment known as Prohibition. By 1982 only a few of the rum-runners were still alive. Fortunately, those I did find were usually willing to talk about their exploits.

The old puritan attitude to drinking has been on the decline since the 1960s. Social disapproval, which kept many old rum-runners quiet, has now largely disappeared. The few surviving veterans of the prohibition era are all quite advanced in years. Moreover, what their neighbours think about their distant past hardly concerns them. Several were anxious to tell their story before the clock ran out on an already long life.

The proceedings of the Royal Commission on Customs and Excise, daily newspapers, and court records, all provided valuable information. But the recollections of the more than 100 survivors of that long-ago era gave me a personal sense of the various players, including smugglers, policemen, coastguardsmen, and liquor barons.

Some of their accounts were difficult to verify and some proved contradictory. Solving the enigma of Ben Kerr, for example, proved to be a particularly challenging task. Old-timers in the Quinte area had variously described Kerr as a friendly, quiet, family man, or as an aloof, icy-blooded killer. In order to resolve these contradictory descriptions, I determined to locate someone who had known him at his home base in Hamilton.

I knew that, from 1926 on, Ben Kerr had travelled with two crew members, Alf Wheat and Jack Morris Junior. Wheat was of the same generation as Kerr and, therefore, long deceased. Jack Morris was a mere teenager at the time and might still be alive. It took me several months, but I finally located him. Fortunately, the man who had travelled the lake with Ben Kerr for three and a half years was more than willing to talk about Kerr and about his experiences while travelling with the King of the Lake Ontario rum-runners.

I sat in Morris's kitchen sipping coffee. Over a floral patterned oil cloth covering a wooden table, Jack Morris had spread a mariner's chart of Lake Ontario. He sketched a lanky finger along the U.S. coastline, pausing to recall the places where, fifty-five years earlier, he, Ben Kerr, and Alf Wheat had delivered their loads of contraband whisky: Sodus Point, Oswego, Thirty Mile Point, and Lone Tree; a litany of place names from a distant, adventurous youth. Of these, only Lone Tree bore no proper place name on the chart. It is located somewhere west of Oswego, but its real location is in the mind of Jack Morris. The other men who met there on that covert, solitary shore are all gone.

Jack Morris's recollections enabled me to get a better grasp on the complex personality of Ben Kerr. He also enabled me to travel vicariously to another time. It was during this era that organized crime first came to Canada. Prohibition was responsible for that, and also for the creation of many family fortunes. More important for Canada, American Prohibition and our response to it provided the conditions for our liquor industry to become one of the largest in the world. Distilled liquors are now Canada's sixth largest export.

Seagrams, Hiram Walker-Gooderham and Worts, and Corby's were all immensely successful at selling their product to the illegal American market. All three expanded enormously during Prohibition. Today, Seagrams is the largest distilling company in the world. Corby's and Hiram Walker are not far behind. This book will explain how this came about. In particular, it will examine the careers of the Hatch brothers – how they rose from being mere saloon keepers to the very pinnacle of the liquor business.

Moving Canadian liquor across the Detroit River and the Great Lakes eventually involved Canadian smugglers and the U.S. coast guard and prohibition forces in a shooting war.

This war on the lakes has been largely ignored by Canadian historians. Fortunately, coast guard records in the U.S. National Archives have preserved it. To these records, I have added the recollections of the few who are still around to remember those days. The war created waterfront heroes; men with more nerve, skill, and luck than the rest. The secret nature of their activities meant, however, that their exploits went largely unrecorded. This book has, among its purposes, the intent to record at least some of those exploits.

ACKNOWLEDGEMENTS

There are many benefits in writing a book such as this. For me, the most satisfying aspect was preserving a folk history while its few remaining custodians were still alive to tell their tales. This book was made possible thanks to the many men and women who vividly recalled the rum-running era. They endured my many questions and answered them with courtesy and patience. I was privileged to meet them and to hear their stories. I thank them all. If some parts of this book are colourful or humorous, then much of the credit for that belongs to them.

I would like to thank the Ontario Heritage Foundation for providing a grant, which helped to defray the cost of research. I must also thank Indra Persaud who typed the manuscript with magic fingers and who brought a lively intelligence to bear on my text.

Writing is lonely work. I believe it was Oscar Wilde who said that the principal enemies of writers are friends, family, and bill collectors. I disagree. My friends were wonderfully supportive and, most important, respected my periodic need for privacy. My family was equally helpful. When the interruptions of daily life threatened to give me a permanent writer's block, my mother, Glady, provided a haven where I could work undisturbed.

Two of my relatives deserve special mention: my nieces Linda and Ren, who are the most enthusiastic people I know. Their interest in the book repeatedly revived my faltering enthusiasm. Wise beyond his years, my son, Bill, provided a sound commentary on my prose. I thank him for that and for listening carefully when I needed a critical assessment.

My thanks also to my editor, Dinah Forbes. She smoothed out the rough edges, cut the grammatical errors, and somehow managed to get inside my head so that the book now reads as I had originally intended.

And, finally, I thank my wife, Milli. For thirty-five years she has supported me in all my endeavours, and no less so in this.

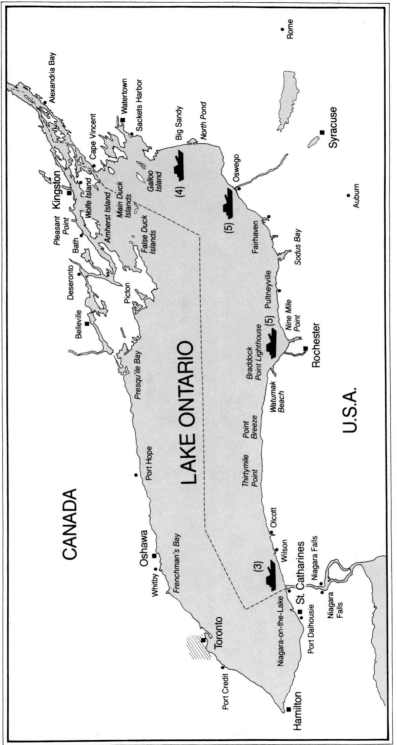

Lake Ontario, showing the number of armed boats at coast guard stations.

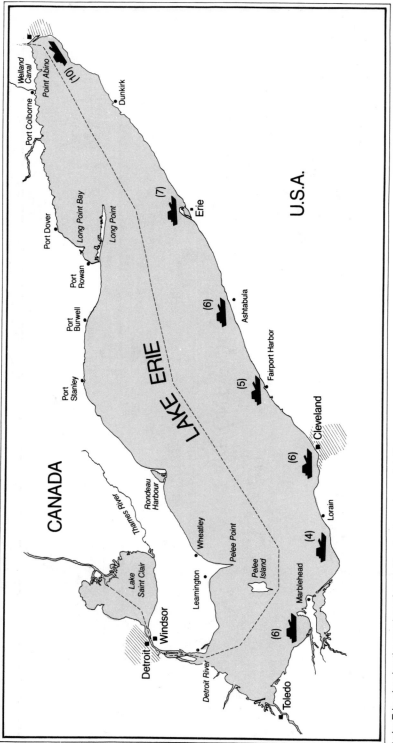

Lake Erie, showing the number of armed boats at coast guard stations

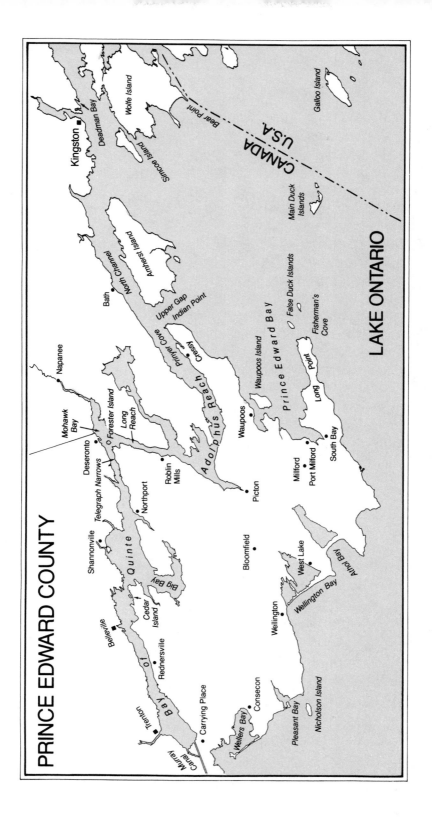

PRINCE EDWARD COUNTY

Murray Canal
Trenton
Carrying Place
Belleville
Rednersville
Shannonville
Napanee
Deseronto
Mohawk Bay
Telegraph Narrows
O Forester Island
Long Reach
Roblin Mills
Northport
Cedar Island
Big Bay
Bay of Quinte
Bloomfield
Picton
Adolphus Reach
Prinyer Cove
Cressy
Upper Gap
Indian Point
Bath
North Channel
Amherst Island
Simcoe Island
Wolfe Island
Deadman Bay
Kingston
Bear Point
CANADA
U.S.A.
Galloo Island
Main Duck Islands
False Duck Islands
Fisherman's Cove
Waupoos Island
Waupoos
Prince Edward Bay
Long Point
South Bay
Milford
Port Milford
West Lake
Athol Bay
Wellington Bay
Wellington
Nicholson Island
Pleasant Bay
Wellers Bay
Consecon

LAKE ONTARIO

1

GOODBYE
JOHN BARLEYCORN

There was a general free distribution of booze in some of the leading Clubs in Rochester yesterday... [T]he Prohibition Act makes it necessary to get rid of all intoxicating liquors by midnight last night.

Rochester *Times Union*
January 17, 1920

Residents of northern New York State are used to cold, snowy weather. But Friday, January 16, 1920, was colder, snowier, and windier than usual. Perhaps that's why, on this last day before Prohibition, so many stayed home rather than brave the elements to enjoy a last legal drink at their favourite saloon.

In the lake port city of Oswego about eighty couples ventured forth to the luxurious Pontiac Hotel, where they danced and drank until well past midnight, the legal drinking deadline. But most Oswego saloons and hotels were empty, or nearly so. Even the historic Clancy and Muldoon's, a watering hole for generations of Irish, was almost deserted. Here, both barkeep and patrons were saddened by the knowledge that the long mahogany bar their elbows had found so familiar would be auctioned off on Monday. With it would go the tall gilt mirrors, the long brass rail, the swinging doors, the stained spittoon – all those worn, familiar things that over the decades had formed the backdrop to their arguments, boasts, gossip, and occasional brawls.

Farther west along the lake at Rochester, the only celebrants were the prohibitionists. At midnight church bells were rung throughout the city's suburbs to announce with jubilation the passage of the Eighteenth Amendment to the Constitution and the arrival of Prohibition. Earlier in the evening a meeting of Baptist, Presbyterian, and Evangelical ministers had been held at the Methodist church to celebrate the victory of their common cause – the eradication of demon rum. Their joy was enhanced by the dejection of their opponents. Procter Welch, proprietor of the Onondaga Hotel in Syracuse, summed up wet sentiments when he told a reporter, "It doesn't seem quite respectful to organize any real celebration of an event so sad as tonight will be."[1]

The members of the Billy Sunday businessmen's club in Syracuse felt otherwise. At their weekly luncheon they held funeral services for "John Barleycorn." Old King Booze had a final ride in his casket on the shoulders of jubilant pallbearers and was preached over by Joseph O. Whitcomb, who shattered precedent by refusing "to say anything good... about the deceased."

On Saturday the editor of the Syracuse *Post Standard* assured his readers that "it is going to be so hard to get a drink hereafter that only a small fraction of the people will have the courage, patience, or price to get it."[2] Seldom has an editor's prediction been proven so totally wrong in so short a space of time. But for the moment, the Women's Christian Temperance Union, the Anti-Saloon League, the Methodist and Evangelical churches, and most of respectable middle class society savoured their apparent triumph. The liquor interests, the hotel and saloon keepers, and the ordinary man – women were not allowed in saloons – could only despair. In Rochester, Fritz Kioster dramatized the plight of the dedicated imbiber by writing a long note to the local newspaper. That task completed, he put his head in the oven and turned on the gas. Poor Fritz, if only he had waited. Two weeks after the start of Prohibition, Canadian and American rum-runners had already started to smuggle booze into New York State and, within months, these early rivulets became a vast flood sufficient to quench the thirst of the most determined of drinkers.

In some centres the social drinker was further comforted by being able to partake of his favourite grog in familiar surroundings. In Oswego most of the old saloons re-opened ostensibly as "soft drink parlours," but in reality they carried on much as before with the same patrons lined up at their usual stations along the bar, one foot firmly planted on the brass rail. The prices were higher and the product not always too reliable, but the law looked the other way, and the saloon remained a social centre for the working man.

It was not so wide open in the larger centres of Syracuse and Rochester. Federal prohibition agents stationed in these cities could swoop down at any moment to seize the beverage being served for analysis of its alcoholic content. If it exceeded 0.5 per cent – the legal limit to remain non-alcoholic – the proprietor would be fined and, on repeated offences, jailed. This unwelcome activity by the federal agents led to the growth of illegal drinking establishments known as "speakeasies" or "blind-pigs." Hidden away in alleys or disguised as private clubs, the speakeasies often enjoyed the protection of local and state police forces. This made enforcement of Prohibition difficult for the federal agency created for the task. Consequently, the 200 prohibition agents who were responsible for all of New York State found themselves totally occupied by patrolling the major cities. But even there they were seldom more than a minor irritant to the saloon-keepers and bootleggers.

In the smaller centres, such as Oswego, the feds were infrequent visitors and posed no serious threat to the numerous booze emporiums in that wide-open city. A former Torontonian, Tom Mowatt, was police chief in Oswego, and while generally regarded as honest and conscientious, he remained strangely blind to bootlegging. Residents eventually concluded their police chief was under orders from his bosses at City Hall to ignore the Volstead Act, which had been passed specifically to enforce the prohibition amendment. Consequently, Oswego remained thoroughly "wet" throughout the fourteen years of Prohibition. In any given year there were always at least 100 places in the city where you could get an illegal drink. Counting women and children, this worked out to one speakeasy for every 230 residents.

The conditions that prevailed in Oswego were fairly typical of the United States overall. Geography and local attitudes made it easier to enforce Prohibition in some states but, generally, liquor was available for anyone willing to pay the price. Canadian whisky sold for between $5 and $15 a quart, depending on the quality of the liquor and the distance it had to travel from the Canadian border. That same bottle cost the distillery, on average, about ten cents.[3] The enormous mark-up between manufacturing cost and the final price to the consumer paid for an army of smugglers, who sprang into existence to supply a seemingly limitless demand. In 1926, one journalist estimated that there were at least 100,000 people engaged in smuggling liquor into the United States.[4] Although some of this liquor came from Europe, the great majority of it originated in Canada, primarily because our long undefended border made smuggling both easy and relatively inexpensive.

After World War I, Canadians had followed the American lead by imposing some form of prohibition on the consumption of alcoholic beverages. But in Canada Prohibition was a provincial matter. The provinces, while they could and did outlaw the consumption of alcohol, had no power to regulate its manufacture. This power resided with the federal government, which chose not to prohibit the production of beverage alcohol. The federal government further assisted Canada's booze industry by ignoring the American demand that Ottawa stop the export of Canadian liquor to the United States. This meant that it was legal in Canada for breweries and distilleries both to manufacture their product and to export it to the United States. Consequently, ordinary Canadians were attracted to liquor smuggling because, while it paid fabulous wages, it was not perceived as a criminal activity.

In the Prairies and the eastern townships of Quebec, farmers made good rum-runners because their knowledge of equipment helped to keep the automobiles and trucks running. There were literally hundreds of back roads criss-crossing the border between the two countries, most with no customs officials or police for miles. The main danger to these smugglers was not the police, but other smugglers who might hijack their load, steal their vehicles, and beat them up or shoot them.

The dangers were even greater for those Maritimers who joined the East Coast smuggling rings. These gangs purchased large schooners, steamers, and other vessels capable of carrying thousands of cases of whisky, which they unloaded to speedboats waiting off the American coast along a strip known as Rum Row, which ran from Boston south to New York City. The crews of these vessels were made up of seasoned sailors drawn from the docks of Nova Scotia, New Brunswick, and Newfoundland. Besides the dangers posed by the stormy North Atlantic, these smugglers were particularly vulnerable to attack from maurauding hijackers who roamed the seas in fast, heavily armed vessels.

In Ontario, the largest volume of smuggling took place on the Detroit River. Small, fast motorboats, operating from government-licensed export docks, regularly dashed across the river, unloaded their cargoes, and returned for yet another load. The men involved in this traffic initially came from around the piers and docks of the Windsor-Detroit area and included dock workers, fishermen, and other "river rats." But the enormous profits soon attracted criminals and gangsters who flocked to the area like sharks to a feeding. Within a short time, gunfire was an almost nightly occurrence on the Detroit River.

The situation on the Great Lakes was similar in that the smugglers were usually recruited from the dock areas of those towns and cities fronting on the lakes. Commercial fishermen were particularly sought after. They had the skills and the knowledge necessary to navigate and to handle the boats on these waters. On Lake Ontario, the rum-runners had the advantage of being close to their sources of supply. There were breweries in Kingston, Belleville, Toronto, and Hamilton, as well as Wiser's distillery in Prescott, Gooderham and Worts distillery in Toronto, and, just north of Belleville, the huge Corby distillery.

Only 20 per cent of the product of these companies was consumed in Canada, the rest ultimately found its way into the United States.[5] In the early days of Prohibition, a large amount got there via Great Lakes ports. For example, a cargo of Corby's whisky might travel by boat through the Welland Canal and then from Port Colborne be smuggled either into Cleveland or, more commonly, into Buffalo, only thirteen miles to the east.

On the lakes, vessels of all types and sizes were used, from twenty-foot fishing boats to eighty-foot cabin cruisers. In the early days, small open fish boats would cross Lake Ontario – a distance of sixty miles – in convoys of perhaps a dozen vessels. Most were under twenty-five feet long and could travel at no more than six or seven knots per hour. These convoys could only travel during good weather and eventually they were displaced by larger and much faster speedboats. The men who operated these expensive mahogany beauties were a select group, regarded with envy and admiration by other sailors. As one old-time lake sailor and commercial fisherman put it, "they were outlaws in a way, but...oh my, they had nerve."[6] They were also well paid. In a single week, a speedboat operator could make more money than a hard-working fisherman earned in an entire eight-month season.

The backgrounds of these highly paid risk-takers were surprisingly diverse. They were drawn from a spectrum of occupations and classes, ranging from ne'er-do-wells to professionals and business people. Nevertheless, they shared a common *métier* and eventually came to know each other through a common sanctuary. Whether they came from Hamilton or Kingston they usually sought refuge from both the lake and the coast guard at Main Duck Island.

This lonely square mile of trees and swamp is located twelve miles south of Prince Edward County, just a few hundred yards north of the international boundary. It is almost directly north of the city of Oswego, making it an ideal spot for smugglers. It was here that the rum-runners would lay over, waiting for darkness or better weather before making their dash for the American shore.

Except for periodic visits from the lighthouse keeper, Main Duck Island is now deserted. Sixty years ago, it was home to a small colony of fishermen, the lighthouse keeper and his family, and the family of Claude "King" Cole, who owned the island. The rum-runners were frequent visitors. Sometimes there were as many as seven rum boats anchored in the tiny harbour waiting to make their dash to the States. Many of the island's fishermen were bachelors or else their wives were on the mainland, taking care of their school-age children. Visitors therefore provided a welcome break in a hard and tedious existence. When bad weather forced a rum-runner to lay over at Main Duck, he would usually be invited to spend the night at one of the fishermen's primitive cottages. Most often the evening would be spent with a half-dozen men playing stud poker by the flickering yellow light of a coal oil lamp. At other times, the hosts – there were usually two fishermen to a cottage – would hunker down by the claw-footed, pot-bellied iron stove, nursing an illegal drink provided by their outlaw guest. It was during these visits that the rum-runners spun their tales, which would be repeated over and over again by their hosts, each telling deepening the details.

Only a few grizzled and greying survivors remain from those long nights at Main Duck. But their eyes brighten at the memories as they recount the tales of daring escapes, coast guard captures, and lives lost, with a clarity that wipes away the years until the drama is as real and as fresh as today's newscast. In the shared memory of these old fishermen and lighthouse keepers, Main Duck Island was Lake Ontario's "rum-runners' roost."

The island was also the scene of the first major raid by the police against Lake Ontario's rum-running fraternity.

2

THE RAID ON
MAIN DUCK ISLAND

The grave yard of Lake Ontario
The Main Duck is widely known
For the score of helpless vessels
On its jagged shores have blown.
>   Willis Metcalfe,
>   *Canvas and Steam on Quinte Waters*

In the cool, early morning hours of May 11, 1921, four police officers and a civilian gathered quietly at the government dock in Belleville. Within minutes they had loaded their guns, search warrant, crowbars, and hot lunches into a large motorboat and by three in the morning were heading east onto the Bay of Quinte.

The civilian was A.H. Kerr, a local boatman brought along as navigator for the expedition. Kerr held the course, his keen mariner's eyes probing the blackness ahead. The boat moved slowly as its prow pushed through the heavy mists rising off the bay, the dull throb of the engine and the soft muttering of the men barely breaking the stillness of the night. Two hours later, the boat was moving much faster, skirting along the eastern shores of Prince Edward County at a steady ten knots. An occasional yellow dot flickering from shore announced a farmer stirring to early morning chores. In another three hours the raiders were making their best time, heading east along Adolphus Reach. As the red sun burned away the last of the morning's mist, they reached the Upper Gap, that stretch of water separating Prince Edward County from Amherst Island. Here the shallow chop of the bay ended and the long, rolling swells of Lake Ontario began.

During this first part of their journey the friendly shores of the county had never been more than two miles distant. Now the land fell away sharply on their right and within minutes they were on the open lake hoping the morning calm would hold. Ahead and to their right they could just make out the two islands called the False Ducks. The presence of these two sentinels, standing guard off the south-east tip of the county, was comforting. The men knew if a storm blew up they could anchor in the lee of False Ducks. Once past them, however, they faced ten miles of open lake before reaching the haven of Main Duck Island.

The raid on Main Duck was led by Licence Inspector Frank Naphan and included two OPP officers and Sergeant Dan Boyd of the Belleville police. Naphan had recently been appointed to supervise the enforcement of the Ontario Temperance Act (OTA) in Hastings and Prince Edward counties. He had heard rumours that rum-runners were using Main Duck as a stopover point, but held no illusions he could capture any of them as the rum-runners' activity was perfectly legal under Canadian law, so long as they went directly to their foreign destination after leaving their Canadian port of exit. If forced by bad weather or mechanical breakdown to put in at a Canadian port, their cargo of alcohol must remain intact and under seal. This was to prevent rum-runners from smuggling their export cargo back into Canada, a manoeuvre known as "short-circuiting."

Naphan had heard that Claude "King" Cole, who owned

Main Duck, had been hauling large loads of booze to the island, where he then broke these into smaller loads before smuggling them into the United States. Under the OTA, the off-loading and storing was clearly illegal.

At first glance, Claude Cole seemed an unlikely candidate for rum-runner. He was already fifty years of age, a grandfather, and a successful businessman. Yet he was one of the earliest and most successful rum-runners on the lake. Starting out as a farmer in the Milford area, he had purchased Main Duck from the federal government in 1905. His first trip to the island had been made in an old sailing scow, when he had taken along a rifle to clear the place of wild cattle. From this humble beginning he had built up large herds of cattle and pigs on the island, as well as a thriving fishing business. In addition to his own two-storey frame house, he had built a dozen fishing cottages, which he rented out to area fishermen, basing their rent on the weight of their catch. This catch, along with that of other area fishermen, he hauled several times a week in his three tugs to the Booth Fish Company in Cape Vincent, New York. At Cape Vincent he owned a second farm, which he and his family used during the winter months.

Cole's business success was due to more than just hard work and rural shrewdness. He was bold, a risk-taker who relished physical danger. Naturally gregarious, he could hold an audience enthralled while he spun tales of his derring-do on the lake. The cheery *raconteur* was also arbitrary and high-handed. If someone crossed him, Cole would simply ban them from the island. This quality earned him the sobriquet "King" Cole. It was a well-deserved nickname, for he ruled Main Duck as his private fiefdom: the fishermen held their tenancy to the small cottages at his pleasure, and no one landed a boat on the island without his permission. In spite of these qualities, the "King" was generally well liked. Even those who disliked him admired his nerve and his business acumen. He was a man difficult to ignore. Not least because of his propensity for the unusual. When he heard the Hamilton Zoo was going to dispose of its wild buffalo, Cole purchased the bull and two cows and had them shipped to Main Duck. For a time this experiment flourished, the cows giving birth to several calves. The herd eventually increased to seven buffalo, all roaming the island in a semi-wild state. In addition to his livestock, Cole kept a string of racehorses on the island. When one of the buffalo gored a valuable pacer, the "King" took his rifle and disposed of the wild animal. This action was greeted with a great deal of approval by the local fishermen, many of whom had had to postpone the call of nature when they found their path to the outhouse blocked by an ill-natured buffalo.

Claude Cole's other activities were more profitable than the buffalo experiment. For a number of years he was particularly successful as a breeder of race horses. He was a regular at many of the tracks around New York State, where his entries were frequent winners. It is probable that his horse-racing activities first brought him into contact with the "fast changers" at Syracuse who operated that city's blind-pigs and speakeasies. However the contacts were made, Cole was soon buying large quantities of Corby's whisky from Belleville and Old Tower beer from Kingston. He would haul as many as 1,000 cases in his old cruising yacht, the *Emily*. At Main Duck he would unload part of this cargo and cover the rest with fish. The *Emily* would then cross the lake to Oswego and from there travel up the barge canal to Syracuse. The fish made an excellent cover, but Cole's real protection came from the money he paid to the various canal and customs officials. This highly profitable arrangement was just getting nicely established when Inspector Naphan and his men made their raid.

The arrival of the Ontario Provincial Police at Main Duck must have caused quite a stir. Occasionally, someone would sail over to visit the Coles or the lighthouse keeper and his family, but normally the two-dozen resident fishermen saw few visitors. They were there to earn a living, and the Spartan accommodations provided by King Cole discouraged overnight guests. The police chatted with the fishermen for a while and were informed that the Cole family was away. Pointed questions from the officers concerning large caches of liquor elicited only shrugs, and finally one of the fishermen suggested that the officers should not delay their departure as "there was weather on the way," meaning a storm was brewing. Inspector Naphan, while still determined to find the cache was also anxious to leave. Outside the harbour a stiff sea was running and the island itself unnerved him. It was covered with some forest and meadow but also with a great deal of swampland. He and his men could not help but notice the hundreds of large black snakes that infested the area.

After a search of the island had turned up nothing, Frank Naphan faced his decision: He and his men could leave empty handed or they could force their way into Cole's padlocked home. In this he had a choice, for Cole had two homes on the island, a newer two-storey frame house, and the remnants of an earlier stone residence. The latter looked more like a root cellar, consisting chiefly of an old stone basement to which a new plank roof had been added. Naphan decided to try the older building first. Taking a crowbar, he forced open the bolted and padlocked door and led his men into the damp recesses of the basement. Once inside, his flashlight picked out wooden boxes, piled to the ceiling, plainly labelled Old Kentucky bourbon. It was like finding buried treasure.

In total, the officer uncovered thirty-two cases of bourbon, a ten-gallon keg of rye, and two five-gallon kegs of straight alcohol.[1] As there was not enough room in Kerr's boat to haul all this booze back to the mainland, one of the fishermen and his boat were hired and the men prepared to load the contraband into the two large motor boats. By this time, all the fishermen were on shore drying their nets. They cautioned Naphan against venturing out onto the lake as a west wind had been blowing since early afternoon, gradually building up a heavy sea. The long fetch along the lake from Hamilton – a distance of 175 miles – means that a steady west wind can build seas exceeding twenty feet. Reluctantly, Inspector Naphan and his men decided to wait it out. Not until late afternoon did the wind abate enough for the intrepid officers to venture forth onto the lake. This time they went directly to Picton, a distance of forty miles. On arrival, the booze was hauled by wagon to the town jail and there unloaded for safe keeping. Finally, about midnight, the weary officers set off by motorcar for Belleville. There were no paved highways in the county in 1921 and, with the speed limit just 25 m.p.h., the trip took more than an hour. The whole expedition had taken over twenty-two hours.

Exhausted as they were, Naphan and his men were nonetheless elated. Their raid on Main Duck had been a complete success – at the time, their liquor seizure was the largest against Lake Ontario rum-runners. All that remained was to convict Cole.

The trial aroused a great deal of interest; spectators were present from Belleville, Kingston, and as far away as New York State. In his defence, Cole maintained he had purchased the liquor for his own consumption and not for export to the U.S.A. He also claimed that the stone building was one of his residences and that he was, therefore, keeping the booze in his own home, which was perfectly legal.

The laws regulating the consumption and sale of booze in Ontario were a confused tangle. It was not legal to buy the stuff in the province, but it was all right to order it from outside Ontario. Moreover, if you had it you could drink it, just so long as you did so in your own home.

Given this legal chaos, the distilleries and breweries could hardly be blamed for setting up warehouses in Quebec so that the product they manufactured in Ontario could be shipped to their Quebec warehouses and then legally sold by the case through the mails to Ontario residents. This came to be known as the "cellar supply."

In essence, Claude Cole argued at his trial that the seized liquors were his "cellar supply." The evidence suggested otherwise. For one thing, he was a man of considerable means and not likely to prefer cheap whisky, and it was widely known that the bourbon whisky produced by Canadian distilleries was aged a very short time – a few weeks at most – and was not of nearly as good a quality as Canadian ryes, which were aged a minimum of two years. It was general knowledge that Canadian bourbon was produced only for the American market; most Canadians thought it best suited for eating through clogged drain-pipes. As well, the large quantity involved was considerably more than one man could consume.

The trial was held in the ancient Picton courthouse and presided over by Magistrate Levi Williams. Despite the heat, the courtroom was packed as reporters and ordinary folk craned in the languid afternoon to catch the words and gestures of the protagonists. Inspector Frank Naphan was there, stiff, stern, and confident, as was King Cole, who was relaxed, smiling, but as occasion demanded, righteously indignant.

At the conclusion of the prosecution, Magistrate Williams ruled that, according to Supreme Court precedent, a man can have more than one residence, and that he can lawfully have liquor in them. The magistrate, therefore, accepted the defence request for a non-suit and dismissed the case. He then ordered that the liquor be returned to Cole's residence by the officers.

It would be a long time before the police would again raid Main Duck in search of illegal liquor. Claude "King" Cole went back to his fish, cattle, horses, and booze businesses.

Ironically, the "cellar supply" defence used by Cole's lawyers would be invalid before summer's end. This fact was already known to those present at Cole's trial that hot May afternoon. During the preceeding month, a plebiscite had been held across the province in which the citizens of Ontario had voted to end the booze supply. The new law was to take effect on July 19, 1921. It was not the first time Ontario residents had faced Prohibition.

3

CLOSING
THE CELLAR DOOR

BUSINESS AS USUAL AFTER SEPTEMBER 16, 1916

Office of James McPartland, ales, wines, liquors, etc., Kingston. After 16th September, I will have a shipping place at 25 Wellington Street, HULL, P.Q. where all mail and telephone orders will be filled as has been done from my Kingston store. There is no law against getting anything in the above lines for personal or family use, and all orders received will be shipped promptly by express or freight from my Hull agency. Money should accompany every order.

(Keep the above address).

Whig-Standard
September 15, 1916

James McPartland's advertisement was similar to dozens that appeared in Ontario newspapers the week before the Ontario Temperance Act came into effect in 1916. At the time there was no such thing as an LCBO or a government liquor store. The government was not then in the business of retailing liquor. That business was handled by local merchants licensed to do so by the province. While fairly numerous, such package-liquor stores were still rare compared to the hotels and saloons that were found on almost every corner. A good many of these were thoroughly disreputable places where there were frequent brawls and the patrons often drank until they could no longer stand. Bartenders would serve any man just as long as he was upright and not throwing punches at fellow patrons. Women were barred from such places, although in some establishments they could be found frequenting the rooms upstairs.

The unsavoury nature of saloons had a great deal to do with the growth of prohibitionist sentiment. But it was the Great War of 1914-18 that finally led to the passage of the Ontario Temperance Act. The cream of Canada's youth was being massacred on the battlefields of Europe. If abstaining from alcohol would help bring the lads home, surely that was a small sacrifice for the civilian population to pay, especially when compared to the sacrifices and horrors being endured by the boys overseas. Prohibition would lead to a more efficient work force – less absenteeism – which would mean more arms and ammunition for the war effort. Prohibition would also mean more money in people's pockets which could be diverted into war bonds. In short, Prohibition would lead to a quicker end to the war and, most importantly, to the return home of Canada's young soldiers.

On September 16, 1916, the Ontario Temperance Act came into force, ending the sale of the old 9 per cent beer in saloons. The law now allowed the sale of only a "near-beer," whose alcoholic content was no more than 2.5 per cent. The sale of whisky – the price was twenty-five cents for a two-ounce shot – was ended. Spirits could be purchased from the local drugstore, but you had to have a physician's prescription to get it, and most medical men were reluctant to issue these prescriptions to patients without some legitimate illness.

In spite of these restrictions, the booze industry suffered only moderately. The OTA contained a giant loophole. Its strict regulations on what a resident could buy within the province did not apply to purchases made outside Ontario. The brewers and distillers squeezed through the loophole by opening sales offices and warehouses in Quebec. The product they manufactured in Ontario was shipped to Quebec and then sold through the mails to customers in Ontario. For the next eighteen months a booming mail-order business was carried on between the liquor agents in Quebec and Ontario residents. It was finally brought to a halt by the federal government in Ottawa.

By the spring of 1918 the war had reached a critical phase. The major European protagonists were approaching human and economic exhaustion; each side throwing all its resources into the conflict in a desperate effort to avoid a calamitous defeat. In this crisis atmosphere, Prime Minister Robert Borden decided that Canada could no longer afford the self-indulgent luxury of alcohol. To implement his decision, the Cabinet passed an order-in-council shutting down the entire Canadian booze industry for the duration of the war: no alcoholic beverages could be manufactured, imported, or exported. The measure was to be temporary and would expire one year following the cessation of hostilities.

For the next twenty-one months Canadians experienced the most severe Prohibition in their history. A huge thirst began to build as the whole country went as dry as the Palliser triangle. The war ended November 11, 1918, but it was not until the last day of 1919 that Ottawa's restriction against the manufacture and importation of liquor finally expired.

Quebec liquor merchants awoke the day after New Year's to a frenzy of orders from all across the Dominion. In Ontario, the OTA was still in force. It prevented residents from buying liquor in Ontario, but it could not and did not prevent them from ordering booze from outside the province. Interprovincial trade was a federal matter, so the Ontario government had no constitutional power to stop it. The result was a torrent of orders quite beyond the capacity of Quebec's liquor merchants to fill. One newspaper reported that "wholesale merchants have turned down some of their best customers because they cannot at present handle any more business and have no idea when they will be in shape to do so. Some of the heads of wholesale houses have broken down under the severe strain and have had to retire from the business."[1] The story went on to note that no less than five boxcar-loads of spirits were leaving Montreal daily for Ontario.

This deluge of booze did not go unnoticed by Ontario's temperance advocates, who renewed their lobbying to shut down the mail-order booze business. Their problem was the federal government in Ottawa, which had the power to regulate interprovincial trade but did not want to offend Quebec. Quebec had rejected Prohibition in a 1898 national plebescite and was now enjoying the financial rewards resulting from its role as the liquor warehouse for dry Ontario.

To placate the prohibitionists, Ottawa agreed to ban the sale of liquor from outside a dry province to the residents of that province, providing a plebiscite was first held and a majority of the voters upheld the measure. The Ontario Government called for a province-wide plebiscite to be held on April 18, 1921. In the meantime, the Montreal and Hull liquor warehouses continued to do a booming business. In Ontario, those families who could afford it began stocking their basements in anticipation of the expected drought. Many private clubs did the same.

Both wet and dry factions began immediately to organize for the plebiscite. The most prominent prohibitionists were Premier E.C. Drury and Attorney General William E. Raney. Raney was an idealistic foe – many would say a fanatical one – of booze in all its forms. A Toronto lawyer, he had been appointed Ontario's attorney general in 1919 after the United Farmers had surprised everyone – including themselves – by getting elected as the government. The United Farmers party was so totally unprepared for the victory, it had neglected to choose a leader. E.C. Drury, a prominent spokesman for farmers' interests from Simcoe County, was persuaded to accept the leadership, which meant he became premier of the province. A life-long teetotaller and prohibitionist but politically inexperienced, Drury and his attorney general set about enforcing the OTA with the zeal of noviciates.

In the early 1920s, Ontario's population was still predominantly rural and small town. These people were the basis of support for the Drury government. Infused as they were with the rural values of thrift and hard work, they tended to view the city and its ways with suspicion. This is not to suggest that all city dwellers were against Prohibition. As the plebiscite of 1921 would show, only about half of urban dwellers were "wet" in sentiment; the other half regarded booze as the greatest social and economic evil of the day, responsible for homeless waifs, abandoned families, and shattered bodies. At a time when there was no unemployment insurance, no medicare, not even an old-age pension system, middle class opinion generally held that the abolition of booze would solve the painfully visible sores of destitution and drunkenness.

It was also a simpler, more conservative age, which sought to protect people from themselves by prohibiting all sorts of supposed vices. In Ontario in 1920, it was against the law on a Sunday to buy a cigar, a newspaper, or ice cream, to play tennis, baseball, or golf, to fish, or take a steamboat excursion. Newspaper editors railed against bobbed hair, dancing, card-playing, and cosmetics. Even on the hottest summer day, women not wearing silk stockings were barred from attending the theatre.

Premier E.C. Drury and Attorney General William Raney were staunch defenders of these attitudes. But it was a moral view that had reached its ascendancy prior to the war and was receeding even as they took office. The war had returned a generation of men bruised and cynical towards the established order that had wrought so stupid and frightful a conflict. In the end, it had become a war of attrition; the side that could afford to waste the most soldiers emerging as the victor. Not surprisingly, the young veterans' faith in the judgements and values of their elders was severely shaken. Their skepticism was reinforced by the war-profiteering that had gone on at home, and by the poverty wages offered by the factories and offices on their return. The economic recession that followed the war added to the general disillusionment with the old order. The old values were further undermined by the increasing flow of people to the cities and by the automobile, which released young people from the watchful eyes of their elders.

The plebiscite of April 1921 was to some extent a barometer of social change in the province. It indicated how well the old values had held. It was also a measure of the organizing skills of the prohibition forces led by the Ontario Referendum Committee. Protestant churches supported the committee throughout the province. Of these, the Methodists were by far the most significant. Their numbers were particularly dominant in rural areas where they provided a solid basis of support for Prohibition.

Premier E.C. Drury and William Raney were Prohibition's most prominent supporters. Raney spoke frequently at rallies sponsored by the Referendum Committee. At the largest rally of the campaign, 12,000 prohibitionists packed a Toronto arena – another 6,000 were reportedly turned away – to hear nine Salvation Army Bands, the Royal Grenadiers Band, the Festival of the Lillies Choir, and the Premier, who took the gathering by storm. Drury asked for a "Yes" vote to stop the importation of liquor into Ontario so that he could enforce the law – the OTA – and put an end to Ontario as a bootleggers' province.

Those opposed to ending the importation of spirits from

outside the province were organized under the "Liberty League." Veterans and labour groups gave it their public support, but those businessmen and professionals who supported the League's cause tended to do so privately. It was difficult for them to come out openly against the forces of God, morality, motherhood, and the government of Ontario. Stephen Leacock, the humourist and professor, was the most prominent and outspoken supporter of the Liberty League. Leacock put his finger on the problem for middle-class "wets" at a rally in Toronto where he noted, "A fanatical minority has captured the ear of the public and the power of the Legislature. They have contrived to throw around them a false mantle of religion and morality. And for the time being the only response is silence...This man trembles for his business, that man for his profession. All, or nearly all, kept silent."

With wit and logic, Leacock went on to attack Prohibition in general, "Prohibition declares it to be a crime to drink beer. The common sense of every honest man tells him that it is not a crime to drink a glass of beer...The attempt to make the consumption of beer criminal is as silly and as futile as if you passed a law to send a man to jail for eating cucumber salad."[2]

On April 18, the voters of Ontario trooped to the polls and voted by a majority of 166,835 to end the importation of spiritous liquors into the province. The *Farmer's Sun* exulted in the victory and even suggested divine intervention was at work in bringing off the desired result. The good Lord, it seemed, had blessed voting day with rain, sleet, and snow, thereby freeing farmers from working the soil and making it easier for them to cast their dry votes. The *Sun*'s comments emphasized the split in the province. The residents of the larger cities – Toronto, Hamilton, Ottawa, Kingston, Windsor, Kitchener, Sault Ste Marie, Sudbury, Port Arthur, and Fort William – had all voted wet.[3] City dwellers resented this imposition of the rural will on a matter that affected their daily lives. Their resentment went unheeded, however, and on July 19, 1921, the importation of booze into the province ceased. Ontario began to dry up.

This legislation still did not stop Ontario's distilleries from manufacturing and exporting their product. These were federal matters, and the Liberal government in Ottawa was a good deal less enthused about Prohibition than was the United Farmers' government of Ontario. Drury decided to stop the export of booze to the U.S.A. using what legal powers the province possessed. The Sandy Act was passed to prevent the transportation of liquor within the province except for export via a common carrier or by order of the Board of Licence Commissioners. If Ottawa would not put a stop to rum-running, then Drury and his attorney general would, or, to put it more accurately, they would try.

The effect of these two pieces of legislation was not entirely what Drury anticipated. Importation of liquor from Quebec to the cellars of Ontario's middle classes was shut off. But these same middle classes, who had previously spurned the lowly bootlegger, now turned to him in increasing numbers. The bootlegger began to achieve social status. Captains of industry and the smart set began talking about "our bootlegger," and his business flourished. The problem of supply became so critical that many rum-runners, who had previously run their loads to the States, now found the increased prices offered by Canadian bootleggers so attractive, they tried to supply both markets. Boatloads of booze ostensibly bound for Cuba or Mexico were, in fact, destined to be landed on a dark, lonely Ontario shore for distribution through a network of local bootleggers.

The cellar door had been shut, but Ontario's drinkers were still getting their supplies, albeit at much higher prices. For the rum-runners, business, while booming, was now more risky. The Sandy Act put the legality of their export operations in doubt. Moreover, many were now engaged in short circuiting and were clearly breaking the OTA.

The Ontario Provincial Police responded to the law breakers with vigour, as did many local law enforcement agencies. Their resolve only strengthened the bootleggers' and rum-runners' determination to protect their profits – by whatever means necessary. Conflict was inevitable. Canada's reputation as the "peaceful kingdom," one that valued law and order over individualism, was about to be severely tested.

4

VIOLENCE
ON THE WATERFRONT

Principals of Toronto's two forest schools are to
carry revolvers. They are this year to sleep on the
school premises in order to make sure that ma-
rauders do not molest the equipment . . . [E]ach
principal is to have a sleeping tent and is to be
provided with a revolver to protect himself.

Daily Intelligencer
May 31, 1921

In 1921, Canada was barely a generation removed from its
pioneer days. The Prairie provinces had only recently been
settled, and even in the East, the bulk of the population was
still rural or small town. Although we had managed to avoid
the excesses of violence so common to the American experience in the settlement of their frontier, our West was still a
raw and rugged place. The North was even more so. Here,
the airplane and the bush pilot were just beginning to awaken
town and city folk in the south to the North's resources and
potential.

In this rural and pioneer society, guns were commonplace.
Lumberjacks, prospectors, trappers, and all those living on

the edges of the frontier, carried guns for survival and protection. In the more settled rural areas, farmers used rifles and shotguns to protect their livestock from foxes and other predators. And for thousands of city men, a vacation meant a trip to the north woods for a spot of deer or moose hunting.

But even though guns were commonplace, Canadians were still essentially a law-abiding people. American Prohibition, and the criminal border traffic it spawned, threatened to change that.

There was a great deal of money to be made smuggling Canadian whisky and beer across our 4,000 miles of virtually undefended border. An ordinary workingman taking a few loads across to make some easy money might find his entire stake wiped out by hijackers. On his next trip – if he had the nerve to stay in the business – he would likely be carrying some "iron" for protection. Violence – especially in border towns – began to increase dramatically. This was particularly true of the Windsor-Essex area of Ontario. Along a fifteen-mile stretch of the Detroit River there were no fewer than thirty export docks devoted solely to the profitable enterprise of smuggling booze across the narrow waters to thirsty Americans. In July 1920, it was estimated that a thousand cases of whisky were crossing the Detroit River every day. Obviously a lot of protection money was changing hands. Cecil Smith, a former Windsor taxi driver, admitted in court in 1921 that during the previous two-years he had paid out $96,000 to various officials to keep the booze flowing.[1] Along Sandwich Street, the main border road on the Canadian side, a number of roadhouses and hotels openly flouted Prohibition, attracting the less desirable elements from both Windsor and Detroit. The law in Windsor looked the other way.

In response to the outraged protests of Windsor's law-abiding community, Attorney General Raney appointed Reverend Les Spracklin to head a special liquor clean-up squad to act independently of police, licence inspectors, and customs agents. Spracklin was young, dynamic, and strong. He also carried a revolver. Three days after his appointment, six roadhouses were raided and two arrests made. The bootlegging community was outraged, especially when they discovered that Spracklin couldn't be bought. His wife and his parents began receiving letters on a regular basis, threatening that he would be beaten up or shot. On Hallowe'en night, unknown assailants fired at a Spracklin squad member who was hiding in a field, keeping the Sunnyside Hotel under surveillance. That same night, a car drove up to the boathouse where Spracklin kept his squad's patrol boat. The occupants of the car fired several volleys into the boat and sped away. A few minutes later the car drew up to the Spracklin residence, where the bootleggers proceeded to fire several volleys through the living room window, narrowly missing young Mrs Spracklin.

A few nights later, Spracklin noticed two men – both badly beaten – lying on the steps of the notorious Chappell roadhouse. Accompanied by two of his deputies, Special Constable Reverend Spracklin gained entry to the locked roadhouse through a basement window and began searching the premises. He was questioning some of the patrons when the owner, Babe Trumble, suddenly appeared. Although the two men had been boyhood chums, they were now implacable enemies. Fired up by alcohol and the sight of his enemy, Trumble began brandishing a revolver, demanding to know how Spracklin had gotten into his home, did he have a search warrant, and advancing on the minister, he shouted, "By God, I'll get you Spracklin! I'll shoot you where you stand!" He thrust his revolver into Les Spracklin's stomach and, fatefully, hesitated. It was long enough for the fighting parson, who had already drawn his own pistol. Spracklin fired two shots, aiming low so as to wound but not kill Babe Trumble. One bullet lodged in Trumble's leg but the other entered his abdomen, severing the femoral artery. He bled to death in just a few minutes.

At the inquest, the coroner cleared Spracklin of any wrongdoing and even praised his courage. Nevertheless, public opinion in the Windsor-Sandwich area was turning against the feisty preacher. His campaign against the road-houses had frightened off much of the free-spending American trade; Reverend Spracklin and his vice-busting squad were bad for business. A petition, demanding he be brought to trial, quickly garnered 2,000 signatures. Spracklin himself favoured a trial to clear the air, particularly as Babe Trumble's widow steadfastly denied her husband had been carrying a firearm on the night of the fateful shooting.

In February 1921, Spracklin was tried for manslaughter. His defence lawyer, R.L. Brackin, in a brilliant piece of cross-examination, was able to extract from Ed Smith, one of Babe Trumble's bootlegging friends, an admission that he had taken Trumble's revolver from his corpse and dropped it into the Detroit River. It took the jury less than an hour to acquit Spracklin.

Despite the verdict, the trial succeeded in putting public opinion on the side of the bootleggers. Thoroughly disillusioned, the hot-tempered Spracklin resigned his commission as a special Ontario constable, and the clean-up squad was disbanded. Jubilant at this turn of events, the bootlegging and rum-running community decided to stage a celebration. They organized the Bootleggers' Ball, even printing up tickets so inscribed, which they sold throughout Detroit and the border cities. Held in a Windsor dance hall, the event was a roaring, raucous, rowdy, and drunken success.

Along the Windsor-Detroit border, life returned to normal. For the rest of the decade, this meant a degree of violence and lawlessness unmatched in any other part of Canada. In Ontario, the Niagara Peninsula witnessed periodic woundings and murders, linked by the press to rivalry between bootleg gangs. At no time, however, did violence in the peninsula equal the Wild West atmosphere that frequently prevailed along the waterfront frontier stretching from Amherstburg to Windsor. On the river itself, running gun battles between rum-runners and pursuing coastguardsmen became a commonplace disruption of area residents' sleep. Even more disturbing to these waterfront residents were the number of stray bullets that shattered their windows or lodged in their walls.

Pitched battles between rum-runners and prospective hijackers occasionally made a mockery of the forces of law and order. One such battle occurred in June 1920 when a party of hijackers attempted to ambush a group of rum-runners near Amherstburg at a spot known as the Indian Burial Ground. Word of the impending ambush seeped out and reached the ears of the Anderson township farmers-cum-rum-runners, whose booze was scheduled for hijacking. A trap was laid. When the hijackers arrived, they found the cases of booze neatly piled on shore ready to be loaded and no one in sight. They immediately began loading the cases into their automobile. The owners of the contraband had positioned themselves in a nearby barn and now opened fire on the would-be hijackers, who sought shelter behind the whisky cases.

For three hours the battle raged. One man suffered a shattered hip, another was beaten and thrown into the river, and the automobile was riddled with bullets. Finally, the would-be hijackers fled and the rum-runners went about their original business of loading the booze onto boats before running it across the river to Detroit. During the conflict an estimated 300 shots had been fired, yet not a single law officer had made an appearance. The residents of Amherstburg could only look on helplessly during the entire affair.[2]

Prohibition-related violence, while not confined to the border cities region, was most prominent there. This was the result of the large influx of American criminals attracted to the area by the enormous profits to be made from smuggling booze across the Detroit River. In many places the river was no more than a mile across, making it ideally suited to rum-running. By the end of the decade, it was estimated that 80 per cent of Canadian beer and 60 per cent of the Canadian whisky exported to the United States got there via the Detroit River.[3]

Fortunately, the violence accompanying the liquor traffic never quite became endemic; periodic crackdowns by the OPP kept the virus from infecting the entire province. Nevertheless, the Ontario Temperance Act, in as much as many people broke it without in any way feeling they were criminals, did foster disrespect for the law and blurred the distinctions between ordinary people and criminals. Was a bootlegger a criminal? Many normally law-abiding citizens thought he was not. Nor, at that time, did the general public perceive a criminal as someone who could accumulate a great deal of money and influence. Criminals had always belonged to the flotsam and jetsam of society, not to the economic elite. Now, Prohibition and the enormous illegal profits it made possible was changing this perception and leading to the emergence of a new phenomenon in Canadian society – the millionaire criminal.

A rum-running family from St. Catharines, a load of Corby's whisky from Belleville, and an unexpected encounter with Toronto police culminated in a shoot-out known as the Gogo Affair. This event would also provide Canadians with their first public glimpse of Rocco Perri, Canada's first millionaire mobster.

5

THE GOGO AFFAIR

> Today's tragic raid was the first time the police
> have come in close grips with the rum runners who
> have been stealing into Toronto under the blanket
> of night and discharging their illegal cargoes of
> whiskey into the eager hands of Bootleggers
>
> *The Toronto Star*
> October 6, 1923

In September 1923, John Gogo and his father, Sidney, left
St. Catharines in their thirty-three-foot cabin boat, the *Hattie C*. At Toronto, they picked up Sidney's brother James, a
thirty-year-old carpenter, and Fred Van Winkle, who had
acted as cook during their many voyages that summer.[1] On
September 30, 1923, the four men set out for Belleville, arriving the next day at the government dock where a boxcar of
Corby's whisky was waiting to be unloaded. Once this was
completed, the *Hattie C* began her return journey. Along the
way the crew broke up and discarded the wooden whisky
cases, repacking the quart bottles into burlap flour sacks,
two cases or twenty-four bottles to a bag. This was standard
practice with rum-runners, as bags could be unloaded twice

as quickly as wooden cases. They would also sink if the cargo had to be jettisoned, whereas wooden cases floated.

The *Hattie C* followed a westerly route along the shoreline of Lake Ontario, arriving at Newcastle on noon of October 2. Here, Sidney Gogo departed by train for Toronto to make arrangements for the cargo's delivery. Two days later, the boat left Newcastle, arriving at Frenchman's Bay that evening. The next day, John Gogo moved the *Hattie C* again, arriving off Woodbine racetrack (known now as the Greenwood racetrack) in the late afternoon. It was a pleasant October day, cool but sunny, and the men joked and laughed while Van Winkle prepared supper in the galley. After supper they talked and smoked, waiting for the city to turn in for the night.

At that time, the Leslie Street spit did not exist and so, shortly before midnight, the *Hattie C* was able to proceed directly into Ashbridge Bay and from there into a shallow, finger-shaped lagoon that reached westward almost to the foot of Leslie Street. On the north shore of the lagoon, a group of men led by Frank Di Petro waited quietly in the shadows beside two automobiles and two trucks that they had driven over the rough ground almost to the water's edge. They were joined there by Rocco Perri and Sidney Gogo.

As the *Hattie C* nosed into the lagoon's north shore, James Gogo threw a line to his brother, Sidney, who tied it to a small tree. John Gogo disengaged the clutch but kept the engine of the boat running. Fred Van Winkle then pushed a gangplank to the shore and, in a matter of seconds, the men were busy transferring the cargo to the nearest truck. In the chill night air the men worked quickly, their muscles strengthened by a pounding supply of adrenalin. They knew they risked arrest by police, but they were more concerned by the prospect of hijackers sweeping down with guns blazing. They hauled the eighty-pound burlap sacks from below decks with relative ease. Their urgency was tempered only by the fragile and valuable nature of the cargo being unloaded.

Each bottle had a bootleg value of eight dollars. In all, there were 2,544 quart bottles of Corby's Special whisky with a street value of over $20,000. In today's terms, this was the equivalent of a quarter of a million dollars.

Less than a mile away, at the Pape Avenue police station, Patrol Sergeant George Hoag received a mysterious phone call – thought to be from a rival bootlegger – advising him of the goings-on at Leslie Street. He immediately dispatched four officers to the scene under the command of Sergeant Bill Kerr. With Kerr was uniformed constable Jim Rooney and plainclothes officers George Fraser and Bill Mitchell. On its arrival at the foot of Leslie Street, the squad car's headlights alerted the bootleggers, who began running away. The officers leaped from the car shouting, "Stop! Police!" Rooney and Mitchell drew their pistols and quickly flushed out four men, including Rocco Perri, who were hiding in the bushes. Sergeant Kerr collared another man crouching in the shadow of the truck. After turning his prisoner over to plainclothes Officer Fraser, Kerr shouted to the other constables to bring their prisoners over to the truck.

At that point, Fraser spotted the dark outline of the boat about thirty feet from shore and called to Kerr that it was backing away. Mitchell began running towards the other side of the lagoon. The other officers hollered to the men on the boat, "Police! Stop your boat!" Kerr shouted, "Bring in the boat, we have you surrounded." He then whistled as though signalling a large force of officers and yelled, "Come on. We have the boat surrounded," hoping to fool them into surrendering. The *Hattie C* continued backing away and was now almost obscured in the shadow of the south shore. Again Kerr shouted, "Stop your engine or I will sink your boat," firing a round from his service revolver for emphasis. It was the first shot fired, and it galvanized the prisoners who began shouting in Italian, "Termate la machina. Tireranno! Tireranno!" Realizing the men on the boat might not understand, Rocco Perri shouted clearly in English, "Stop the engines or you will be shot." The bow of the *Hattie C* was swinging westward, away from the lagoon's only entrance, when Kerr ordered, "Fire low to sink it." All four policemen opened up with their .32-calibre service revolvers.

A hail of bullets raked the *Hattie C*. Inside the cabin, a bullet bounced off the engine, striking Sidney Gogo on the finger, another burned his neck, yet another ripped through his coat. In the back of the small cabin, James Gogo collapsed to the floor, his jaw shattered. He looked up to see his nephew, John, slump forward. The engine stopped. The shooting stopped. It had lasted about a minute.

By this time, officer Bill Mitchell had crossed to the south side of the lagoon and had reached the *Hattie C*, which was drifting in towards shore. He boarded the boat and shone his flashlight through the frost-covered cabin window. Inside, James Gogo lay to the rear of the small cabin, blood from his jaw seeping over the pine floor. Sidney Gogo was holding his son John in his arms, while Fred Van Winkle crouched beside him. A .32-calibre bullet had entered John's chest, passing through his heart and lung before lodging against his spine. John Gogo was twenty-three years of age, a muscular 190-pounder in the prime of life, but he died within minutes.

News of the arrests and shooting spread quickly. It was the first time a rum-running vessel had been captured by Toronto police and the first time they had killed a rum-runner. At 4 a.m., just three hours after James and John Gogo reached St. Michael's Hospital, the *Toronto Star* dispatched reporters to the homes of Fred Van Winkle and James Gogo. Awakened in the early morning by reporters, both women protested that their husbands were innocent of any wrong doing, but their reactions were otherwise quite different. Mrs Gogo rushed straight to the hospital, where her husband was listed in stable but critical condition. Slim, blonde, and with stylish bobbed hair, Mrs Van Winkle was primarily concerned about the possibility of bail.

The story was headline news. Sidney Gogo, Rocco Perri,

and six other men were charged with "the illegal transport of liquor on the waters of Lake Ontario." Bail was set at $3,000 for each man. Sidney Gogo was the exception; the magistrate showed compassion for the father of the slain man by setting bail at just $2,000 and allowing him to post his boat, the *Hattie C*, to secure bond.

Three days after the shooting, the attorney general's department announced that an inquiry would be held not only into the death of John Gogo but also into the bootlegging activities of the men arrested. The Crown attorney specifically mentioned Rocco Perri, noting that he was particularly well known among the Italian communities in Guelph, Hamilton, and Niagara Falls. The inquiry was a shrewd political move. It appeased both wet and dry sentiments at the same time. Wets could hope the investigation into the shooting of young John Gogo would constrain police action against bootleggers; drys expected the investigation to expose the big-time booze merchants, and possibly lead to their prosecution.

During October, the inquest, conducted by Chief Coroner Dr George Graham, dominated the pages of the *Toronto Star* and, to a lesser degree, of the *Globe*. It was revealed that one of the men arrested by police was an ordinary labourer walking home from a nearby house party. This unhappy soul was quickly released and the charges against him quietly dropped. It was clear from the newspaper accounts that the testimony of the police differed sharply from that of the men arrested. The smugglers claimed the police had not shouted any warning before opening fire on the *Hattie C*. They further claimed the police had used their flashlights to direct their fire into the boat's cabin. The four officers firmly denied these accusations, insisting they had yelled several times to stop the boat before firing at its hull in an effort to sink it. A marine expert then testified that a .32-calibre bullet could not sink a boat as heavy as the *Hattie C*. Other than that, the police testimony stood up quite well.

The smugglers were far less credible. They maintained their destination had been the United States and that they had put in at the foot of Leslie Street only because damage to the boat had made it hazardous to cross the lake. The same marine expert who had picked a hole in the police's account then testified that the damage to the boat was slight and could not have affected its seaworthiness. The smugglers could not explain why they had doused all the lights on the *Hattie C*, contrary to marine law. Nor could they satisfactorily explain why they had kept the boat's motor running. Their testimony was at times evasive and often contradictory. It was pretty clear their real destination was the foot of Leslie Street, and that their cargo was for distribution to Ontario bootleggers. This was short circuiting – a clear violation of the Ontario Temperance Act.

One of the witnesses called at the hearing was William Turnbull, secretary of Consolidated Distilleries of Montreal, which owned the distillery at Corbyville. Turnbull stated that the order for the whisky had come in the mail from an A.D. Geon. He did not know Geon, or where he lived, and admitted the name might be false. The shipment was consigned to the *Hattie C* for delivery to Geon in Havana, Cuba. Normally, a shipment to Cuba would not be subject to the Canadian excise tax of $9 a gallon, yet Corby's had paid some $3,000 in excise taxes on this shipment. Why was this paid? Turnbull answered that once the tax was paid and the whisky loaded on the *Hattie C*, the boat could go anywhere. Evidently, the distillery officials knew, or at least suspected, that the real destination of their whisky was back into Ontario.

The inquest made public the methods used by Canadian distilleries, rum-runners, and bootleggers to evade the Ontario law against the sale of liquor to its residents. However, the chief coroner's primary responsibility was to rule on the death of John Gogo, and here the forces of law and order suffered a considerable set-back. Dr George Graham concluded that the police officers were not justified in shooting John Gogo or in firing at the boat. He went on to note that the OTA was a provincial act and its breach, therefore, was not a criminal offence. The police were not justified in using their firearms in enforcing the act. This ruling seemed to prohibit Ontario police from using firearms to apprehend bootleggers and rum-runners, a view reinforced by the Crown attorney's decision to lay charges of manslaughter against all four police officers.

The ensuing trial took place during November and, once again, the Gogo affair dominated Toronto newspapers. In the end, the jurors were unable to arrive at a verdict; seven jurors were for acquittal, while five believed the officers to be guilty as charged. Whether consciously or not, each of the jurors must have been influenced by their attitude to Prohibition, which was the major political and moral issue of the day. In this sense, the split in the jury reflected the division of opinion within the province. In a plebiscite held a year later, Ontarians were almost equally divided on the issue; 585,000 voted to retain the Ontario Temperance Act, and 551,000 voted to replace it with a system of government-owned liquor stores.

With almost half the population opposed to the OTA, it was clear that a too-vigorous enforcement of Prohibition would precipitate a serious backlash. As well, Dr Graham's decision at the Gogo inquest made it abundantly clear to police that the use of firearms against bootleggers, other than in self-defence, would result in more police officers being prosecuted. Unwelcome as this development was to law-enforcement agencies, it did help defuse the violence inherent in the whisky-running and bootlegging business. The gangland killings, which were so prominent a feature of the booze business in major American cities, never developed to the same degree in Ontario, although periodically the Windsor area threatened to emulate Chicago and Cook County. Even in Windsor, the normal practice for American rum-runners was to leave their weapons behind when coming to Canada to pick up a load. Later, as hostilities between smugglers and U.S. prohibition forces heated up, many rum-runners flouted Canadian law by arming both themselves and their boats.[2]

Another factor discouraging violence in Ontario, although not on the Detroit River, was the relatively light penalties for major infractions of the OTA. At the time of the Gogo shooting, a common drunk would be fined a minimum of $200. Yet Sidney Gogo and Frank Di Petro, who were caught smuggling over 2,500 quart bottles of Corby's Special whisky received a sentence of only thirty days or a fine of $1,000. Di Petro paid the $1,000 fine, while Sidney Gogo elected to serve the thirty days. The OTA did not discriminate much between large-scale smugglers and the town drunk found in an alley with a bottle in his pocket.

The Gogo affair also pointed up the difficulty in nailing "Mr Big," who in this case was Rocco Perri. Although it could not be proven at the time, subsequent events leave no doubt that Perri was the real buyer of the boatload of booze being shipped on the *Hattie C* to A.D. Geon of Havana, Cuba.

Perri, who had been arrested along with the others found at the scene of the shooting, was subsequently charged with violating the Ontario Temperance Act. He offered an ingenuous explanation for his presence at the foot of Leslie Street while the whisky was being unloaded: "I run into Frank Di Petro on York Street about eleven o'clock," he said, "and Frank asked me how to get to Leslie Street, so I show him." Later, the police discovered that Perri owned both of the large Marmon touring cars seized near the boat. Nevertheless, the Crown attorney's office decided they had insufficient evidence, and the charges against Rocco Perri were dropped.

At the inquest, Rocco had been put on the stand, where

his answers to Crown Attorney Dewart's questions suggested Perri's real occupation and the reason he was present
at the foot of Leslie Street the night of the shooting:

Dewart: "Where do you work?"
Perri: "I am a traveller for the Superior Macaroni
Company."
Dewart: "Do you drive trucks in your business?"
Perri: "Yes."
Dewart: "Do you ever carry anything other than
macaroni?"
(Perri grinned and hesitated.)
Dewart, prompting: "A little liquor perhaps?"
Perri: "Can you prove it?"
Dewart: "No, I am expecting you to admit it."
Perri: "No, I don't."[3]

This denial was to be expected, but a considerable amount
of circumstantial evidence suggested otherwise. Why, for example, did Rocco's common-law wife, Bessie Starkman, post
the large bail required to free Sidney Gogo and Frank Di
Petro? Nor did the Perris' life-style jibe with Rocco's claim to
be merely a macaroni salesman. Bessie Starkman was the
possessor of a lavish and expensive wardrobe, including a
full-length sable coat. She and Rocco owned a beautiful
mansion in one of Hamilton's most exclusive neighbour-
hoods. Moreover, although Perri had never been convicted
of any crime, the daily newspapers covering the Gogo inquest noted euphemistically that Rocco Perri was well
known to police departments throughout the Niagara Peninsula.

If there was any doubt about Rocco Perri's role in the Gogo
affair, it was dispelled a year later when he granted an interview to *Toronto Star* reporter Dave Rogers. A suave, im-
maculately groomed Perri admitted to Rogers that there was

some foundation to the popular description of him as King of Ontario Bootleggers.[4]

During the interview, both Rocco Perri and Bessie Starkman made a number of incriminating statements, perhaps in the belief that the law could not or would not touch them. After all, they had been in the bootlegging business for eight years with no serious trouble from the law. The talk on the streets was that Rocco had bought off the top police officials in Hamilton, including some of the judges. These rumours were supported by the resignation, earlier that year, of licence inspector Arthur Paxton after phone calls had been traced from his home in Mimico to a Hamilton liquor dealer.[5] An investigation had been conducted by the attorney general's department but the name of the Hamilton bootlegger was not disclosed.

With their new wealth and connections in high places, Rocco and Bessie apparently believed themselves immune from the ordinary workings of the law. In their interview with the *Star* reporter they demonstrated a fatal hubris. After admitting he was a bootlegger, Perri went on to defend his occupation: "The law. What is the law?" he asked scornfully. "They don't want it in the cities. They voted against it. It is forced upon them. It is an unjust law. I have a right to violate it if I can get away with it."

He claimed to be against guns in his business: "My men do not carry guns. If I find that they do, I get rid of them. It is not necessary. I provide them with high-powered cars. That is enough. If they cannot run away from the police, it is their own fault. But guns make trouble, my men do not use them."

A gracious and expensively gowned Bessie Starkman interjected, "You have heard that there is honour among thieves, but maybe you do not know that there is such a thing as principle among bootleggers. Yes, we admit that we are bootleggers, but we do our business on the level."

Rocco Perri warmed to this aspect of his business. Picking

up on Bessie's theme he added, "There is no business, I don't care what you name, in which honesty is a more important factor than in the bootlegging business. I mean accredited bootlegging. The man who does not play the game as it should be played will not get very far. Pure liquor, fair prices, and square dealing. Those are the requisites of the trade." The reporter began to wonder if he hadn't mistakenly wandered into a university lecture on business administration.

The atmosphere changed when Dave Rogers brought up the matter of two murders, attributed by police to the Italian bootleg ring and believed to be part of a struggle to control the bootleg business. Rogers asked, "Who killed Joe Baytoizae and Fred Genesee?"

Perri was jovial. He smiled at Bessie. "Rocco Perri did it, I suppose. Everything that happens they blame on Rocco Perri. Why is it? Maybe because my name is so easy to say; I don't know, it is amusing."

Rogers pressed the issue. "It has been said that these two men met death at the hands of an Italian bootlegging ring. You are the recognized leader of the Italian population of Hamilton. Have you not some theory to advance in respect to such an extraordinary sequence of murders?"

Perri became more serious. He had consented to this interview. He knew that tomorrow it would be on the front page of the *Toronto Star*. He answered cautiously. "How came these two men to be killed? I know not, but from what I have read, I would say Joe Baytoizae was put out of the way because he was a squealer. He was a Polack. I have been told that he was a stool pigeon...He said too much. He has paid the price. That's what I think, but I don't know."

Perri had moved on to dangerous ground. Rogers pressed his advantage. "There is a report that Baytoizae and Genesee were killed in connection with a bootleg war."

Rocco Perri was silent. Bessie Perri reached forward and patted him gently on the back. "You tell them, Rocco, that there is no war. You are the King of the Bootleggers. That is what they say. You should know." It was a revealing moment. Advised by his wife, Rocco Perri responded with abrupt emphasis, "There is no bootleg war."

For a brief moment, Dave Rogers had caught a glimpse of the real brains behind Ontario's bootleg king. Only later, when Bessie was brought before a Royal Commission and forced to testify under oath, would the extent of her influence be known. For now she had helped Rocco through a difficult interview – an interview to which he should never have consented.

The next day a large photograph of Rocco Perri dominated the front page of the *Toronto Star*. The headline proclaimed, KING OF BOOTLEGGERS WON'T STAND FOR GUNS." It was sensationalist journalism at its most effective and caused a near riot at the newsstands where the issue quickly sold out. The regular newsstand price was two cents, but by the end of the day scalpers' copies were selling for two dollars each.[6]

Perhaps Rocco thought he was now a celebrity. He had certainly managed to put the spotlight on his activities, but both he and Bessie had made statements they would later regret. They had miscalculated and eventually would be brought to account for their public indiscretion. For the time being, however, they basked in the publicity, and continued to rake in enormous profits.

6

THE SHORT
TRIP TO MEXICO

Canadian whiskey can be bought...for one hundred and twenty dollars a case. Single quarts cost fifteen dollars. There is plenty of liquor and there are plenty of purchasers and the price seems to be no deterrent.

> Ernest M. Hemingway, *The Toronto Star*
> June 19, 1920

In January 1920, the Licence Board of Ontario announced an across-the-board price increase. Henceforward, a forty-ounce bottle of Seagrams v.o. would cost $3; a quart of Usher's Black Label Scotch, $3.50; a dozen pints of beer, $1.85; and a forty-ounce bottle of Concord wine, 75 cents.[1]

These prices seem wonderfully cheap, but inflation was still present, manifesting itself as soon as the booze crossed the lake to the American shore. Once there, a case of Canadian whisky was automatically worth at least $100 and sometimes as much as $250.[2] That fifty-mile trip across the lake was one of the most expensive in the world.

Who reaped these incredible profits? How were they divided up? And how were Canadian brewers and distillers able to export their products "legally" to the United States?

Generally speaking, a $3 bottle of Canadian whisky would sell in northern New York for from $7 to $9. As you went further inland, the costs and risks involved in transporting it increased the price. Hijackers were the greatest risk; so much so that some loads unintentionally changed hands several times before reaching their destination. As a consequence, a quart bottle of Canadian whisky would fetch $12 by the time it finally arrived in the big apple, New York City.[3]

The prices charged by the local bootlegger to his American customers was common knowledge, as were the selling prices of the Canadian manufacturer. But the commission paid to the men taking the physical risks, the rum-runners, was not widely known. Avoiding hijackers and the U.S. coast guard and the border patrol was made easier if a man kept his own counsel. As a consequence, rum-runners, especially those who were successful, tended to be pretty tight-lipped about their work.

An interesting court case exposed the export system devised by Canadian distillers to avoid openly breaking American prohibition laws while maintaining multi-million dollar sales in that huge and profitable market. During the course of the trial, testimony was given that detailed the commissions paid to the men who actually took the risks and ran the booze across the lake. The case resulted from the arrest of George R. Woodward of Toronto, ostensibly for an infraction of the Ontario Temperance Act. In reality, the charge was an attempt by Attorney General Raney to stamp out rum-running in Ontario and to destroy the brewing and distilling industries in the process.

On the evening of April 21, 1922, George Woodward and his mechanic, Charles Faulkner, piloted *Le Voyageur 15* into Belleville harbour and tied up at the government dock. Woodward had reason to be in good spirits. Since April 13, when he took *Le Voyageur 15* out of dry dock in Toronto, he had made three successful trips across the lake to Oswego, each time taking 200 cases or 2,400 bottles of Old Crow bourbon whisky in his thirty-foot cabin cruiser. In the morning, he would take yet another load, making four loads in just eight days.[4]

At 5 a.m. the following morning, two OPP constables arrived at the docks and silently stationed themselves in the cabin of the *City of Dresden*, an old steamship docked opposite Woodward's boat. From here they were also able to observe the two Grand Trunk Railway boxcars standing nearby. A little after 7 a.m., five workmen began transferring the wooden cases of Old Crow bourbon from the boxcars into the cabin cruiser. At this point, the redoubtable Inspector Naphan – the invader of King Cole's fiefdom at Main Duck Island the previous year – arrived on the scene and, with the assistance of the two constables he had posted on the *City of Dresden*, proceeded to arrest Woodward and place his boat and cargo under seizure.

How could they do this? As far as Woodward knew he was not breaking any Canadian law. He was one of several men who picked up boatloads of Corby's whisky every week. Captain John S. McQueen, the grizzled old lake sailor who owned the *City of Dresden*, was regularly taking as many as 4,000 cases a trip in the very steamship on which the two policemen had lain in wait. Woodward could not have known that he was being arrested in order to test the OTA. Under the act it was legal for a "common carrier" to take liquor from Canada for export. Attorney General Raney intended to challenge Woodward's status as a common carrier by proving that Woodward's declared destination – Mexico was shown on the manifest – was beyond the capability of his small boat. If the Crown succeeded, then the hundreds of small boats used in liquor-running would lose their status as common carriers. Almost all the smuggling in the Windsor-Detroit area was done in small boats. If he succeeded against Woodward, Raney would deal a heavy blow to Ontario's liquor-export business.

At the trial Woodward was first on the stand. It soon became evident the Crown attorney was trying to prove Woodward was short circuiting his loads back into Ontario. To prove his real destination was the U.S.A., Woodward had to name names and give details. He admitted being approached the year before by an American bootlegger, Sam Smith of Buffalo. Smith and his partner, Fred O'Leary, supplied a number of speakeasies in New York State and needed reliable rum-runners. A deal had been struck. Woodward bought *Le Voyageur 15* in Toronto on October 1, 1921, for $2,500, putting up $500 of his own money and borrowing the rest from O'Leary and Smith, who took a lien on the boat as security for their loan. Over the next several weeks, *Le Voyageur 15* had taken seven loads across the lake to Oswego. Woodward always timed the ten-hour trip so as to arrive about midnight. In Oswego he would be met by O'Leary and his crew of roustabouts who would transfer the 200 cases to waiting trucks in about ten minutes.

The Crown attorney asked Woodward why he didn't follow the usual route to Oswego, which was east to Deseronto and then south through the Upper Gap and on past Main Duck Island to Oswego. Woodward explained that the lake was too rough at the Upper Gap. Therefore, he went west along the Bay of Quinte to Trenton, then through the Murray Canal to Brighton Bay, and from there across the lake to Oswego. The Crown's line of questioning implied that Woodward's real destination was not the U.S.A. at all but some quiet cove in Ontario, and that was the real reason for his heading west toward Toronto.

If the Crown succeeded in convicting Woodward on such flimsy circumstantial evidence, then the police would be encouraged to seize every boatload of whisky where there was the slightest suspicion it could be short circuited. The Woodward case could set a precedent that would imperil a system that allowed Ontario distilleries to export more than 80 per cent of their production to the "dry" United States.[5] It was probably this danger to the distilleries that led to a most unusual event. The American bootlegger Fred O'Leary actually took the stand in a Canadian court in order to convince the judge that he was the real buyer of the booze exported on *Le Voyageur 15*.

In his testimony, O'Leary stated that the previous year he had travelled to the offices of the Consolidated Distilleries Company in Montreal. There he had met their salesman, Harry Hatch, with whom he had left $20,000 to cover future orders. It was arranged that these orders would be made out to the American Import Co. of Mexico City, which was owned by O'Leary and Sam Smith. The American Import Co. had no offices in Mexico City and, in fact, had never transacted any business there. It was simply a legal fiction set up to satisfy Canadian distillery executives, who did not wish to be seen openly selling to dry America. William Hume, plant manager at Corbyville, confirmed this in his testimony.

Mr. John Munroe, chief clerk at Corby's, was next on the stand. He testified that the orders from the American Import Co. went directly to Montreal where they were approved by Harry Hatch and then sent to Corbyville to be filled. Munroe took care of the paper work, including the B-13, the federal Government's form dealing with items for export. He would show Mexico City as the destination and the American Import Co. as the consignee. At this point, the Customs and Excise people took over, making sure the load actually went on board the designated vessel and giving its captain a copy of the B-13 form. This made it all legal as far as the Canadian government was concerned. In this way, hundreds of boats cleared from Canadian lake ports every month, all listed as sailing for some distant port – Mexico City and Havana, Cuba, were popular choices – and most arrived back the next day or the day after, ready for another load. To paraphrase Churchill: Never in the history of human commerce had so few travelled so far in such a short time in the interests of so many. Canadians – true friends always – were striving unstintingly to preserve their American cousins from the evils of Prohibition.

The system revealed at Woodward's trial was clever, and it worked well. The American bootlegger hid his identity from American federal agents behind a dummy foreign company. By selling to a Cuban or Mexican company, the Canadian distillery was breaking no Canadian or American law. As there was no Canadian law against exporting liquor, even the rum-runner was not breaking the law.

Unfortunately for all of these parties, the Ontario provincial government was determined to stamp out rum-running, which it regarded as a moral plague. The trial of George Woodward was one of a number of attempts to close the legal loopholes that made rum-running possible. In this effort, the Ontario government ran counter to the position of the federal government, which had no desire to end whisky exports. Consequently, the legal status of the business was contradictory, and its moral and ethical status was ambiguous. Nowhere was this better illustrated than in the remarks of George Woodward's defence attorney, who openly admitted his client was a smuggler and went on to state in court, "smuggling is the seeming foundation upon which the city of Windsor, for instance, is built. If smuggling were criticized there, the critic would be run out of town, because in smuggling there is much profit."[6]

This must be one of the most unusual defence arguments ever put forward in a Canadian court of law. It implied that a great many Canadians were not only tolerant of rum-running, but actually supported it. It was, after all, good for the economy.

In his judgement delivered a few days later, Magistrate S. Masson outlined a view that found a ready acceptance with many Canadians. "Though it is admitted that [the liquor] was intended to be smuggled into the U.S.A., I cannot see that that prevents a common carrier [Woodward] from carrying it to the United States under any of our statutes. THERE

IS NO BURDEN CAST UPON US TO ENFORCE THE LAWS OF THE UNITED STATES."[7] Magistrate Masson then dismissed all charges against George Woodward. The whisky companies, the rum-runners, the American bootleggers, all could breathe more easily: The system had survived.

But what sort of profits did George Woodward stand to lose if rum-running had been outlawed? During their testimony both Woodward and O'Leary affirmed that the rum-runner received $1.50 for each case delivered. In other words, Woodward made $300 on each load. From this he had to pay wages to his mechanic – the usual rate was $50 each trip – plus the expenses of operating the boat. His net profit of about $200 a trip does not seem much for having to brave the open lake in a small boat for upwards of twenty hours, a good part of it after dark and, once in American waters, without benefit of running lights. As well, there was always the risk of being captured by federal agents, although, during the first five years of American Prohibition, this risk was very slight.

To translate Woodward's net profit of $200 into today's money, we would have to multiply it by at least ten. In those days $10 would buy a man's suit or two women's dresses or a room at a good hotel for a week. The local high school principal earned about $2,500 a year, and the magistrate who tried Woodward, only $2,000.[8] If he made just one trip a week, George Woodward could make more in a single summer than the magistrate earned in an entire year.

As time went on, and the risks to the rum-runners increased dramatically, many would desert the business, forcing the American bootleggers to pay higher commissions to those remaining. By 1929, the commission on a case of whisky had risen to $8, and beer brought $5 a case.[9] This meant that the profit on just one load of 100 cases was sufficient to buy a brand new Chevrolet roadster, with cash to spare.

With luck, nerve, and a thorough knowledge of the lake, a

rum-runner who owned his own boat could accumulate a small fortune. Ben Kerr of Hamilton, one of the most diligent of the owner-operators, built up a bank account reputed to be in the range of $45,000.[10] He also owned a large home in one of Hamilton's more affluent neighbourhoods and a number of boat-houses that earned him rental income.

In 1926 Ben Kerr's records were seized by the Ontario Provincial Police. They revealed that he averaged one trip a week across Lake Ontario during October, November, and December 1925, taking seventy to ninety cases each trip.[11] As his mark-up was $7 a case, his average gross profit each week was $560. Other evidence indicates he made much higher profits. At one point in 1925, he was taking as many as 1,200 cases of ale across the lake in his boat, the *Martimas*. At that time his mark-up on ale was $2 to $3 a case for a gross profit of $2,400 to $3,600 each trip.[12]

Much bigger profits could be made by multi-boat operators. The four Staud brothers, operating out of Rochester, were able to accumulate over a million dollars between them. George Staud invested his money conservatively and consequently avoided losing it during the economic collapse of the 1930s. His brother, Midge Staud, was less wise. Midge, who was the boss of the outfit, entrusted his considerable fortune to his older brother, Karl. Karl, alias The Bishop, was the bookkeeper of the organization. In that favoured position, he was able to embezzle Midge out of a cool million dollars, which he invested and lost in the stock market. When Midge discovered the loss, he stormed over to their offices, knocked Karl down a flight of stairs and jammed his revolver against his temple. Karl pleaded successfully for his life, claiming, "I can't help myself Midge. I'm just a crook."[13]

The millionaire status achieved by the Staud brothers was earned as much by their bootlegging activities as it was by rum-running. By combining the two aspects of the business, they practised an early example of what the modern businessman calls vertical integration.

Depending upon the scale of their operations, American bootleggers could make enormous profits. Their Canadian equivalents made less because their market was smaller. Even so, the large-scale operators, such as Rocco Perri and Bessie Starkman, were able to accumulate huge profits. Rocco Perri began his bootlegging career in a tiny Hamilton grocery store in 1916 where he sold whisky at fifty cents a shot in the back room. By 1925, Perri was known as Canada's Al Capone. As a result of his high public profile, he was subjected to a detailed investigation by the 1927 Royal Commission on Customs and Excise. The investigators uncovered several bank accounts opened by Bessie Starkman under various names, which revealed the two had over $900,000 on deposit.[14] They owned speakeasies, hotels, a fleet of boats and trucks, and their expensive Hamilton mansion.

One of the major problems for the large-scale bootlegger was obtaining the necessary product. They could not legally purchase from any of the twenty-nine breweries and six distilleries located throughout Ontario. To circumvent the OTA, the bootlegger had to pretend he or, in some cases, she – Bessie frequently placed orders – was an American and that the order was for delivery to the U.S.A. The supplier pretended to believe him. In fact, the success of the whisky and ale companies largely depended upon their ability to develop a network of customers among American and Canadian bootleggers.

Few were more accomplished at this art than Harry and Sam Bronfman, two brothers from an immigrant Russian Jewish family that settled in Saskatchewan in the 1890s. Today, the Bronfman family is one of the richest in the non-Arab world, ranking right up there with the Rothschilds of Europe. Their holdings include some of the world's most prestigious real estate, including a majority interest in Toronto's Eaton Centre. The Bronfmans have interests in every continent except Antartica, and in Canada their interests are omnipresent. But of all their holdings, the family jewel is Seagrams, the largest distilling company in the world and the origin of the family's great wealth.

The Bronfmans got their start by taking advantage of the loopholes in Canada's prohibition laws. They developed a thriving mail-order booze business during World War I, and when Prohibition arrived in the U.S.A., they quickly moved into whisky manufacturing. Harry Bronfman set up the Yorkton Distributing Company, which purchased ten one-thousand gallon redwood vats and a machine that could fill and label a thousand bottles an hour. Harry was nothing if not brash. With no experience as a distiller, he set about producing the first batch of Bronfman distilled whisky. The result was a disaster. Instead of the desired amber colour, the product was a dirty blue. This was unfortunate for Harry but fortunate for future chroniclers of the Bronfman saga because Harry Bronfman decided the vats were to blame and stubbornly refused to pay for them. The result was a court case that laid bare the profits being reaped by the Bronfman distillery.

The equipment, including the vats and the bottling machine, had cost $3,200. To produce 800 gallons of whisky, Harry Bronfman had mixed 100 gallons of aged rye whisky, 318 gallons of overproof alcohol, and 382 gallons of water. The total cost including tax was about $5.25 a gallon. There are two gallons to a case, so the production cost of a case of whisky was $10.50. On average, the price to the rum-runners was $50 a case. Sales from the Yorkton plant ran between 8,000 and 10,000 cases a month. At a profit of $39.50 a case, the Bronfmans were netting between $316,000 and $395,000 in gross monthly profits.[15] Office and sales expenses reduced these profits marginally, but it is still clear that the really big profits were in distilling, not in bootlegging, and certainly not in rum-running.

There is a saga similar to that of the Bronfman brothers which has been kept hidden from the public for more than half a century. It is the story of Herb and Harry Hatch, who created a liquor empire that, in its time, was the largest in North America, larger even than Seagrams. In spite of their achievements, the Hatch brothers and the story behind their rise to wealth and power has remained largely untold. This is due almost entirely to the personality of Harry Hatch. He shunned publicity, seldom granted interviews, and never allowed questions about his personal life. He was equally averse to being photographed. On the five occasions one of his horses won the King's Plate, Harry Hatch declined to go to the winner's circle, frustrating attempts by newsmen to photograph him or to ask him questions. Paradoxically, he did things that drew the public's attention, then, having done so, he declined to be interviewed or to comment. Harry Hatch, one of Canada's richest and most prominent citizens, remained an enigma to the public.

His brother Herb was more open and gregarious, but Harry managed to keep him out of the public eye. He did not want Herb talking about their rise to wealth during Prohibition when they had done business with bootleggers and rumrunners.

On their way to the top, Harry and Herb Hatch had known and dealt with all manner of unsavoury individuals: men like Ben Kerr, the lean, taciturn rum-runner from Hamilton; the violent Staud brothers from Rochester; and Rocco Perri, the self-proclaimed King of the Bootleggers, as well as a host of other characters of dubious backgrounds and pursuits.

7

FROM BAR ROOM
TO BOARD ROOM

Harry C. Hatch...only recently was listed among
Canada's wealthiest citizens...His career and his
rapid rise to wealth are full of romance.

The Globe
December 5, 1928

Few dynasties have had less auspicious beginnings than the
liquor empire of Hiram Walker-Gooderham and Worts.
With sales revenue exceeding a billion and a half dollars
annually, it is currently one of the largest distilling companies in the world. The two founding brothers of this multina-
tional empire, Herb and Harry Hatch, began their careers in
the liquor trade bartending at hotels in the heart of the Tyen-
denega Indian Reserve, east of Belleville.[1]

Their father, Bill Hatch, had been in the hotel and saloon
business most of his life. For many years the family lived in
rural Prince Edward County, where Herb was born in 1882
and Harry two years later. In the early 1890s, Bill Hatch
moved his young family to Deseronto, a thriving lumber and
factory town of 3,200 people. Not only was there more
money to be made in Deseronto, but Herb and Harry could

also get a better education there. They had started their schooling in the tiny hamlet of Roblin Mills, where the single-room school went only as far as senior fourth (equivalent to grade eight). At Deseronto, there was a continuation school, which enabled the brighter students to complete senior fifth (grade ten). In a province where less than five per cent had any high-school education, this was a distinct advantage.

In 1898, his formal education completed, Herb went to work at the Deseronto Iron Works. This began an education of a different sort. At the turn of the century, foundry workers, who toiled sixty to seventy hours a week in searing heat and deafening clatter, did not talk to one another in the soft, modulated tones of English country gentlemen. They were more likely to communicate in shouted obscenities. Herb Hatch spent five years in this atmosphere, acquiring in the process a notably blasphemous vocabulary. Once angered and in full flight, Herb could redden the ears of a stevedore. It was an ability he shared with Sam Bronfman, the mercurial boss of Seagrams. Their successes did not moderate either man's vocabulary or temper.

Later, on one trip to Calgary, Herb needed to cash a cheque for $10,000 but discovered he was not carrying any identification. The local bank manager had never met Herb Hatch and, quite naturally, was unwilling to cash his cheque. Herb exploded. His ears ringing from the tirade, the unfortunate banker retreated to his office and hurriedly telephoned his superior in Toronto. The Toronto executive asked for a description. "He's the most foul-mouthed man I have ever heard. He's called me every four-letter name in the book." No further identification was needed. "That's him," was the superior's response. "Give him all the money he wants."[2]

Harry Clifford Hatch was quieter and less explosive than Herb. More urbane and sophisticated, he avoided the verbal excesses that were Herb's trade mark, confining his use of expletives to those occasions when they were most effective in helping him achieve his ends.

The two men began their apprenticeship in the liquor business as bartenders; first at the Oriental Hotel in the town of Deseronto where they worked for their father. In 1904, Bill Hatch decided to join the thousands of optimists migrating to Canada's raw, unsettled West. The two sons remained behind to take care of their mother, obtaining bartending jobs at the Shannonville Hotel on the Tyendinaga Indian Reserve. Before this establishment burned down in the 1970s, it was known primarily for its brawls and 400-pound female strippers.

Eventually, the two brothers and their mother joined Bill in Indian Head, Saskatchewan, where he had purchased a farm and a hotel. Herb Hatch took on the responsibility of running the farm, while Harry joined his father in coping with the boisterous sodbusters who stormed into the saloon after weeks, sometimes months, of parched isolation on prairie farms.[3]

Harry Hatch had served his apprenticeship in the dingy, smoke-filled, and frequently violent atmosphere of the small-town Canadian hotel. Naturally tough and aggressive, even Harry must have been daunted by the maleficent prairie saloon. Its most conspicuous features were stench and filth. The floors were unplanked, consisting of sawdust and hard-packed prairie soil, odiferously seasoned with tobacco juice, cigar butts, stale beer, and the manure tracked in on the boots of customers. Alcohol was frequently the only amenity in such institutions and it was usually quaffed in quantities that quickly rendered the customers either senseless or highly belligerent.

The Hatch family appears to have prospered modestly in Saskatchewan, but they must have missed the relative comforts of Ontario. In 1908 Bill Hatch sold out and moved to Oshawa, where he leased the Oshawa House at the corner of King and Centre streets. Here Herb and Harry tended bar. In the little leisure time he had available, Harry played amateur hockey, aggressively. It was in Oshawa that Harry met and married Elizabeth Carr and decided, at the age of twenty-seven, to strike out on his own. He and his bride moved to Whitby where Harry opened a package liquor store on Dundas Street in 1911. It was hard scratching for the young couple. On his first day of business, Harry Hatch took in a paltry $8.40.[4] But he had taken the first step on the path that would lead him to the very top of the whisky distilling business.

As a result of Harry's shrewdness and sales ability, the Whitby venture prospered and, after just two years, Hatch sold out and relocated in Toronto. At this point Herb decided to join his younger brother and they formed their first partnership, opening a package liquor store at 433 Yonge Street. Harry then negotiated the right to handle Watson's Scotch whisky. He also made contacts with Scottish distillers, one of whom, Duncan MacLeod, was the owner of Bullock Lade Scotch. MacLeod would later play an important role in helping the Hatch brothers raise the money to purchase their first distillery.[5]

As well as managing his liquor-store operations, Harry also travelled old Highway 2 between Toronto and Montreal as a "drummer" or travelling salesman. At this he was a master. The sheer force of his personality usually won the sale, and Harry loved to win. Like most good competitors, he was a shrewd judge of his opponent's weakness and he combined this talent with intelligence and considerable ingenuity. He kept a large hypodermic syringe in his sample case. If a customer preferred a deep amber colour to his whisky, Harry would simply inject the requisite amount of caramel colouring through the cork into the sample bottle and, *voilà*, present the customer with his favourite whisky.[6] He carried a complete range of colouring chemicals in his sample case and seldom lost a sale.

Hatch could also turn an apparent set-back to his advantage. In 1916, when the passage of the Ontario Temperance Act closed down the saloons and package liquor stores,

Harry and Herb were suddenly put out of business. Sensing where the money could be made, Harry immediately relocated to Montreal, where he and Herb went into the mail-order business. As the Bronfman brothers had done, Hatch had shrewdly anticipated the enormous profits to be made by selling booze through the mails to residents of Ontario. The Hatch brothers had already built up a large clientele in Toronto and the new venture was an immediate success. This enterprise was interrupted in 1918 when the federal government decided to shut down the liquor distilleries for the duration of the war. Herb and Harry returned to Toronto where they were briefly in the retail tire business. When Ottawa lifted its ban on the manufacture of alcohol, Herb and Harry returned to Montreal and re-entered the mail-order liquor trade.

Herb threw in with Larry McGuiness, a handsome, black-haired Irish-Canadian, with whom he formed Hatch and McGuiness. Harry went into partnership with Pud Woods, forming Woods Ltd. Pud Woods had connections. He was the son-in-law of Abe Orpen, a big-time Toronto bookie, gambler, and owner of a number of race tracks, including Kenilworth Park in Windsor, Dufferin Park in Toronto, and later the Hillcrest, Long Branch, and London race tracks.

Both outfits purchased liquor from various Canadian distilleries, stored it in warehouses, and then sold it through the mails to Ontario buyers, just as had been done before the wartime interruption. They also combed the illegal liquor market to the south, soliciting orders from American bootleggers. Harry Hatch's sales success brought him to the attention of the Montreal tycoon Sir Mortimer Davis, founder of the Imperial Tobacco Company. Sir Mortimer was also the president and owner of the Canadian Industrial Alcohol Company, which owned and operated both the Corby and Wiser distilleries.

In 1920, passage of the Volstead Act had eliminated the legal

American market for Canadian distillers. The smuggling of Canadian whisky across the border to American bootleggers had begun almost immediately, but some of the big distilleries, especially Corby's, were slow to get involved. As a consequence, sales at Corby's had plummeted. This placed Sir Mortimer Davis in a quandary. He was a member of several of Montreal's most exclusive clubs and had been honoured with a knighthood by King George v for his philanthropic contributions during the war. His social status would certainly suffer if he involved himself in business dealings with whisky smugglers and bootleggers. Still, he could hardly ignore the slumping fortunes of Corby's, made all the worse by the shutting down of the mail-order booze business in Ontario in 1921.

Both Woods Ltd. and the firm of Hatch and McGuiness had begun selling to American bootleggers at the very beginning of Prohibition. When he heard of the passage of the Volstead Act, Harry Hatch is reported to have said, "Herb, that Volstead Act will make us millionaires." Herb inquired how it would do that, and Harry explained, "Well, you know we got it. They ain't got it."[7]

Anxious to revive his flagging liquor sales, Sir Mortimer hired Harry Hatch as his sales manager. As part of the deal, Herb Hatch and Larry McGuiness were to continue their sales efforts in the United States but, henceforward, would channel their orders through Harry. The Canadian Industrial Alcohol Company would pay the firm of Hatch and McGuiness a dollar for every case of whisky they sold. What bonus system Sir Mortimer offered to his new sales manager is not known, but he did promise shares in his company to both Herb and Harry.[8]

In 1921, when Harry joined the Canadian Industrial Alcohol Company, sales at its Corbyville operation were down to 500 gallons a month. Within two years, Hatch had increased sales to 50,000 gallons a month. The *Toronto Star* noted that

Hatch had achieved this thousand-fold increase by finding "a market for the output in foreign countries."[9] Put less euphemistically, the *Star* was saying that the remarkable increase was due to Hatch's ability to sell Corby's whisky to American bootleggers on a grand scale. To do this he had to organize a system that would guarantee delivery to his American buyers. The Bronfman brothers had solved their delivery problem by selling to American bootleggers, who sent fleets of cars across the long, undefended Prairie border to the plant in Yorkton, Saskatchewan. With the rear seats stripped out, each car could carry from twenty to sixty cases. This method worked fine on the Prairies, but wasn't suitable for Ontario. The Canadian Industrial Alcohol Company's two plants were located on waterways, Corby's on the Bay of Quinte and Wiser's at Prescott on the St. Lawrence River. Clearly, boats would be needed. A few boat owners had seized the opportunity and were already buying loads of booze and hauling them across the lake. Claude "King" Cole of Main Duck Island was one of these independents. But the Hatch brothers needed to organize smuggling on a scale large enough to ensure delivery of the immense production of the Corby plant. They decided to visit a relative, Big Maudie Hatch of Whitby.

Big Maudie had made his money in manufacturing but loved the company of fishermen, and over the years he had loaned money to scores of them, taking mortgages on their fishing boats as security. Their plan was simple. Buy Big Maudie's mortgages, most of which were in default, and then recruit the fishermen to run the booze across the lake. Big Maudie reluctantly agreed. These open fish boats were the genesis of what would come to be known as "Hatch's Navy."[10]

Word spread quickly throughout the American bootlegging fraternity that Hatch could deliver the goods, and in large quantities. Their emissaries began appearing at Corby's offices in Montreal. They came with briefcases stuffed with cash, prepared to do business. Once the money had been deposited with Corby's, they could forward their orders from the U.S. to Montreal where Hatch would approve it. A clerk would then send it on to the plant in Corbyville to be filled. Most of the orders were for 100 to 200 cases. These would be sent by CNR freight to Whitby, or some other port, where they would be picked up by a "common carrier" – a rum-runner operating a boat, often just a converted fishing craft.

The necessary government forms would be completed by the customs officers in Belleville and would accompany the shipment. The excise permit would show whether duty had been paid, and customs form B-13 would list the goods, their value, their destination – usually Cuba or Mexico – and the name of the boat. The captain of the vessel signed the form, but no oath was required and no penalties were specified for false information. The 1927 Royal Commission on Customs and Excise would later conclude that most of the names given for the boats were false. This didn't bother the customs officers, who generally displayed considerable enthusiasm at furthering Canada's liquor exports. The outside inspector had the key job of seeing that the whisky was actually loaded onto the boat and that it sailed out of the harbour, ostensibly for a foreign port. As the customs inquiry would show, the outside inspector was frequently on the payroll of the liquor exporters.

Herb Hatch set about augmenting his navy by recruiting the independent rum-runners. These sturdy entrepreneurs were particularly numerous at the eastern end of Lake Ontario, where organized crime had never bothered to move in and take control, preferring instead to concentrate its violent efforts in Detroit and other large metropolitan centres. The man hired to recruit the independent operators was J. Earl McQueen. Originally from Amherstburg, near Windsor, Earl McQueen and his pretty Scottish bride, Patricia, had settled in England after the war. It is probable that Herb

Hatch, who was frequently at the Corby plant, heard of Earl McQueen through Earl's father, Captain John S. McQueen, who ran large loads of Corby whisky to the States in his steamboat, the *City of Dresden*.

In order to persuade McQueen to join them, Larry McGuiness was dispatched across the Atlantic.[11] The hearty Irishman succeeded in his mission and, in 1921, Earl moved back to Canada. He and his wife, Pat, rented rooms at the New Queen's Hotel in Belleville, not far from the waterfront. Later biographies were very specific about Earl McQueen's distinguished war record and business achievements, but vague about his activities in Belleville. That period was dismissed simply as "when he was associated with Corby distilleries." Earl himself was more candid and jokingly recalled that his job was "sales manager in charge of exports."[12] Later he purchased Black's Cold Storage on South Front Street, converting it into Black's Wholesale Fish Dealers and Boat Houses. As a fish buyer, McQueen was in an ideal position to meet the commercial fishermen in the area and to recruit them into "Hatch's Navy."

The job of recruiting and organizing the rum-running fleet on the eastern end of Lake Ontario required a special blend of qualities. He was a competent, well-organized businessman, yet the fishermen recognized Earl McQueen as one of their own. At thirteen he had gone to sea with his father, and by 1915, when he joined the Canadian Army, he was not only an experienced Great Lakes sailor but a mechanical engineer as well. From the army he transferred to the British Royal Navy, where he rose to the rank of Lieutenant Commander, a considerable achievement considering the negative attitudes of the British towards colonials. During his four-year naval service, he mastered the techniques of undersea diving and ocean salvage. At the Battle of Zeebrugge off the Belgian coast, McQueen was in command of a rescue ship and distinguished himself for coolness and competence under enemy fire.[13]

McQueen recruited many of his rum-runners from among the 400 commercial fishermen who operated between Bowmanville and Main Duck Island.[14] These men appreciated Earl McQueen's competence as a sailor and his record during the war; they also enjoyed his company. Earl, or "Cap" as everyone called him, was all business during working hours but spent the evenings with his buddies and his ever-present mutt, Toby.[15] His vivacious wife, Patricia, would frequently join this otherwise all-male fraternity. "Beanie," as Earl called her, was a gracious hostess who could frequently match her husband's abilities as a raconteur. At these gatherings the McQueens were lively and generous hosts. While spinning tales of his adventures on the Great Lakes or the Atlantic Ocean, Earl could put away a quart of rye with little apparent affect, a feat silently noted and approved in the macho world of his fishermen friends.[16] Earl's stature with these tough, hardworking men was further enhanced by his willingness to run the same risks they did. For several years, he took loads of Corby's whisky across Lake Ontario in his forty-foot powerboat, the *Ullacalula*.[17]

Fishermen were not the only men recruited by McQueen. In any port town there was always a quota of "wharf rats," men who hung out around the docks and who knew boats. There were also more substantial business types, entrepreneurs who had the cash to buy a boat or two and hire the wharf rats to drive them. Belleville had both types in abundance as did Kingston, Port Dalhousie, and Port Colborne. During those early years the runners ran few risks and the money was good. A few, notably Ben Kerr, salted their earnings away in anticipation of leaner times. They were the exception. Most would play out their personal version of the roaring twenties by blowing their money on big cars, small hip-flasks, fast women, and slow horses. Archie Goyer, the Belleville barber and rum-runner, usually carried a couple of thousand in his pockets and liked to bet the whole works on a single horse. He always bet his nags to win and, to his impoverishment, they seldom did better than place or show.[18] Damon Runyon would have approved.

Herb Hatch and Larry McGuiness made additional arrangements with a number of men who would later achieve notoriety for their rum-running activities. In Port Colborne they hired Amos "Nick" Vandeveer, a bespectacled commercial fisherman who seems to have carried out much the same role at the eastern end of Lake Erie as McQueen did on Lake Ontario. Nick owned several boats, all engaged in rum-running, and was instrumental in convincing his father, Aaron, and several relatives to join him. He also recruited Bill Shepherd and Shaddy Anderson – Port Colborne residents who smuggled booze on a smaller scale than did the Vandeveers.[19]

The arrangements made with these men varied greatly. Some of the rum-runners remained independent and carried loads for a number of distilleries and breweries. In some cases Hatch and McGuiness owned the boats outright and simply hired men to drive them. Larry McGuiness stated that, at one point, they owned forty-two boats, some of these on the Great Lakes, others on the Atlantic seaboard, and a few on the Pacific.[20]

Hatch's Navy was so successful that Sir Mortimer Davis began planning a major expansion of the Corby plant. He also prepared to go public with an issue of shares in Canadian Industrial Alcohol. The proceeds from the sale of shares would be used to pay for Corby's plant expansion and to retire long-term bank indebtedness. About this time Harry Hatch approached Sir Mortimer reminding him of his promise to give him and Herb shares in the company. Sir Mortimer is said to have replied, "You must have misunderstood me. I had no such intention."[21] As far as the Hatch brothers were concerned, Sir Mortimer Davis, member of the Mount Royal Club, the St. James Club, the Montreal Hunt Club, the Montreal Jockey Club, and Knight to His Majesty King George V, was a two-bit welcher.

Harry Hatch continued in his position of sales manager

but resolved to buy his own distillery. He had two options. Either start up his own, as the Bronfmans were about to do in Montreal, or buy an existing unprofitable one. He chose the latter course, probably because he and Herb lacked the money to build one from scratch.

Hatch turned his attention to the prestigious but inactive Gooderham and Worts distillery. Located on sixteen acres near the downtown, the old, white stone building is still a Toronto landmark. The distillery had been idle for eight years, its equipment increasingly antiquated, its stock of aged whisky totally depleted. Hatch reasoned that the Gooderhams would be anxious to sell, particularly as there was still a $500,000 mortgage on the property on which payments had to be made.

The Gooderham family were prominent members of Upper Canada's unofficial aristocracy. Their roots in Canada went back to 1832, when their grandfather had migrated from England to York, as Toronto was then known. When he arrived, the Gooderham patriarch promptly made the largest deposit to date by an immigrant in a Toronto bank. Within two years he had become Toronto's largest taxpayer. Thereafter, the Gooderham family never lowered its eyebrows.

Late in 1923, Harry Hatch decided to make an offer to the two brothers who controlled Gooderhams. Sir Albert and William George were both on the board of directors of the Bank of Toronto, but William George held the real power. He was president of both the Bank of Toronto and Gooderham and Worts Ltd. Moreover, as the elder brother, he was the acknowledged patriarch of the clan and controller of the family fortune. As befitted a leader of the colonial aristocracy, William Gooderham was an avid sportsman, a philanthropist, and an unyielding British imperialist. In 1916, he and his brother had stopped producing alcohol as a gesture of support for the war effort. Later they had used the distillery's equipment to produce acetone for the military, but had insisted they receive no profit from doing so. William

Gooderham was not an easy man to approach. A contemporary writer noted that "he was reserved...and peremptory in dealing with presumption."[22] Harry Hatch, the former bartender, wisely chose not to approach the great man directly. Instead, he made his offer through William's son, Eddie, a contemporary of the Hatch brothers, who shared their love of yachting. Initially, the elder Gooderham coldly rejected the Hatch offer, believing Harry was merely fronting for his employer, Sir Mortimer Davis. In his eyes, Sir Mortimer, as a Jew and as a Montrealer, was beyond the pale.

William Gooderham's intransigence evaporated once Harry Hatch convinced him that the future Gooderham and Worts would be in direct competition with Sir Mortimer. To assist the young entrepreneurs in this worthy endeavour, Gooderham even arranged for the Bank of Toronto to loan Hatch part of the money used to buy the Gooderham and Worts distillery.

On December 22, 1923, Harry Hatch and William Gooderham signed a deal. Under the agreement, Hatch would get the distillery, the land, the equipment, and most important, the trade mark and the use of the name Gooderham and Worts. For these assets, Hatch agreed to pay $1,500,000, of which $500,000 would be covered by the new company assuming a mortgage on the property. Of the $1 million that remained to be paid, $250,000 was put up by the Hatch brothers from their own personal funds. Further money was raised by selling shares to a group of Toronto investors headed by William H. Mara, president of a Toronto brokerage firm. Eddie Gooderham took out shares in the new company instead of cash, and Duncan MacLeod of the Bullock Lade distillery in Scotland bought a large block of shares. The Bank of Toronto financed the balance.[23]

The new company, Gooderham and Worts Ltd., did not offer shares to the general public and so was not required to make public its financial dealings. As part of the package arranged by Hatch, Duncan MacLeod, Eddie Gooderham, and William Mara all assumed seats on the board of directors and Harry Hatch took the positions of president and chairman.

By purchasing the assets of Gooderham and Worts, Harry Hatch demonstrated what modern management calls good marketing sense. The antiquated distilling and bottling equipment was at best a dubious asset, but the old and respected name of Gooderham and Worts was the ticket to penetrating markets thirsting for good Canadian whisky.

Gooderham and Worts is a very old firm; the original incorporation took place in 1845. Perhaps because the aging of whisky improves its quality, whisky drinkers appear to equate the age of a distillery company with the quality of its product. This is why whisky manufacturers display their firms' founding date so prominently on their products, often stretching the truth a bit in the process. There is a rule here: the older the company, the more conspicuous the founding date. A bottle of Gooderham and Worts Bonded Stock has a large red seal printed on its label with the year "1832" boldly imprinted over the seal. It would seem that Gooderham and Worts was founded in 1832. Not so: 1832 was the year they went into the grist-mill business and incorporated the earlier firm Worts and Gooderham. In the whisky business, clearly, older is better.

Hatch knew this. He also knew that Americans, drinkers of bourbon whisky, were less able than Canadians to distinguish between good rye whisky, which is aged and mellow, from the cheap variety, which is young and raw. This was important because Gooderham and Worts had not a single drop of aged whisky and, when Hatch tried to purchase aged spirits to make a good blended whisky, he found no one willing to sell.[24] American prohibition had created such a demand for Canadian booze there was no surplus available. Canadian distillers needed every drop of aged spirits they could get their hands on and were still unable to keep up with the burgeoning demands of their neighbours to the south. In fact, there was such a shortage, it became common practice for American bootleggers to "cut" Canadian whisky by adding alcohol and water. One gallon of Canadian whisky would yield anywhere from two to four gallons of saleable booze, with a commensurate increase in profits.

Hatch's inability to find anyone willing to sell him aged whisky created a serious problem for Gooderham and Worts. Under Canadian law, whisky had to be aged two years before it could be sold. In the meantime, Gooderham and Worts had to make payments on its loans, pay its employees, purchase raw materials, and meet the multitude of costs involved in a manufacturing enterprise. Ironically, the money to do this came, at least in part, from the president of the Canadian Industrial Alcohol Company.

Sir Mortimer Davis had been quite annoyed with Harry Hatch when he quit. First, because Hatch took Jack Crump with him. Crump was Corby's master blender, and as neither Herb nor Harry knew much about making whisky – their specialty was selling it – they needed Crump to set up production. Second, because Harry was going into competition against the Corby and Wiser distilleries. But the third and most important reason for his anger was that Harry had the contacts with the American bootleggers and Herb the control of the rum fleet, both of which were necessary to maintain sales and profits at Canadian Industrial Alcohol. When Harry Hatch left as sales manager, Sir Mortimer had to build a new network of buyers. In the meantime he had little choice but to continue to fill the orders coming in from Hatch and McGuiness and to pay their commission of $1 a case.[25] The plant at Corbyville was producing 50,000 gallons a month, about 17,000 cases. The commission on the sale of this whisky was augmented by the additional $2 to $3 charged the American buyers on every case delivered by the Hatch rum-running fleet.

These monies to Hatch and McGuiness were used to finance production at the old Gooderham and Worts distillery. Harry Hatch's next problem was selling the whisky without waiting the required two years. Sir Mortimer Davis was already moving to sell Corby's production to large coastal rum-runners, operating from the islands of St-Pierre-Miquelon, intending, no doubt, to cut off sales made through Hatch as soon as the coastal operators could move all of Corby's production. Before this happened, Hatch had to find a way around the federal government's two-year aging requirement or face bankruptcy.

With his usual directness, Harry Hatch went to Ottawa, where he held meetings with assistant deputy minister Taylor and with the minister of customs, Jacques Bureau. Hatch wanted the ministry to exempt Gooderham and Worts from the requirement that Canadian whisky be aged a minimum of two years. Hatch argued that the government had granted a similar dispensation to all Canadian distillers in 1920 when they had gone back into production following the conclusion of the war. Gooderham and Worts had not reopened after the war and therefore, Hatch argued, they should now be granted the exemption the other distilleries had earlier enjoyed. It is possible that Hatch took with him a large sum of money to be handed over to a Liberal Party bag man, as this was a common practice, attested to by former auditor general Maxwell Henderson, who was employed first by Hatch and later by his arch rival, Sam Bronfman of Seagrams. Henderson states that both Liberals and Conservatives expected heavy contributions from the distilling companies, and that it usually benefitted the distilleries to pay up.[26]

On April 1, 1924, Jacques Bureau was able to advise Hatch that the government, by order-in-council, had granted his distillery an exemption, good until December 31, 1924. Gooderham and Worts, a highly respected name in whisky circles for more than three-quarters of a century, could now distil bourbon or rye whisky on a Monday and export it on a Tuesday.[27] With that problem solved, Hatch turned his attention to improving and enlarging the distillery in order to cope with the flood of orders from both Canadian and American bootleggers.

Herb Hatch and Larry McGuiness were dispatched to Niagara Falls, New York, to set up an office under the name Hatch and McGuiness that would act as a sales agency in forwarding orders on to the plant. Rocco Perri and Bessie Starkman were among the many bootleggers who were soon phoning in large orders to Gooderham and Worts.[28]

Why American and Canadian drinkers would pay bootleggers sky-high prices for whisky and bourbon of such youthful vintage can only be explained in terms of the available alternatives. In Ontario, the alternatives consisted of native wine, a 2.5 per cent near-beer, and, especially in smaller centres, the liquor supplied by portable-still operators. This latter product, known as moonshine or, more tellingly, swamp-whisky, varied greatly in quality, depending upon the skill and experience of the still operator. This homebrew was not aged; the furtive distillers, constantly in danger of being raided by the police, sold the product as soon as it had cooled sufficiently to be bottled. There was no lack of buyers for swamp-whisky and the bootlegger's price reflected this.

The near-beer, on the other hand, was safe, consistent in taste but, unhappily for the consumer, nonintoxicating. Drinkers complained you could imbibe a barrel of the stuff with no effect. Consequently, when the underground telegraph flashed the message that a certain hotel would be serving stronger stuff – which, of course, was illegal – the customers lined up eagerly at the bar quaffing all the "good stuff" they could until the proprietor, noting their growing state of inebriation, shut off the supply. Their frantic tippling over, the customers returned reluctantly to sipping their near-beer and to passing opinions on the quality of the real suds they had so quickly consumed.[29]

Before World War II, native wines were derived solely

from the hardy *labrusca* grape, which differs sharply in taste from the *viniferas* of Europe. Best suited to ports and sherries, the *labrusca* leaves a foxy aftertaste as table wine. Still, if he persevered, a serious wine drinker, who anesthetized his taste buds, could reach the desired state of insensibility. Some of these wines had an alcohol content as high as 28 per cent. The major barrier to their widespread consumption was the Ontario government's regulation allowing each winery just one retail outlet for the entire province. This effectively restricted wine sales to Toronto, the Niagara Peninsula, and London. There were no wineries east of Toronto until late 1926. In October that year, a group of Toronto businessmen opened the Belleville Wine Company, intending to capture the eastern Ontario market. The ending of Prohibition in 1927 resulted in government liquor stores being set up throughout the province. This ended the Belleville Wine Company's geographic advantage in supplying eastern Ontario and it quickly went bankrupt.

In the United States, Prohibition was more severe. No beverage with an alcoholic content greater than 0.5 per cent could be sold other than by medical prescription. Distilleries were not allowed to produce for export and consequently, most legitimate U.S. distilleries had closed down altogether. As a result, Americans were largely dependent on Canada for their supply of properly distilled spirits. As Canadian distillers were initially unable to supply the demand, the underworld had moved quickly to fill the vacuum. Not surprisingly, their methods of manufacture paid little heed to sanitation. All too often the product they unleashed on an unsuspecting American public was poisonous. In Chicago, for example, the Genna brothers, who controlled the south side, operated the biggest bootleg plant in the city. Ostensibly their company was licensed to handle industrial alcohol, which they purchased legitimately from federal sources. Token amounts were sold to legitimate industrial users but the bulk was redistilled, coloured, and flavoured to imitate bourbon, whisky, rum, or whatever liquor the market required.

Ethyl alcohol is rendered unfit for human consumption by the addition of certain toxic chemicals, chiefly wood (methyl) alcohol, and as such is then sold for industrial use. Unfortunately for their customers, the Gennas' grasp of chemistry was somewhat less than adequate. Although their redistilling process removed much of the wood alcohol, enough remained to render their whisky lethal; consumed immoderately, it contained sufficient poison to cause blindness and even death. Attempts to improve the flavour and colour of their product added still further to its health hazards. Fusel oil, which contains toxic amyl alcohol, was added for flavour and coal-tar dyes for colour. Only the sturdiest of constitutions could survive frequent exposure to such noxious libations.

Bath-tub gin, moonshine, swamp-whisky, needled beer, all were used to slake the nation's thirst. Needle beer was the safest of these concoctions. It was made by adding raw alcohol to the near-beer allowed by law. Problems sometimes arose when the raw alcohol had not been properly denatured and contained quantities of wood alcohol. Organized crime had little or no concern for sanitation – dead rats were found in every one of a hundred barrels of mash confiscated by one Chicago policeman. Deaths from alcohol poisonings in the U.S.A. shot up from 1,064 in 1920 to 4,154 in 1925. Little wonder Canadian whisky, no matter how raw, commanded premium prices.

Viewed from this perspective, the efforts of Harry Hatch can be seen as truly humanitarian. By reopening and expanding Gooderham and Worts, he was indirectly providing well-paying jobs for fishermen in the export liquor trade and, more important, providing American drinkers with a safe alternative to the noxious concoctions of the U.S. underworld. It seemed he also laboured to save Ontario drinkers from the evils of swamp-whisky. Early in 1924, Toronto police arrested a man by the name of Richards in whose car was found fifteen cases of Gooderham and Worts whisky. Richards admitted the invoices he carried made out to customers in Niagara Falls, New York, were fraudulent; the people did not exist. The Crown argued that the whisky was paid for in Canadian money by a Toronto syndicate who intended to distribute it locally. The liquor was confiscated and Gooderham and Worts fined $1,000.[30]

Fines of this magnitude came to be regarded as part of the cost of doing business. Grant Springs Brewery of Hamilton, for example, was fined six times for various breaches of the OTA between April 1922 and January 1923. The fines totalled $2,700, but did not effect any change in the company's policy.

It was during these years that the Canadian distilling industry, prodded by the impetus of American Prohibition, embarked on a large-scale expansion. In 1924, the same year that the Bronfmans began construction of their new distillery at Ville LaSalle and Harry Hatch reopened Gooderham and Worts, the Canadian Industrial Alcohol Company began construction of a new facility at Corbyville capable of producing 10,000 gallons a day, making it one of the largest distilleries in the world.[31]

Fortunately for the Canadian distilling industry, the profits more than justified this enormous expansion. In the summer of 1926, Harry Hatch, who loathed publicity, agreed to an interview with the *Financial Post* after which the paper reported, "It is learned on good authority that the company's earnings...are running...at the rate of $1,440,000 a year."[32] Considering that Hatch had paid just $1,500,000 for Gooderham and Worts, his gamble in purchasing the long-closed facility had paid off handsomely. Financial analysts began referring to Harry Hatch as the man who put the dividends into alcohol.[33]

In November 1925, the directors of Gooderham and Worts voted to make available to the investing public 20,000 shares at $100 each. This would raise $2 million for the company to be used to expand and modernize its distillery and help the Hatch brothers keep up with their booming American export business. No financial information was released, which served merely to heighten public interest and fuel demand for the shares. The day they came on the market, the shares traded at a $20 premium.[34]

The price of Gooderham and Worts shares kept rising, perhaps because the investment community was starting to believe that Harry Hatch had the Midas touch. His reluctance to divulge information about Gooderham and Worts's profits stirred the rumour mills to exaggerated guesses, which in turn drove the price of shares to inflated heights. Less than a month after the stock began trading, the *Financial Post* was complaining that "Nothing whatever is known of Gooderham and Worts's financial position. Rumours of large profits and split-ups lack official confirmation. Belief in the industry is that insiders are trading in stock, but even this is not known for certain. The shares are closely held and whatever game is being played is within an inner circle."[35]

In a circumspect and cautious manner, the *Financial Post* was warning its more perceptive readers to stay away from Gooderham and Worts stock. The use of the word "game" strongly implied they believed the price of the stock was being manipulated to the advantage of the insiders, who controlled a large percentage of the total shares. When stock is closely held – meaning a large amount is owned by a few people – it is easy for the holders to drive the price of shares up artificially by buying and selling among themselves. The unwary public sees the price going up day by day and is drawn in to buy shares at an artificially inflated price. Whether Gooderham and Worts insiders were manipulating stock value is not definitely known, but someone at the *Financial Post* was suspicious. At the time the article was written, the stock had risen to $192, an increase of $72 in just thirty days.

The latter half of the 1920s saw the stock market climb to dizzying heights with stock prices bearing little relation to their real earning power. Playing the market became a national pastime involving people in ordinary jobs with modest incomes as well as the rich and famous. In such a climate, reason gave way to enthusiasm, caution to reckless optimism. It was an ideal atmosphere for shrewd, hard-nosed Harry Hatch, who could orchestrate the market for his company's stock like a maestro. Just one year after its issue at $100 a share, the stock was trading at $350; a phenomenal increase even for those heady days. (The stock was actually trading at $35 a share by mid-October 1926, but as Gooderham and Worts had earlier split the stock at ten for one, one share of the original $100 issue was worth $350.)[36] Fortunately for the investors, the company was making excellent profits, which were wisely being ploughed back into modern equipment, enabling the company to further increase its production and its earnings.

Harry Clifford Hatch was not just another quick-buck artist; he was planning for the long term. Already, he was preparing for his next move; one that would make him president of the largest distilling empire in Canada, and one of the largest whisky manufacturers in the entire world. Nor were the Hatches the only ones to profit from the booze business. These were halcyon days for the whole industry – the legal and illegal parts of it alike.

8

EASY MONEY DAYS

Farmers on the shore make more money selling unloading privileges than working the soil. About the only way to obtain information is through quarrels among the bootleggers. It seems that nearly everyone will aid the bootleggers. Of course they are well paid in coin and liquor. Even officers of the law will aid them.

> Commander E. Jackson,
> Oswego Coast Guard Station,
> January 12, 1925.

When he wrote the above passage in a letter to his superintendent, George Jackson had good reason to complain. For five years he and his fellow officers had been trying to stem the flow of booze into the Oswego area with nothing more than a few surfboats and one motor lifeboat. All along the lakes the story was the same; not one of the sixteen coast guard stations of the Ninth District had boats or equipment capable of stopping the whisky and ale smugglers from Canada.[1] Nor had a long and honourable tradition of saving lives and property prepared the coast guard for the radically different task of stopping the deluge of smuggling, which had begun within weeks of the passage of the Volstead Act.

The coast guard's inability to deal with smuggling on the Great Lakes was just one of a number of factors that made the first five years of American Prohibition so easy for the rum-runners. Public opinion also favoured the smugglers, particularly in New York State, where Al Smith presided as governor for most of the decade. Smith was openly opposed to Prohibition and in 1923 signed into law a bill repealing the Mullen-Gage Act. This act had been passed to provide practical state enforcement of the Volstead Act. By revoking it, Smith relieved state and local police from any direct responsibility for enforcing Prohibition. This left that onerous and unpopular task to federal agencies, including the coast guard, the customs service, the border patrol, and a new agency set up under the Treasury department with the specific task of enforcing the Volstead Act. Only 200 of these federal agents were allocated to enforce Prohibition throughout the entire state of New York. As they were posted to the larger cities, where their efforts would yield maximum results, the rum-runners could usually avoid them by landing at small towns or along lonely rural beaches. Even when tipped off by rival bootleggers, the federal agents were seldom able to capture the rum-runners. Their equipment consisted primarily of hand-guns and automobiles, adequate for apprehending land-based smugglers but useless against the rum boats. In the cities and towns, where they were a nuisance, the feds could often be bought off. During the first eight years of Prohibition, no less than one-quarter of those hired on as Prohibition agents were subsequently dismissed for larceny. The men recruited into the new service were, in the words of one Treasury man, "a most extraordinary collection of political hacks, hangers on, and passing highwaymen."[2]

By contrast both the customs and border patrol services were staffed by career officers, many of whom had served long and honourably at a difficult job. The border patrol was an arm of the customs service organized solely to prevent violations of the customs laws, including not only the smuggling of alcohol but also of furs, jewels, and narcotics. It was a tall order; barely a hundred officers of all ranks had the task of patrolling the entire length of the Canada-U.S.A. border.

The prevalence of bribery among customs and border patrol officers is a matter of conjecture. Some observers contend that corruption was widespread, others that it was minimal and confined to a few hot spots such as the Detroit-Windsor area. All agreed that it did exist. Considering the hostile attitude in border towns to Prohibition, the low pay of the officers, and the generous bribes offered them by the bootleggers, it was inevitable that many would be on the take. In the early 1920s, a border patrol officer worked a minimum nine-hour day, six days a week, for $1,680 a year, and from this wage he was expected to provide for his own uniform. At that time, the Bureau of Labor Statistics estimated that the minimum salary on which a family could live decently was $2,260 a year.

The profits available to large-scale bootleggers enabled them to offer bribes only a saint could refuse. When a young boatswain commanding a crew of two and a thirty-six-foot picket boat succeeded in capturing a black ship (a term coined by the coast guard to denote rum-running vessels) on Lake Erie, the rum-runners offered Bo'sun Walter Buettner $300 if he would set the three of them free and return their boat. Buettner refused. They kept increasing the offer until Buettner found himself turning down $3,000, an amount much larger than he earned in an entire year. The young officer later admitted, "It did tempt me."[3]

Most officials could be bought off more cheaply. When the deliveries were made on a regular basis, it was common at certain ports to pay the local customs inspector $20 for each load delivered safely. Of course, the whisky exporters and

American buyers tried to keep such payments to the minimum consistent with ensuring safe passage of their goods. Independents such as Ben Kerr and Charlie Mills elected not to pay any graft at all, relying on their ability to outsmart the law. Large-scale operators usually opted to put some officers on the payroll. Given the profits involved, it was cheap insurance.

When everyone played the game the system worked smoothly. One group of whisky smugglers ran loads across Lake Ontario for several years with just one mishap, and it resulted when a smuggler tried cheating the system. The group consisted of a dozen open fish boats and two dozen fishermen led and coordinated by Wes Kaiser.[4] As Kaiser owned and operated a fish-buying and storing business in the village of Consecon in Prince Edward County, he was strategically placed both to make contact with the fishermen and to use his docks as a departure point for trips to the States. During the fair weather months from April through October, Kaiser and his fishing associates would cross the lake an average of six to eight times a month. The number of crossings was limited by the weather as the boats were, on average, only twenty-five feet long. They made fewer and fewer trips in the fall when Lake Ontario gets increasingly stormy and dangerous.

A typical trip would begin with each open fish boat taking on twenty-five to thirty cases of whisky at Wes Kaiser's docks. Each cardboard case had five three-inch diameter holes on the top, sides, and bottom, and contained twelve quart bottles of either William Penn whisky or Old Crow bourbon, each bottle wrapped in excelsior and lead. In the early days of prohibition, Corby's had used wooden cases, which, of course, would float on water. This posed a problem for the rum-runner who, when pursued by a coast guard cutter, usually tried to jettison his cargo. If the cases floated, the coast guard could not only seize them as contraband, they could also use them as evidence to convict the rum-runner. With their holes and lead-wrapped bottles, the cardboard cases frustrated the coast guard by sinking almost immediately. In the easy money days from 1920 to 1924, the wooden cases continued to be used simply because the coast guard, not being equipped to catch rum boats on the Great Lakes, posed no danger.

By late afternoon the fish boats would be loaded up and underway, travelling on a compass heading of 190 degrees, almost due south. Once darkness had set in, the convoy could steer by the lights of Rochester, which would be clearly visible. Travelling at only six or seven knots an hour, it could take the men as long as ten hours to cross the open lake before arriving at the customs dock a few miles west of Rochester.

Joe Large who made his first trip in 1927 at the age of fifteen, remembers being scared the whole time. They were most afraid of storms. These would come slowly, preceded for at least an hour by a gradual increase in the long, slow roll of the lake. This gave the men a chance to lash everything down, don their sou'westers, and if necessary, jettison some cargo – always a last resort.

Most of the fish boats were painted a dull grey, and with their low silhouette, they were almost invisible. Once they had crossed into U.S. waters, the boats doused their running lights. Even on moonlit nights they were invisible beyond a few hundred feet. To further frustrate the coast guard hunters, each ship in the convoy carried an L-shaped exhaust pipe, which was attached to their regular exhaust while in American waters. This device diverted the exhaust under water, effectively muffling the noise of the engine. The fleet now moved in ghostlike silence across the lake. Small wonder the coast guard was never able to intercept the Consecon convoy during a crossing.

Sometime after midnight, when they were about three miles away from the customs dock, the fishermen reduced the speed of their boats to steerageway. One of the boats would then leave the convoy and head for the customs dock. This was the lead boat, chosen earlier, whose captain had the job of making sure that the coast was clear. He would tie up at the customs dock and stroll into the office where, as it was after midnight, only one officer would be on duty. It was the job of this man to know where the coast guard cutter was that night so he could advise the fishermen-smugglers whether it was safe to land. If it was, he would nod to the fishermen, who would then lay a $20 bill on the counter, usually with the comment, "Why don't you get yourself a haircut?" The customs officer pocketed the twenty before switching on the big light on top of the guardhouse. It had a shield all around, except for a small area facing directly out to sea, and so would not be noticed by the townspeople.

Three miles out, the convoy was waiting for that light; it was the signal for them to come in. Also waiting for that signal was the driver of a large truck, parked in the shadows with its engine idling. As the truck rolled down to dockside, the customs officer left; it was time to get his haircut. (The only time the convoy came to grief happened when a lead man tried to pocket $15 for himself by paying the customs officer only $5. The customs man alerted the coast guard cutter and the convoy had to jettison its cargo. One man wasn't fast enough and was caught with some booze still on board. He went to jail.)

Over 3,500 quart bottles of whisky would be transferred from the fish boats to the truck in under an hour. The job completed, the truck, disguised one night as a furniture van and something else the next, rumbled off towards Rochester. Beside the driver in his slouch cap sat a heavily armed guard; his job was to fend off hijackers.

By this time the fishermen's convoy was already back on the lake headed for Consecon. Unloaded, they could make better time and would arrive back in the early morning. At Consecon, an envelope awaited Kaiser and the other skippers, containing $2 for each case of whisky safely delivered. After deducting the cost of his gasoline, the skipper and his mate would each net between $20 and $25 for their long night's work. Between trips, they went back to laying their fish nets.

During the half-dozen years that he made these trips, Joe Large learned that the man leaving the envelopes was Foy Maidens, outside customs inspector for Belleville harbour. In this position, Maidens had to be present to supervise the loading of whisky aboard the export boats and was therefore in constant contact with the rum-runners.

A dapper man, who drove a new model Essex sedan each year while most of his fellow customs officers travelled by bus, Maidens must have acquired a considerable amount of money from his position as contact man for the Consecon smuggling operation. As the man in charge, he probably received a dollar on every case delivered safely to the other side. Testimony at the Royal Commission on Customs and Excise about similar organizations indicated that a dollar a case was a fairly standard commission. The enterprising Maidens also earned profits from his 50 per cent ownership in a rum-running boat.

A successful rum-running operation invariably depended on the collusion of some public officials. For three years, Claude Cole ran large loads of beer and whisky in his cruiser, the *Emily*, all the way up the New York State barge canal to Syracuse. Old-timers who knew Cole state that he paid off certain officials, which is why he was never caught.[5] Cole never said which officials he bribed, but the capture of the rum-runner *Semaj* suggests how it was done.

On the morning of September 24, 1923, customs collector John Pallace of Rochester and his two assistants, while driving parallel to the canal, noticed a tug struggling to free the fifty-eight-foot cruiser *Semaj*, which had gone aground near Battle Island about six miles south of Oswego.[6] Suspicions aroused, Pallace and his men boarded the Canadian vessel and discovered 350 cases of beer. James Monahan from Oswego and three men from Syracuse were arrested. They had no difficulty in posting $4,000 in bail money.

Further investigations revealed the *Semaj* had entered the canal about 1 a.m. and had passed through Oswego locks 8, 7, and 6 without any of the lockmasters investigating the motorboat's cargo. It was also rather curious that the lockmasters had been on duty at such a late hour. Was it dedication to duty, or were other considerations involved? Possibly, the lockmasters were augmenting their state wages by helping to turn the canal into a bootlegger's highway. The furor resulting from the arrests spurred a clamp-down by federal officials. Claude Cole – and many others, no doubt – stopped hauling booze to Syracuse via the canal.

The *Semaj* was one of the very few captures made on the Great Lakes system before 1925, and it was made in a canal, not on the open lake. The first black ship captured on Lake Ontario was a four-masted schooner appropriately named the *Maple Leaf.*[7] During the summer of 1923, the *Maple Leaf* had been engaged in the innocuous tasks of hauling hay to Oswego or making YMCA excursion trips around the Bay of Quinte. If the purpose of these activities was to lull the coast guard and customs officials, they certainly worked. When the little schooner docked at Oswego about 10 p.m. on the evening of November 12, no one took the least notice of her. When he was queried by the press, Oswego coast guard commander George Jackson explained that he had not informed customs of the *Maple Leaf*'s arrival because there was nothing suspicious about the vessel. Had the bootleggers not been so incredibly incompetent, Jackson would never have been asked the question.

Below decks the seventy-foot schooner carried an enormous load, fully 2,000 burlap bags of Canadian beer, each bag containing twenty-four quarts and weighing about seventy pounds. Forty-eight thousand bottles was a lot of beer in one boat.

At least twenty-five men were needed if the cargo was to be unloaded before daybreak. The captain decided to recruit his amateur stevedores from the waterfront's speakeasies and blind-pigs. That was his first mistake. Fortified by an evening's drinking, and knowing the owners needed the ship unloaded before dawn, the roustabouts demanded outrageously high wages. The captain refused and a wage dispute ensued. Finally, well after midnight, a settlement was reached. The men would get $1.50 an hour, roughly four times the going rate. The work finally got underway, albeit somewhat fitfully. The cargo was not so much transferred to the waiting trucks and wagons as it was consumed en route. Residents of the area were awakened by the sound of trucks, horse-drawn wagons, and, above all this din, the roistering shouts and oaths of men who had reached nirvana. After years of paying outrageous prices for inferior booze, the system was now rewarding *them*. Not only were they getting free beer of excellent quality, they were being paid to drink it.

The captain threatened to call the whole mess off and sail back to Canada. Realizing their party might come to a premature end, the men agreed to stop drinking and start working. But they demanded another pay increase. With daylight fast approaching, and time running out, the captain ruefully agreed to $2 an hour. Even so, progress was fitful. When loaded the wagons tended to sink their wheels into the soft soil. Valuable time and manpower was wasted in getting the wagons unstuck and moving.

The sun rose, the city awoke and stirred to its daily business. Men and women on their way to work noted the *Maple Leaf* still at its moorings, the trucks and horse-drawn wagons still clattering down the road loaded with burlap sacks of beer. Incredibly, they were carrying on the operation in broad daylight. Perhaps the laxity of the law in Oswego had led the bootleggers to conclude that they were immune from arrest. But even a corrupt law enforcement department must maintain some self respect. This was going too far.

Hurrying by on his way to work, Customs Inspector C.J. Cusack could not believe his own eyes. For a moment he paused, stunned in disbelief, then recovering, he rushed to the site, shouting at the men to halt the unloading. The elderly Cusack carried no weapons, nor was he physically imposing. He was ignored and the unloading continued. Cusack cajoled and implored them to stop, all to no avail. Finally, he headed for the customs office and a telephone to summon the Oswego police chief, Tom Mowatt. Mowatt could have been there in no more than fifteen minutes, but his orders were to leave violations of the Volstead Act to the feds. This case was slightly different because smuggling, while a violation of prohibition law, was also an indictable criminal offence and, moreover, Mowatt knew that a certain element of public opinion would be clamouring for his hide if he failed to make an appearance. Half an hour later, the Chief arrived. This immediately provoked a mass exodus, the stevedores running off in all directions, clutching what personal supplies they could manage. An enormous bear of a man, Mowatt was not someone to trifle with. Incredibly, he did not recognize any of the miscreants and none were arrested.

For awhile the law looked like it was going to take itself seriously. Federal agents from Syracuse forty miles away showed commendable haste by arriving about noon. Aboard the *Maple Leaf* they seized 168 bags of Canadian ale and a paper indicating the captain had been paid $500 for his services and would receive a further $500 when the job was successfully completed. This was for just one trip, and compares with the $54 a month paid to a coast guard recruit.

A trail of empty beer bottles, wagon tracks, and gossipy neighbours led the Federal agents to the barn of George W. Buskey. Inside, neatly stacked, they found 548 bags of Canadian beer (13,152 quart bottles). Buskey claimed to have no idea how so much beer had gotten into his padlocked barn, and his thespian abilities almost convinced the agents of his innocence. Nevertheless, they arranged for the transfer of the beer to a safer place in town. During the transfer, no one noticed that one of the trucks being loaded had not been hired for the job. The enterprising and, no doubt, elated trucker drove off, his drinking problems solved for some time. The other truckers later complained that, en route to Oswego, residents along the way kept snatching bags of beer from their vehicles.

Once the 548 bags of beer had been removed from Buskey's barn and the agents had departed, the bootleggers returned to the barn and picked up – as rumour has it – an additional 500 bags the agents had failed to find. This cache was immediately trucked to Syracuse, the original destination of the entire load.

Meanwhile, back in Oswego, a few thirsty lads were attempting to break into Sayer's Grocery, where the seized beer had been stored, and were busy kicking in the cellar windows when Constable Hageny arrived in the police patrol car, firing his revolver in the air and calling out "Halt, Police!" The miscreants fled down West First Street into the woods with Hageny in hot, if somewhat winded, pursuit. The law maintained its batting average; the men escaped.

Shortly thereafter, the police, and the other law enforcers on the case began to shed their Keystone Cops image by tracing the trucks used in the original unloading of the *Maple Leaf* to none other than George Buskey. Still protesting his innocence, Buskey was arrested and charged with the unlawful possession of intoxicating beverages. Such a charge meant, at most, a fine of a few hundred dollars. But the farce continued. Two months after his arrest, a federal court dismissed all charges against Buskey. He was the only person ever charged in the imbroglio.

The *Maple Leaf* was later sold at public auction and, if the usual practice was followed, was bought back by its original beer-smuggling owner for a fraction of its real value. The police claimed not to know the identity of the boat's owner, although the $500 receipt found on board named the captain as one Joseph Jessup. A thousand dollars for one trip was a lot of money to pay unless the man receiving it was also providing the boat. In other words, it is highly probable that the captain of the vessel was also its owner. But the police did not know of any Joseph Jessup, and it is likely he did not exist. At that time, all Canadian boats over ten tons' displacement had to be registered in Ottawa. A twenty-minute check during research for this book revealed the owner to be James M. Ferguson of Kingston.

Three years after the capture of the *Maple Leaf*, Captain Ferguson and his seventeen-year-old son were caught trying to smuggle beer into Oswego on board the schooner *Pinta*. Neither the police nor the press connected Ferguson to the *Maple Leaf*, consequently, when he was brought before the magistrate, Ferguson was released as a first offender.[8] Still, he hadn't gotten off all that lightly. Lacking the $1,000 required for bail, he had had to wait seventy days in the Oswego jail for his case to come to trial. Ferguson's lack of bail money was not the norm, most rum-runners carried large amounts of cash and, in the easy-money years, few spent much time in jail.

George Jackson, commander of the Oswego coast guard station, complained bitterly to his superiors, implying that the courts were hostile to officers enforcing Prohibition. In one letter he cited an example to make his point: "I arrested a prisoner last summer with a load of ale...He was fined $1.00 in court and as his carfare was $1.15 home, a collection was made in the court room and carfare paid to him."[9]

It seemed that nearly everyone favoured the bootlegger. An honest coastguardsman – and the great majority of them were honest – found himself very unpopular in the community. Americans, having expended enormous energy to bring about the prohibition amendment, seemed to have exhausted their moral will in the process. The dominant attitude of the 1920s seemed to be let's relax, forget the war, and have fun.

Trouble was, they'd passed this darn prohibition law and, once passed, it was near impossible to get rid of as it had been written into the Constitution.

So many factors – the coast guard's lack of equipment, the poor pay of the customs and border patrol officers, the easy corruptibility of the federal Prohibition agents, combined with a public opinion generally hostile to Prohibition – meant that rum-running and bootlegging carried few risks. Given all this, and in view of the enormous profits to be made, the estimate of one source appears quite credible. The source, reputedly reliable and quoted anonymously in *Maclean's* magazine, claimed that at least 100,000 North Americans were engaged in smuggling booze into the United States during 1925.[10] Of these 100,000, most were land-based smugglers who relied on trucks, automobiles, and, occasionally, on horse-drawn wagons and sleds. Only a small number were involved in crossing the Great Lakes, as to do so required a knowledge of boats, navigation, and seamanship possessed by few Canadians. Even during the easy-money days, the lake smugglers were following a hazardous occupation. By crossing the unpredictable and frequently violent lakes in small boats, often dangerously overloaded with contraband booze, they pushed their luck to the outer limits, sometimes with fatal results.

9

DANGER
ON THE LAKE

With three weeks gone there are still no traces of
the "Sea Hawk" and it is almost finally established
that the quartette perished in Lake Ontario. One of
the men was...Harry Gunyo, of Brighton

Daily Intelligencer
February 6, 1928

Death on the lake was easily the greatest danger faced by the
rum-runners. Harry Gunyo and the Americans who died
with him were not amateurs but seasoned sailors who had
been running beer across the lake for at least a year. Only a
few months earlier, they had barely escaped the sudden violence of the lake. On the return leg of a trip to Rochester,
they had encountered a heavy storm. The *Sea Hawk* was
disabled, and for hours the men bailed out the cruiser in the
numbing November cold. The next day, exhausted and half-
frozen, they were spotted by Captain Redfern, piloting the
Cobourg ferry to Rochester. The rum-runners were rescued
and the *Sea Hawk* returned to Rochester for extensive repairs. On January 18, 1928, the *Sea Hawk* left Rochester on
what was to be her final voyage. Caught in a vicious storm,

the boat was apparently driven onto a reef that tore the fifty-foot cruiser in half. Jim Lovelace, a Prince Edward County constable, found the wreckage in Pleasant Bay, frozen in thirty feet of ice and snow. In the spring, two of the missing men floated to the surface; the others were never found.

The fate of Gunyo and his companions was repeated by many others, and illustrates the dangers posed by the lake. In the 1920s there were no marine weather forecasts on radio for fishermen. The survival of the rum-runners required that they know boats, navigation, and, most important, be able to gauge the weather with little or no equipment. But many rum-runners were just week-end sailors. Crossing the lake in a small boat, loaded to the gunnels with valuable contraband, seemed an easy enough route to riches, but a moderately rough sea with three- to four-foot waves quickly dispelled such illusions. Only those who were experienced sailors or fishermen remained in the game.

Wes Thomas, lighthouse keeper at Main Duck for thirty-three years, remembers two young greenhorns taking a load of Tower beer from Kingston across to Oswego. On the way to Main Duck a hard blow came up, and the one lad was soon bailing for all he was worth while the other steered the boat as best he knew how. As they neared the island, the driver of the boat pointed to three huge waves bearing down on them. The lad doing the bailing saw the waves and fainted dead away. The experience so terrified the novice smugglers, they traded their boat and load of beer in exchange for passage back to Cape Vincent, New York, on Claude Cole's big, sixty-two-foot tugboat.

Not all novice smugglers were as fortunate as those two young men from Cape Vincent. Jack Copping's encounter with the lake had a different ending. During the summers of 1927 and 1928, Copping, originally from Rochester, made a great many friends and charmed some of Belleville and Picton's best-bred young ladies. Tall, slim, and friendly, the young American had inherited a substantial estate, but bad investments and a taste for high living had left him nearly broke. He turned to rum-running as a last chance to recoup his squandered inheritance.[1]

To the proper young ladies of small-town Ontario, Copping provided a romantic escape from the staid young men their parents deemed acceptable. With the manners and connections to pass their fathers' stern muster and the wisdom to keep his real purpose obscure, Copping provided the ladies with just a hint of mystery and danger beneath an exterior of faintly dissolute gentility. The fishermen and rum-runners of South Bay and Picton saw him differently. Jim Hutchinson, an experienced mariner and the best-known whisky smuggler in South Bay, was convinced Copping's inexperience with boats and the lake would end in tragedy.[2]

By 1928 a massive offensive of the coast guard had driven many rum-runners to safer pursuits. Copping decided he could avoid capture by using a hydroplane, a type of boat then becoming popular with boat racers. Drawing on the remains of his inheritance, he purchased the *Wasp*. The folks of Prince Edward County had never seen anything quite like it. Powered by two converted Liberty aircraft engines, each generating over 500 horsepower, the *Wasp* could flash across a calm body of water at speeds in excess of sixty miles per hour. This was double the speed of the coast guard's fastest cutters. Gerald Mouck, a farmer in South Bay, remembers that when Copping opened up the throttle, Mouck was thrown forcibly back against the seat, unable to hear anything over the roar of the engines.

In early October 1928, Jack Copping and two companions, John Arroway and John Viviamore, set out for Oswego with a cargo of fifty bags of beer. Following behind, in a much slower boat, came the veteran rum-runner, Jim Hutchison. Shortly afterwards bad weather forced the group to put in at Fisherman's Cove off Long Point at the southern tip of Prince Edward County. For two days the men waited in this small cove for the weather to improve. Finally, on

Thursday afternoon, October 4, they decided the winds had abated sufficiently to chance a crossing. Hutchison and a companion followed Copping and his friends.

Out near Main Duck Island, Jim Hutchison noticed that the stern light of the *Wasp* appeared to be receding – the boat was gathering speed. Hutchison knew that accelerating into heavy waves was foolish, as the bow of the boat could plough under or, even worse, the hydroplane might flip. That is probably what happened. The stern light disappeared, and Jim Hutchison could find no trace of the men or their boat.

The next day, the body of Jack Copping washed up at Long Point. Ken McConnell, who found it, remembers Copping telling him at Long Point a few days earlier, "This is my last trip. I'll never do this again."

A few days later, John Arroway's body was found on Gull Bar, just west of Long Point. Seven days after the accident the last of the three bodies was found floating in the water near Kingston. A good many lives were lost on the lake in circumstances similar to those that claimed the lives of Jack Copping and his companions. Around South Bay and Picton, the old-timers still tell his story.

The most dangerous part of Lake Ontario is near its eastern end. Captain E.P. Bertholf described this danger in a letter to coast guard headquarters in Washington: "Mexico Bay [east of Oswego]...is subject to sudden and very severe squalls of wind and rain from southwest to west...alternating with strong southeast winds and, under such conditions, the average gasoline launch, when disabled, is but a toy at the mercy of the elements; likely to founder with all on board before it reaches the beach...It is generally conceded a condition of weather prevails in that section during certain seasons not found elsewhere on the Great Lakes."

Captain Berthalf went on to explain that these sudden storms happened because, at its eastern end, the bottom of the lake rises 1,700 feet in just fifteen miles. The Salmon River valley splits this rise, frequently causing strong currents.[3]

During the nineteenth century, the most common vessels on the Great Lakes were schooners and steamships of 100 to 500 tons' displacement. They were much smaller than modern lakers but dwarfed the average black ship, which were seldom larger than four or five tons. The rum-runners might have opted for another occupation had they been familiar with the toll taken of the hundred-tonners in the previous century. In 1883, for example, no fewer than forty vessels and 672 lives were lost on Lake Ontario.[4] It has been estimated that fully two-thirds of these losses took place in a small stretch of water at the eastern end of the lake between Wellington and Main Duck. The large number of sudden storms and resultant sinkings has inspired writer Hugh Cochrane to dub the area "the Marysburg Vortex" and to compare it to the Bermuda Triangle. The rum-runners were on the edges of this storm centre everytime they put in at Main Duck Island.

Lake Erie has its counterpart to the Marysburg Vortex in the twenty-two-mile scythe-shaped shard of land known as Long Point. Scores of vessels have gone aground on the dreaded shifting sand bars off its south shore, driven there by the gales that come roaring out of the southwest, unimpeded till they reach Long Point. When the wind rises, captains make for the quiet of the north shore and the lee of the wind. But the north shore is a treacherous haven. It, too, has shifting sand bars, and when the wind backs treacherously to the east or northeast, as it often does, the haven becomes a deadly trap.

Such a fate awaited the *City of Dresden*, which left Belleville harbour in November 1922 loaded with 1,000 cases and 500 kegs of Corby's Special Select whisky and Old Crow bourbon valued at $65,000. In charge of the vessel was Captain John Silvester McQueen, father of Earl McQueen, and at age sixty-six still a tough old seadog. Captain McQueen had bought the *City of Dresden* back in 1914 and had replaced her power plant with a boiler from one tug and a steam engine from another. The result was a vessel seaworthy under normal conditions but underpowered in a heavy sea.

November and December are the months when the Great Lakes are angriest. McQueen and his crew had the misfortune to be caught in a ferocious November storm just off Long Point in Lake Erie. For two days the Captain and his five-man crew laboured to save the vessel, its precious cargo, and their own lives. Finally, on Saturday evening, November 18th, the old steamer was driven onto a sand bar on the south shore of Long Point and began to break up.

Three women, alerted by the *City of Dresden*'s wailing whistle, hitched up a horse and buggy and raced to the beach. They arrived in time to see the crew lower a lifeboat, which capsized immediately. A second lifeboat was lowered, and the crew, including Captain McQueen and his twenty-one-year-old son, Peregrine, climbed into it only to be dumped into the waters as the lifeboat rolled over. In the frantic struggling that followed, both McQueens went under, the elder man managed to grab the boat's painter. Other crew members joined him and, eventually, the lifeboat was righted and the crew climbed in. The oars had been lost during the upset, leaving both men and boat at the mercy of the sea. A strong undertow kept the boat off the beach while the cresting breakers gave her a merciless pounding.

At this point two of the women, Pearl Rockefeller and her niece Viola Blackenbury, came to the rescue. They waded out into the chilling breakers, gesturing to the men to throw them a line. One finally did, and the two women, frequently buried by the cresting waves, gradually pulled the lifeboat to shore. Captain McQueen, delirious with fever, was put to bed in the Rockefeller's home. Peregrine's body was found the next day.

While the rescue was going on, men from nearby Port Rowan, hearing the distress signals of the *City of Dresden*, dropped their usual Saturday night activities and headed for the beach. Over the years, they and their fathers and their fathers before them had often reaped the benefits of salvage from Long Point's hazards to shipping. But never such a bonanza as this. With furious activity they set about retrieving the steamer's valuable cargo. By Sunday morning not a single bottle could be found. A week-long investigation by the OPP failed to uncover a single cache. One farmer seemed particularly suspicious to Inspector Edmonds, who kept dropping by his farm to make unannounced searches, even going so far as moving all the hay in the barn. "Thank God it didn't rain that week," the farmer later confided to a friend. "I had the eavestroughs of that big barn lined with bottles all the way around."

The sinking of the *City of Dresden* was both a financial and a personal tragedy for Captain John McQueen. Grief-stricken at the loss of his youngest son, the old mariner decided to retire from sailing. His eldest son, Earl, continued in the trade, encountering only occasional misfortune.

One of Earl's bad breaks occurred almost a year to the day the *City of Dresden* sank. His forty-foot motorboat, the *Sonora*, had successfully delivered a load of liquor to the Rochester area and was returning home when she ran into a dense fog. Although these fogs are common occurences during the fall, they are hazardous to mariners lacking sophisticated direction-finding equipment. Captain Al Wilson and his two-man crew were all experienced mariners, nevertheless, they were soon totally lost and, at 4:30 a.m., the *Sonora* smashed onto some rocks. A heavy sea was running, which sent breakers crashing over the disabled cruiser. It was mid-November, the air temperature was near freezing; if the men stayed with the boat they faced death by exposure. All were strong swimmers and decided to swim to what they perceived through the fog patches to be the higher ground of the shoal. All three men believed they were well out in the lake, marooned on a rocky outcropping. In fact, they were just a few hundred yards from the mainland.[5]

For crew member George Keegan, swimming for his life was becoming a familiar experience. Just two years earlier he had been a sailor aboard the *Oliver Mowatt* when the old schooner had been rammed during the night, near Main Duck, by the steamer *Key West*.[6] The captain and two crew members drowned, but Keegan and one other man swam to safety.

The *Sonora*'s crew was more fortunate; all three crew members made it to shore and were able to start a fire and get through the night in reasonable comfort. In the morning they discovered they had gone ashore at McLellan's Point, four miles west of Colborne. Earl McQueen was able to salvage the 4,500-pound motor from *Sonora*, but the boat itself was a total loss. His insurance policy provided coverage only to midnight November 14, as winter storms made insurance coverage prohibitively expensive after that date.

The fate suffered by the *Sonora* and the *City of Dresden* illustrates the risks involved, even for experienced mariners, in venturing onto the lakes after October. Commercial fishermen minimized these risks by confining their activities to inshore fishing during the months of November and December.

One of the early rum-runners who followed the fishermen's example was Charlie Mills, a slender, sandy haired American from the Niagara Falls area. Mills had been one of the first men in the U.S.A. to fly hydroplanes and for many years was a highly paid stunt pilot and barnstormer. He flew under suspension bridges, raced against speedboats, and was involved in at least two crashes. In one of these, he was flying his hydroplane just fifteen feet above the Niagara River when a gust of wind caused the primitive craft to flip over and crash into the water.[7]

By 1922, Mills had moved from the crowded, overly competitive business of stunt-flying into the easy money of rum-running. No one would ever question his courage, but Charlie Mills was wise enough to realize he was too inexperienced a mariner to cross the lake in the stormy season. Consequently, after October each year, he contented himself with what he called "shore work." Operating out of Deseronto for beer and from Belleville for whisky, he hauled 1,000-case loads in his fifty-five-foot cruiser, the *Adele*, to various points along the Ontario shoreline, such as Picton, Point Anne, the shore between Trenton and Belleville, and Prinyer Cove, known locally as "Booze Bog."[8]

During the summer, the soft-spoken Mills (his nickname was "Gentleman Charlie") was a frequent visitor at Main Duck Island, where he was noted for his generosity and free spending. He liked to carry large sums of money and recklessly flashed wads of $100 bills in front of his fishermen friends. Some of them could not resist the high wages he offered and joined him in his smuggling activities. The fishermen, hard pressed to make a living from the lake, were convinced Gentleman Charlie was a millionaire, one guessing his worth to be an even $3 million.[9] In fact, Mills spent money as fast as he made it. At one point he had a girlfriend and house in Belleville, three large boats, several fancy automobiles, and a wife, beautiful house, and airplane in Sanborn, New York. The free-spending Mills was also a gambler, losing heavily to such card sharps as Martin Lowery, also a rum-runner. It seemed that Charlie Mills was cautious and careful only when it came to the lake.

The Hamilton plumber and boat builder, Ben Kerr, was Mills's opposite in almost every respect. Where Mills was gregarious, Kerr was reserved and wary. In contrast to Mills' easy-come-easy-go philosophy, Kerr was a trader and an investor concerned with building his capital base. He owned thirty boat-houses in Hamilton, which he rented out, laying down strict conditions to the renters and administering intimidating tongue-lashings to anyone abusing his property. Mills was a gambler who frequently lost, whereas Kerr was a high-class billiard player who almost always won. Billiards was one of his few diversions. A perfectionist himself, he did not tolerate carelessness in others. He made sure the work-men sent by Corby's to load whisky from the boxcar to his beautiful mahogany speedboat did so with the utmost care. A family man, Ben Kerr kept in daily radio contact with his attractive blonde wife, Louisa May. He was one of the very few rum-runners on Lake Ontario to make use of radio, then a rather novel technology.[10]

In the early years, Kerr ordered whisky from Corby's and beer from Dow Ale. The ordering would be done through a front organization in the U.S.A. such as Hatch and McGui-ness of Niagara Falls. Kerr would be named by them as the carrier and the destination given as either Cuba or Mexico. The order would be approved by Harry Hatch in Montreal and would then be forwarded to the plant at Corbyville. The load, usually a full boxcar, would be shipped by CNR to Whitby, where Kerr would transfer as many as 1,200 cases to his forty-two foot cruiser, the *Martimas*. He would then deliver the load to a prearranged spot on the shore near Rochester. The real American buyers, not Hatch and McGuiness, who were merely sales agents, would pay Kerr's commission in cash at the time of delivery. Secrecy was vital to the success of these operations. There was always the danger a rival organization might tip off the feds or try to hijack the load and the money for themselves. To discourage this, Kerr, his men, and the American bootleggers were heav-ily armed and maintained the strictest secrecy.

One legal problem arose from the need to have a fully completed B-13 form signed by Canadian customs, which indicated the port of destination, number of cases, consignee, value of shipment, and so forth. Kerr's boat could not handle a whole boxcar load in one crossing, and the B-13 had to be made out to equal the exact amount he was taking on each trip. He did not often know in advance how big his loads would be. It depended on the weather, how much the Ameri-can buyer could handle, and which boat he would be using. The customs officers solved this problem by graciously signing a number of blank B-13s, leaving Kerr to fill in the destinations, number of cases, dates of departure, and other trivia.

This system worked well until, for some unknown reason, Kerr shifted his operations from Whitby to Belleville. This change may have resulted from the 1927 Royal Commission inquiry, which, among other things, put a stop to the signing of blank B-13s by customs officers. The proximity of the Corby plant to the government docks at Belleville made it feasible for Corby's to deliver small loads that coincided with the capacity of Kerr's boat. The B-13 could be correctly filled in and signed by customs on the day Kerr loaded.

From Belleville, Kerr travelled east on the Bay of Quinte and then south, sometimes stopping in at Prinyer Cove, locally known as "Booze Bog," where the residents gave him a wide berth. The local lads were of the opinion that Kerr would not hesitate to use his big revolver on anyone found snooping around his boat. From Booze Bog, he would travel directly across the lake except when the weather turned bad and then, like so many rum-runners, he would put in at Main Duck, where lighthouse keeper Wes Thomas was often his host. Thomas remembers Ben Kerr as a quiet man who spoke fondly of his wife and daughter and justified his occupation by his need to support them. He told Thomas, "At the end of the War, we were nearly starving. You know, Wes, I make $500 to $1,000 every trip. Hell, I can't make that plumbing."

An outdoorsman himself, the friendly lighthouse keeper was particularly impressed with Kerr's ability to forecast the weather, a skill he may have acquired from his father who spent many years as a fish and game inspector. The skill was a great asset, particularly when Kerr decided to challenge the lake in all seasons, including winter.

Unlike Lake Erie, Lake Ontario does not freeze over during the winter, which enabled the rugged and the foolhardy to carry on smuggling all year. Kerr appears to have been the first rum-runner to have made winter crossings of Lake Ontario. Although others would follow his example, few, if any, survived at it as long as the intrepid plumber.

Winter weather presented a whole new set of problems for the smugglers. Thin ice, no thicker than a pane of glass, could cut through the wooden hulls and send boat, cargo, and crew to the icy depths with no warning. To guard against this, fishermen adopted the practice of nailing barn metal – granary steel, they called it – to the prow of their boats. This galvanized metal was adequate for the thin ice of late fall, but Kerr needed protection from the heavy shore-ice that builds up in winter, through which he often had to guide his ship. Kerr enclosed the entire hull of his boats with tonkin, a heavy gauge, rust-proof steel.[11]

Another danger arose from the formation of ice on the decks and cabin, which raises the centre of gravity and can cause a boat to turtle. To guard against this disaster, the crew had to keep chopping the ice off the boat, particularly during a winter storm when the boat was most vulnerable and the ice build-up most rapid. But the greatest danger from ice lay in the large floes that drifted in open water and, with their masses largely submerged, were difficult to spot on dull, overcast days. To avoid them required constant vigilance on the part of the helmsman. As Kerr was frequently on the lake for two or three days at a stretch, fatigue added considerably to all the risks.

Jack Morris Jr. started working for Kerr in 1925 when he was just seventeen. Now in his mid-seventies, he recalls most vividly the sensation of constant cold. The boats had no heating system, so the men dressed as warmly as they could, except for their feet. The danger of slipping off the deck made it necessary to wear running shoes even in winter. The rest of their clothing was more suited to the elements and included heavy mackinaw shirts, long johns, woollen trousers, and sheepskin coats which reached down to their knees.

Among the rum-running fraternity an expensive sheepskin coat was a badge of success.

By 1925 Ben Kerr could afford a closet full of sheepskin coats. He owned and operated three fast boats: the *Lark*, the *Voyageur*, and the *Martimas*.[12] Of these, the *Martimas*, while the slowest, was capable of hauling as many as 1,200 cases of ale in a single trip. Forty-two feet long, fairly beamy, and with a high freeboard, she was well suited to the early days of rum-running when reliability and carrying capacity, rather than speed, were the important qualities of a black ship. Kerr used the *Martimas* to deliver beer to the vicinity of Rochester. By late May 1925, he had made eighteen such trips, grossing on each one between $2,500 and $3,500, less expenses. His expenses included $50 each for his two crew members and the cost of oil and gasoline for the *Martimas*. He did not bribe the customs or federal agents and openly boasted he could outwit the feds any time. The customs men had been trying to catch him for three years, but he always appeared where least expected. They regarded him as the most daring rum-runner on the lake.[13]

The circumstances that enabled Ben Kerr to flout America's prohibition laws were rapidly changing. At the end of April 1925, a new boat arrived at the Charlotte coast guard station in Rochester harbour's east basin.[14] Up to that point, the station did not have any vessel capable of catching black ships. But coast guard picket boat *CG-2330* was designed specifically for that purpose. With a length of thirty-six feet, she was big enough to handle the lake in most weather, yet small enough to follow the black ships into shallow coves. Her top speed of twenty-four knots was faster than that of most boats the rum-runners used. As well as the crews' usual complement of revolvers and rifles, *CG-2330* mounted a .30-calibre Lewis machine gun. This weapon gave the coast guard a big edge over their opponents.[15]

The new boat was placed under the command of Bo'sun Mason B. McCune, a career officer who had spent his entire adult life in the service. This tall, blond, thirty-five year old was one of three brothers, all of whom were members of the coast guard on the Great Lakes. Over the next few years, they would terrorize the rum-running community by catching more than thirty of them on Lake Erie, Lake Ontario, and the Niagara River.

The arrival of *CG-2330* did not go unnoticed by Rochester-area bootleggers, who, no doubt, warned Ben Kerr of the new danger. But Kerr was a man supremely confident of his own abilities, contemptuous not only of the corrupt and amateurish federal agents but of his rival rum-runners as well. He could not bring himself to take his new opponents seriously, and he continued to operate the *Martimas* in the Rochester area despite her lack of speed.

There was another factor working against Kerr of which he was probably unaware. The Standard Brewing Company of Rochester was producing beer and ale, which was legal providing these products contained no more than 0.5 per cent alcohol. According to rumour, the Standard Brewery was manufacturing a 9 per cent beer with the paid cooperation of certain local treasury agents. A Rochester group calling itself the Committee of Twenty-Five had charged that the Standard Brewery was producing beer of a higher alcoholic content than was allowed under the Volstead Act. It further charged that local politicians were "interested in the brewery and are active in keeping out Canadian ale in order to have a monopoly of the business in the Rochester area." It also charged that bootleggers handling Standard's products had little to fear from "local authorities," implying the collusion of federal officers.

The American bootleggers who purchased the ale delivered by Kerr were in competition with the Standard Brewery. The owners of the brewery decided to infiltrate their rivals and then tip off the feds as to Kerr's arrival. The feds could then protect the source of their graft money and refurbish their tarnished image as crime fighters, all at the same time.

Kerr delivered to a number of customers at various points along the lake from Rochester east to Pultneyville, New York.[16] At Rochester, he delivered regularly to a group led by Butch Shank and Mae Davis. Shank owned a cottage near the lake in a shantytown area known as the Oaklahoma settlement. According to curious neighbours, Mae Davis arrived at Butch's cottage every afternoon by taxi and stayed until late in the night, when she departed the same way. While she was at the cottage, which served as a wholesale liquor store for area bootleggers, Mae Davis handled the money and seemed to be in charge.

On the evening of May 26, 1925, Andrew Wiedenmann, collector of ports and customs duties, was patrolling the shore in an automobile together with a number of federal agents when he spotted Kerr's boat. The cargo of *Martimas* was being unloaded into a dory that was attached to shore by a cable. When the dory was filled, the men on shore were hauling it in and carting the beer to the nearby cottage. Wiedenmann flashed a signal to Mason McCune, who was patrolling off shore in *CG-2330*. Both groups closed in on the smugglers. A cordon of thirteen federal agents surrounded Butch Shank's cottage, while Wiedenmann sent to town for a search warrant. Mae Davis was arrested as she reached for a fully loaded .45 automatic. Dressed in overalls and a slouch hat, Davis had been mistaken for a man.

Warned by those on shore, Kerr immediately cut the cable attached to the dory and headed for the open lake, with Mason McCune in hot pursuit. As the faster *CG-2330* closed in on him, Kerr ordered his men to toss the rest of the beer overboard. Two shots were fired across the bow of the *Martimas*, but Kerr kept on. McCune then raked the hull of Kerr's boat with the .30-calibre Lewis machine-gun, eight shots finding the mark. By this time the faster picket boat had overtaken the *Martimas*, and Kerr slowed his boat. As McCune drew up alongside, he realized that Kerr's men were on the other side throwing bags of beer overboard. He ordered them to stop, punctuating his command by firing a round over their heads from his service revolver. They stopped. All that remained on the *Martimas* were eight cases of Dow ale. Had Mason McCune acted a second or two more slowly, Kerr's men would have dumped the last of the incriminating ale.

Aboard the *Martimas* McCune seized one repeating shotgun, a Winchester rifle, and an automatic revolver, all fully loaded. At Butch Shank's cottage, Collector Wiedenmann seized 600 cases of Dow ale, eight cases of Corby's whisky, two automatic shotguns, two rifles, a double-barrelled shotgun, and an automatic pistol. The dory was found to contain another sixty cases of ale.

The arrests and seizures were hailed by the Rochester *Democrat-Chronicle* as the end of the Lake Ontario rum ring. Kerr, whom they labelled "King of the Rum-Runners," was quoted as saying, "The rest of the rum-runners are too yellow to come over here very often." He knew that the truth was quite different and may have been grandstanding, or he may have been trying to take the heat off his fellow rum-runners.

The evening following Kerr's arrest, someone unknown set off two bombs in the Standard Brewery, which did considerable damage.[17] The Rochester newspapers saw this as a retaliatory action for the brewery owners' complicity in the capture of Kerr and associates. The next day, the commissioner set bail for the prisoners at the unusually high figure of $60,000: $10,000 for Kerr, $10,000 each for his two crew members, and $5,000 each for the six Americans.

The following day brought more bad news for the rum-runners. In addition to the fast picket boats, Congress had also authorized the design and building of a new class of cutter. In April, the first of these new hunters had arrived on the Great Lakes. Now, in the late afternoon sun of May 29,

CG-142 glided into Rochester harbour.[18] District Commander Ralph Crowley proudly announced that three more of the new cutters would soon be cruising Lake Ontario.

The rum-runners' easy money days were coming to an end.

10

END OF
THE EASY MONEY

Captain F.G. Dodge of the Coast Guard...soon
will have 28 rum-hunting speed boats in operation...The government announcement that smugglers would be hunted down relentlessly...resulted
in an immediate increase in prices. Previously
whiskey prices were so low that bootleggers were
making small profits. The price of Canadian whiskey was raised $5.00 a case by wholesale boot-
leggers, and the retail price was increased by 50
cents a quart to $7.00.

> *Associated Press*, Tacoma, Washington,
> Oct. 10, 1924

Ben Kerr was an outdoorsman. He found jail almost unbear-
able, but it did give him the opportunity to reflect on his
misjudgements and to resolve that never again would he let
himself be captured.

Kerr was tried in Rochester during September 1925. His
lawyer had succeeded in getting bail reduced to $4,500 and,
after posting the money, Kerr had returned to Hamilton.
Earlier, his two crew members, Clark and Elliott, had

pleaded guilty and had received sentences of just sixty days. But Kerr was still being called the King of the Rum Runners – a title he now denied – and the press made much of his beautiful home, reputed wealth, and his many successful smuggling trips before being apprehended. He had good reason to expect a much stiffer sentence. Yet, on September 18, he pleaded guilty. Sentencing was scheduled for the following week. In the interim, Kerr got wind of a rumour that the state prosecutor was preparing to charge him with manslaughter.

The possibility of a manslaughter charge arose from a conversation between Clark and Elliot with a Rochester lawyer while they were serving their sixty days. The crewmembers told the lawyer that the previous summer, while running a load to Oswego, they had felt something strike the *Martimas* amidships. Using the ship's searchlight, the rumrunners had probed the rainy blackness, picking out two men in a small boat. For a moment one of the men had stared back, then both men and boat had disappeared beneath the waves. The lawyer, George Forsyth, knew the two men who had drowned. They had been pleasure fishing off Main Duck and had decided to return to Oswego despite the heavy sea and the warnings of the local fishermen. Apparently, they had not seen the *Martimas* in the blackness and had collided with the larger ship, wrecking their stern. The *Martimas* had violated maritime law by running without lights (as most rum runners did while in American waters). As captain, Ben Kerr was therefore criminally negligent in causing the deaths of the two Oswego men.

Once he had connected the deaths of the two men to the rum-runners tale, George Forsyth called for the state to bring manslaughter charges against Ben Kerr. The Rochester newspapers published the story, alerting him to this new danger. Kerr decided to forfeit bail and not appear for sentencing. The office of the United States Attorney General began extradition proceedings against him.

Most of the Americans who had been arrested with Kerr received sixty day sentences, but John "Butch" Shank, who owned the cottage used as a beer storehouse, was sentenced to a year and a day at the federal prison in Atlanta, Georgia. The charges against Mae Davis, the gun-toting lady bootlegger, were dropped, supposedly for a lack of evidence, but possibly because she had been the one who tipped off the police, or perhaps because of the prevalent chauvinist attitude toward the "gentler" sex.[1] Meanwhile, at the border, Ben Kerr defiantly announced he was returning to the ale fleet. The coast guard and the Attorney General's office responded by putting a price on his head.

Kerr did return to the lucrative trade of running booze across the lake, but with a different attitude. He was now more wary of his opponents, more determined that the coast guard would never capture him again. As far back as October 1924, Kerr had known that the coast guard was deploying some of its fast new picket boats to Lake Ontario. On the sixth of that month, picket boat *CG-2207* had arrived at Oswego. A local bootlegger had immediately sent a telegram to the rum-runners in Belleville apprising them of the new danger. Yet Kerr, even though he owned much faster boats, had continued to operate the comparatively slow *Martimas*, partly because its capacity to carry large loads earned him big profits, partly because the boat was less than a year old, but also because, in his self-confidence, Kerr had underestimated his opponents. Several experienced rum-runners had made the same mistake during the summer of 1925 and, like Kerr, had ended up in American jails. Ironically, Kerr, the first to be captured, had also been one of the first to appreciate the new danger and to prepare for it. Several months before his capture he had ordered a new boat, one that would be too fast for any picket boat. He had placed the order with Jack Morris, a second-generation boat builder who could produce the finely crafted boat Kerr demanded. Unfortunately, the small Morris Boat Works would take almost a year to build the new boat. In the interim, Kerr continued to use the *Martimas*, a costly gamble as events proved.

The strengthening of the coast guard had been announced in April 1924, when Congress had voted an extra $13 million for the force over and above its regular budget of $10 million. About $8 million of this extra money was to be used for the construction of 203 seventy-five-foot cutters, costing $35,000 each, and 103 picket boats, costing $6,800 each. Money was also allocated for a radio station at Buffalo to co-ordinate the activities of the rum chasers. A machine shop was also to be built at Buffalo; its sole purpose would be to keep the new fleet serviced and operational.

The cutters, or six-bitters as they came to be called, were designed to cruise for a week at a time. They carried a crew of eight and mounted a one-pound cannon on the foredeck, a weapon that could literally blow a black ship to pieces. Accurate over a distance of two miles, this gun compensated for the six-bitters' top speed of only fifteen to sixteen knots.

The smaller picket boats were designed for day runs and came in two designs: a thirty-five-foot, single-cabin, open cockpit type, numbered *CG-2200* through *CG-2229*, and a double-cabin, thirty-six-footer, numbered *CG-2300* through *CG-2372*. Both types carried a crew of three, mounted a .30-calibre Lewis machine-gun, and could make twenty-four knots. When they first appeared on the Great Lakes, only a few black ships could match their speed, and even fewer could outrun them when carrying a cargo of booze.

When Congress first announced these additions to the coast guard's fleet, rum-runners on the Great Lakes had reason to hope that few, if any, of the new boats would be deployed to the lakes. The main battle against rum-running was being fought on the Atlantic along the northeastern coast between New York City and Boston, the area known as Rum Row. Here, large mother-ships, carrying thousands of cases of booze, would anchor just outside the international three-mile limit and await the arrival of contact boats, usually fast motorboats capable of carrying a hundred cases. Several hundred of these contact boats, owned by New York and Boston bootlegging rings, regularly dashed across the three-mile gap between shore and ship. They hauled an estimated 100,000 cases of booze into the United States every month. The coast guard could not seize the supply ships as long as they remained in international waters, but they could follow them and they could also do their best to intercept the contact boats. But even when a coast guard cutter was in the area, the contact boats could usually outrun them. The faster ones could dash across the three miles to the coast in under five minutes, giving the patrol boat little time to detect let alone apprehend them. The coast guard estimated that, despite their best efforts, they intercepted less than 5 per cent of the contact boats.

To turn the logistics of the chase in their favour, the United States had pressed Britain, who controlled Canada's international affairs, to establish a twelve-mile limit in North American waters. After three years of negotiations, a treaty was signed in early 1924. Instead of a new twelve-mile limit, both parties agreed to "an hour's steaming distance from shore," a decision that weighed heavily against the contact boats. The faster the black ship, the further from shore it had to travel to be in international waters. This gave the pursuing coast-guard ships a greater distance in which to catch the contact boat or blow it out of the water. This treaty, together with the transfer of twenty destroyers and two mine sweepers from the Navy, turned the tide against the Atlantic smugglers. By the summer of 1925, the coast guard was able to report that Rum Row had been dispersed.[2] This achievement made possible the diversion of some of the new boats and men to other areas, in particular, to the Great Lakes.

The first indication that coast guard headquarters realized the extent of smuggling activity on the lakes was their decision to reopen Big Sandy Station, near Woodville, New

York, at the far eastern end of Lake Ontario. The station was reopened in September 1924 for the specific purpose of curtailing smuggling. In spite of being woefully ill-equipped for the task, the men of Big Sandy were soon catching rumrunners. One of the first to be arrested was Tony Kane, one of the most persistent smugglers on the lake.

On the political front, the U.S. government, after much pressure, was able to obtain limited cooperation from the Canadian government of Mackenzie King. The resulting agreement, signed in June 1924, put a stop to one of our best waterfront jokes. No longer could twenty-foot open fish boats, loaded with Canadian booze, clear for Cuba, Mexico, or other impossible destinations. Henceforward, if a boat was too small or unfit for the destination stated, no clearance would be issued. The United States also wanted Canada to forbid the clearance of liquor boats to its shores, but Prime Minister King refused, fearing that voters would see him as toadying to the Americans. Consequently, the rum-runners were able to state openly their American destination rather than pretending they were headed for Cuba, even though doing so meant they had to pay an excise tax of $9 a gallon.

More damaging to the rum-runners was the seemingly innocuous Article Four of the Agreement, which called for an exchange of information between the two countries. In practice this meant that Canadian customs officials phoned their American counterparts whenever a vessel carrying booze cleared a Canadian port for a stated destination in the U.S. This information put the coast guard crews on the alert and led to many arrests and seizures. The rum-runners quickly developed new ways to avoid the problems posed by these clearance procedures.

In August 1924, Commander E.J. Clemons of the Charlotte coast guard station captured the black boat *Rowdy* when it entered Rochester's harbour with a broken steering cable. On board the *Rowdy*, Clemons and his men seized sixty-five cases of Canadian ale and its owner, Fred Fricke, a

Rochester policeman. Decent, law-abiding citizens were understandably shocked that an officer of the law should engage in such illegal activity, and Fricke inflamed public opinion still further by telling the press that he had purchased the contraband from one of several large boats that plied the lakes, selling their wares to operators of smaller boats. The story was pure fantasy, but it spurred Collector Wiedenmann of Rochester to announce that, "he had ordered his men to seek out Lake Ontario's rum fleet."[3] How they were going to do this without boats was not explained.

In fact, Fricke had purchased his beer from King Cole at Main Duck Island.[4] Cole had realized that some rum-runners would not want to buy beer from the breweries and have their departure reported to U.S. officials. So he had set himself up as an exporter, buying large amounts of beer and whisky and hauling it to Main Duck, where he stored it in his two homes and sold it off, illegally, in small lots to various rum-runners.[5] This service was used by those rum-runners of eastern Lake Ontario who could afford to pay King Cole his mark-up, but it was not available to runners anywhere else on the lake. In other places, different tactics to circumvent the law had to be developed. Charlie Mills liked to delay his delivery for several days after his clearance. He would do this by stopping over for a visit with friends at Amherst Island, or some other spot where he was relatively safe from the OPP. After two or three days, the coast guard would assume he had landed, and Charlie would slip in on a dark night and make his drop. But, eventually, most rum-runners came to rely almost entirely on the only other resource they had to keep out of the clutches of the coast guard and American jails – the speed of their boat. It took some time for these new, fast boats to be built and even for the rum-runners to fully realize their need of them. In the meantime, the coast guard had a field day in its new ships.

By the spring of 1925 five of the new picket boats were on the Great Lakes. Two of these were assigned to Sault Ste

Marie, the other three went to the Ninth District for Lakes Erie and Ontario.[6] Of these three, one was assigned to district headquarters in Buffalo and one to Niagara, where Maurice, the eldest of the McCune brothers, was posted. In the following six months Maurice McCune captured no fewer than seventeen rum-runners.[7]

The third of the picket boats, *CG-2207*, was assigned to Oswego, where Merle McCune, the youngest of the three brothers, cruised the waters south of Main Duck with such success he became recognized as the ace hunter on the lake. His brother Mason was at Charlotte station when *CG-2330*, the first cabin picket boat on Lake Ontario, arrived in Rochester. Mason McCune wasted no time in proving the worth of these fine boats by capturing the *Martimas* and Ben Kerr.

To harrass the rum-runners still further, two six-bitters were sent to the Ninth District, one to be based at Erie, Pennsylvania, and the other at Buffalo. The effect of these new boats on the rum-runners of Lake Erie was both immediate and dramatic.

More picket boats were assigned to the lakes during this transitional period. In the spring of 1925, the first seventy-five foot cutter arrived. Roaming Lake Erie on *CG-121*, Captain U.F. Engman managed four major captures that first summer, including the dramatic arrest of Nick Vandeveer and the seizure of his forty-four-foot launch. Maurice McCune, the oldest of the three brothers, was second-in-command of *CG-121* at the time.[8]

On the evening of June 11, 1925, Captain Engmen, commanding *CG-121*, spotted a large black motorboat about twelve miles north west of Erie. He immediately gave chase. Three cannon rounds were fired across the black ship's bows as a warning but, instead of heaving-to, the captain, Nick Vandeveer, shouted that he would not stop. Rather than fire on the rum-runners with his one-pounder, Captain Engman ordered two crewmen to fire at the boat with rifles. The chase continued for several miles while the six-bitter gradually closed the gap between the boats. Her twin Stirling 200-horsepower engines were whining at maximum revs as *CG-121* drew alongside and three crewmen leaped down onto the smaller black boat. Boarding in a fashion reminiscent of pirate days, they smashed the windows of the pilot house, trained their guns on Vandeveer, who was at the wheel, and when he still refused to stop, sent in a crew member to shut off the engines.

Aboard Vandeveer's boat were 608 cartons (7,296 twenty-two-ounce bottles) of Frontenac ale and two men: the crewman, twenty-nine-year-old David Marr of Port Colborne, and Nick Vandeveer, age thirty-two, also of Port Colborne. The bespectacled Vandeveer was the owner of three boats and had been at the trade for several years. He would prove an implacable enemy of the coast guard, as infamous on Lake Erie as Ben Kerr was on Lake Ontario.[9]

The previous August, the Department of Justice had announced that whisky smugglers would no longer be charged under the Volstead Act, which treated the activity as a misdemeanor, but under the Tariff Act, which treated it as an indictable offence. The Volstead Act provided penalties for first offenders with fines of up to $1,000, or prison sentences of up to six months. But, under Section 593 of the Tariff Act, smugglers could be fined up to $5,000 and receive lengthy prison terms.[10] Marr and Vandeveer were charged under the Tariff Act and bail was set at an unusually high $5,000 each. Vandeveer's financial worth was demonstrated by the apparent ease with which he raised the bail money. After his release, he returned immediately to the rum fleet.

Few of the captures were as dramatic as those of Amos Vandeveer or Ben Kerr. More typical was the first capture achieved on the lakes with the new picket boats, which took place in September 1924, shortly after *CG-2205* arrived in Buffalo. While anchored on the east side of Buckhorn Island in the Niagara River, J.J. Daly and his crew spotted a suspicious-looking boat, which they easily outran and seized with-out a shot being fired. Aboard the thirty-four-foot motor-boat they seized 162 cartons of ale and arrested Tom Davis of Chippewa, Ontario, and the teenaged Ed Ackerman of Buffalo. It was later discovered that the boat belonged to William Barber, a well-known rum-runner from Niagara Falls, New York.[11]

Captures during 1924 were, however, few and far between. It was not until 1925 that picket boats were in regular patrol on both Lakes Erie and Ontario. Shortly thereafter the battle began to shift in favour of the coast guard.

Not long after Kerr's arrest, Mason McCune, while com-manding *CG-2330*, cooperated with customs patrol officers in a joint sea-and-land operation off Nine Mile Point that netted nine prisoners, two cars, two trucks, 420 cases of Cosgraves ale, and a thirty-six-foot motorboat. The rum boat, the *Sparkley*, was painted entirely black and had a maximum speed of about fifteen knots.[12] It was typical of the rum ships used in 1925; later boats would be much faster.

Mason McCune assisted in one more major capture dur-ing 1925. Again, it was a joint land-and-sea operation near Nine Mile Point. The customs patrol officers arrested three men and seized a quantity of Canadian ale, two cars, and one truck. McCune and his crew seized the boat and 125 cases of Frontenac ale, and arrested the boat's captain and crew.[13]

Meanwhile Mason's brother Merle McCune was begin-ning the series of arrests that would earn him so much un-wanted attention from the bootlegging community. He was then thirty-two years of age, stockily built with a determined set to his square jaw. Since his early teens, Merle McCune had been set on joining the coast guard. For several years he substituted for any coastguardsman who went on leave until, finally, in 1917, he was taken on full-time. It was a demand-ing and dangerous job, involving the rescue of people from the lake. But it was rewarding, and the service was much appreciated by both mariners and the general public. Prohibition changed all that. The job of enforcing the new law was unpopular with large segments of the public. But Merle McCune, like his brothers, was a career coastguardsman. He would do his job and duty regardless of the damage to his personal popularity.

The bootlegging fraternity quickly discovered that Merle, like his brothers, could not be bought off, and he was soon the recipient of threats against himself and his family. As a consequence, he bought a .32-calibre Colt automatic and, during the prohibition period, never answered the door of his home without the revolver in his hand.[14]

Merle had an uncanny ability to locate and apprehend black ships, which eludes rational explanation. When *CG-2207* arrived at Oswego, he had already spent seven years at the station and was thoroughly familiar with the coves and inlets around the eastern section of the lake. Other officers had the same knowledge but none was as successful as Merle at catching smugglers on Lake Ontario. Mason might have done as well, but he was promoted to station commander at Charlotte and so spent more time on administration. Maurice was highly successful, but he operated in the narrow confines of the Niagara River, where the task of actually finding rum-runners was much easier than on the lake. All three of the brothers had great determination and integrity, which, combined with good intelligence and a sound knowledge of boats and the waters they served on, made them worthy opponents for the wiliest of rum-runners.

In the late summer of 1925, these qualities helped Merle McCune capture the clever and cautious Charlie Mills. On the night of September 3 at about 2 a.m., Mills and his son were about five miles west of Oswego in the *Winnifred S* running in a westerly direction about seven miles from shore. The *Winnifred S* was running without lights; yet, somehow, Merle McCune spotted her and gave chase. When Mills tried to escape, McCune fired five tracer bullets and, as they drew abreast, two shots from his revolver. Realizing he was beaten on speed, Charlie Mills surrendered. He and his son, Edwin "Bud" Mills, were handcuffed and taken aboard the picket boat. The rather shabby *Winnifred S* was found to contain only fifty cases of William Penn whisky and Old Kentucky bourbon, a surprisingly small load for a thirty-six-footer, suggesting that Mills had already delivered part of his load.

In the early days, most captures of rum ships were made near shore, often on the strength of tip-offs from rival bootleggers. The customs patrol officers would have an idea where the landing was to take place and, when they found the smugglers, would signal the coast guard, who had been forewarned and were cruising in the general area. The challenge for the coast guard crew was not just to find the rum ship but also to catch it before its contraband could be dumped overboard.

On the night he arrested Charlie and Bud Mills, McCune had to find a dark grey boat, cruising well out on the lake with no running lights. To add to the difficulty, visibility was near zero; it rained steadily all during the evening of the capture. Nevertheless, Merle McCune was able to locate his elusive quarry.[15]

Paul Lobdell was just sixteen when he joined the coast guard in 1924. Merle McCune had recently been promoted to bo'sun's mate and Lobdell frequently served under him in patrols on *CG-2207*. They would usually start the patrol about 10 p.m., with Merle determining where and when they would go. Paul Lobdell remembers Merle's great instincts: "He could almost smell 'em." He also credits the rum-runners, some of whom he recalls were "real foxy guys."[16]

For Charlie Mills, his capture was the turning point in his career, both personally and financially. He had already lost his younger son, Chester, who had developed an infected appendix on one of their trips across the Lake. Charlie, thinking it just sea sickness, had kept on. The appendix had ruptured and Chester had died. Charlie's wife, Maime, could not forgive him, and their already troubled marriage had come to an end. When Mills came before Commissioner Bulger at Oswego, both he and Edwin were charged under the Tariff Act and their bail set at $3,000 each.

Later that month, Charlie Mills returned to Belleville after a successful trip across the lake. He had a Friday night date with his girlfriend, Jennie, but she was out when he arrived. Upset, he began drinking and was driving around Belleville, trying to find her, when he crashed his light coupe through a fence and into a hedge. At 1:30 a.m. there was no one around to help push the vehicle out onto the street. After some kicking of tires and muttered curses, the inebriated Mills noticed two men about a block away and called to them for assistance. They turned out to be Constables Evans and Franks. They seized some American cigarettes and a flask of whisky from his car and threw Mills into jail. He spent the weekend in the county lockup and on Monday was fined $200 and ordered to pay for the fence and hedge.[17] It had not been a good month for Charlie Mills.

Mason McCune was also fairly effective that summer, managing three major captures in *CG-2330*. Of these, the arrest of Ben Kerr and the seizure of the *Martimas* was the most important and dramatic. But the capture of the *Sparkley* a month later involved the arrest of a rum-runner who, while never as successful as Ben Kerr, was certainly more colourful. He gave the court the name William Sheridan, but at other times called himself Bill Sheldon, or John Woover. None of these was his right name, but it didn't matter very much, everyone knew him as "Wild Bill."[18]

After a stint in the infantry during the war, William Sheldon – the alias he used most often – returned for a time to his trade as a boilermaker, but gradually drifted into the more adventuresome life of smuggling. For Wild Bill was not a rum-runner in the traditional sense, but an old-fashioned smuggler who carried anything in his boat from diamonds to Chinese aliens. Of Italian ancestry, his six foot three inches was topped by a mass of thick black hair, streaked with grey like the peak of some glacial mountain. To the police, he was a friendly giant who never carried guns and relied solely on his guile, knowledge of the lake, and skill with a boat to escape arrest. These qualities were clearly not sufficient. By the end of the decade, Wild Bill held the dubious distinction of being the most frequently captured rum-runner on Lake Ontario.

In the summer of 1925, he was thought to be a first offender. That fact, and perhaps his room-filling smile, may have influenced the judge, who fined him only $750 and set him free. The light sentence no doubt encouraged Wild Bill – he returned immediately to the rum fleet, only to be captured again in less than two months.

Neither Charlie Mills, nor Ben Kerr, nor Nick Vandeveer, was so foolish as to blame his capture on bad luck. They had each been in the game for several years and knew its character was changing. In 1923, only two captures had taken place on the two lakes, one the comedy of errors involving the *Maple Leaf* at Oswego and the other, an insignificant seizure of a twelve-foot skiff and a small quantity of liquor. In neither case were any prisoners taken. But the arrival of the six-bitters and picket boats on the lakes signalled a new era in rum-running. The number of captures began to climb steadily until, by December 1925, fully twenty-three major seizures had been made, most involving prisoners and several involving shoot-outs.[19]

In July 1925, Harry Smith, collector of customs at Buffalo, announced that rum-runners in American waters who refused to stop would be fired upon and risked having their boats blown up. He further warned that they risked a fine of $5,000 and up to five years imprisonment.[20] Then, to emphasize the seriousness of the conflict, the coast guard announced that, in order to combat smuggling, all stations on the Great Lakes were to remain open that winter. No one could remember a time before when the stations had been kept open past December.[21]

The easy days of smuggling were clearly over. To survive, the rum-runners would have to develop better tactics and strategies. One man had already done so. Harry Hatch had followed the development of the coast guard closely and, when the picket boats and cutters arrived on the lakes, the rum-running fleet organized by Herb Hatch and Larry McGuiness was ready.

11

GIRDING FOR BATTLE

Practically all 6-pounder guns have been replaced by modern 3-inch and 4-inch guns...All the small craft are now armed with rifles, pistols, and machine guns...Experiments have been carried on by various vessels in the use of star shells at night for target practice...In the course of the year, all cutters...have held great gun target practice and small arms target practice.

Coast Guard Annual Report, 1924

The coast guard's annual report for 1924 contained for the first time a section dealing with ordnance or gunnery. It was also the first year the report dealt with the problem of enforcing the Volstead Act. The 1924 report signalled a dramatic change for a service whose primary function had previously been the saving of lives.

This was the same year that Harry Hatch revived the production facilities of the Gooderham and Worts distillery at Toronto and his brother, Herb, bought the mortgages on a large number of fishing boats on the Great Lakes and seconded their skippers into the rum fleet. Hatch's Navy, as

these boats and men came to be called, would be easy prey
for the armed vessels the coast guard was assigning to the
lakes.

The Hatches had a number of options to choose from to
get their product to market. They could rely on the ocean-
going vessels operating along Rum Row on the East Coast, a
prospect less viable now that the three-mile limit was being
increased and the coast guard reinforced by the transfer of
twenty destroyers from the U.S. Navy. A more practical
alternative existed in the Windsor-Detroit area, where scores
of fast speedboats crossed the Detroit River daily. Despite
the concentration of border patrol officers in this area, literally millions of gallons of Canadian booze were shipped
across every year. Corruption of police, border patrol, and
customs agents was so widespread, systematized, and effective that, by the middle of the decade, the Border Cities area
had effectively displaced Rum Row as *the* booze funnel into
the United States.

The Hatches, like most of the large distillers, did not rely
solely on any one method to get their product to market. If
anything they were more versatile than their competitors
and, unlike them, they developed a system that enabled
Gooderham and Worts to export huge amounts of whisky
from Great Lakes ports with almost no interference from the
coast guard. At Whitby, Hatch and McGuiness had the
Heyden Boat Works install twin Packard engines in several
of these open fish boats. So equipped, each boat was able to
haul an enormous quantity of whisky. On average, a twenty-
five-foot fish boat could carry twenty-five to fifty burlap bags
of booze. But they devised a system whereby each boat could
take several times that much. A large fish net was slung on
each side of the boat running from bow to stern. Each net
was loaded with bottles of booze, the weight of which was
greatly reduced because the whole load was under water. The
method was a closely guarded secret; all loading was done
after dark, after which the fleet proceeded across the lake

where the fish nets and their valuable cargo were deposited on the sand bars off Olcott, New York. When they were certain the coast was clear, the American buyers would go out and retrieve the nets. Commercial fishing had never been so profitable.

This system had two major advantages. First, it enabled each boat and crew to transport several times the amount carried by the traditional method. Second, it rendered seizure of the whisky by the coast guard almost impossible. Should a cutter come across the boats, each skipper was able to cut the nets free in a matter of seconds, allowing them to sink to the bottom of the lake. The nets were marked so that they could be retrieved later. One method of marking the sunken cache was to attach both a buoy and a large piece of salt to the net. Once the salt melted, the buoy would float to the top where the smugglers could retrieve both it and the net full of booze. This system, while it helped the fishermen-smugglers avoid arrest, could be expensive. A lot of time could be spent in finding and retrieving the loads, some of which would be either irretrievably lost or found by rival smugglers.

To reduce this cost, Herb Hatch and Larry McGuiness had Tom Heyden design a boat they called the master cruiser. Powered by twin Packard engines, the first of these was forty-four feet in length and had the firepower and speed to defeat the coast guard picket boats. Herb hired Slim Humphreys of Whitby to command his new boat and to test out new ones as they were completed by Heyden Boat Works. All told, Slim Humphreys tested nine of these boats, two of which were stationed on Lake Ontario. One was kept at Whitby, the other may have been stationed at Toronto but, in any case, was not posted to the eastern end of the lake, an area dominated by independents.

Spray, the name Hatch gave his master cruiser, was not built to blow the picket boats out of the water, although that was possible, but rather to lure them away from the fishing fleet. Hatch knew full well that open warfare with the coast guard would have drawn more attention to the lakes and would have led to the deployment of even more cutters and picket boats.

The system worked extremely well. One former resident of Whitby remembers flatcars, loaded six cases high with Gooderham and Worts whisky, sitting on the old Nip and Tuck railway siding. The siding ran from Port Whitby for a distance of about a mile where it hooked up with the CNR spur line. The old Nip and Tuck was frequently full of flatcars, all loaded with good Canadian whisky. At dusk the fishing fleet would be sitting out in the harbour waiting for nightfall so they could come in and load up. During the night, the noise from the unloading and the breaking open of the wooden cases could be heard all the way to Heyden's shore, three-quarters of a mile away. In the morning the flatcars would still be there, but all the booze would be gone. The man who remembers all this was just a young boy at the time. His fondest memories are of the broken wooden cases, which he and his chums used to make into rafts, on which they floated through idyllic summer holidays.

In the ensuing years, as the coast guard fleet expanded to a veritable armada, many independent operators decided the route to survival lay in joining Hatch's Navy. In return for protection they agreed to carry only what they were told.

One of the largest independents to come to this decision was Rocco Perri. He had moved into the liquor export business in 1921, putting his bootlegging operations into the capable hands of Bessi Starkman while he developed the export business. Much of Rocco's fleet of fifty fishing boats operated on Lake Erie and were used to run booze both to the States and also back into Canada. Once Rocco had put his boats under Hatch's control they were sent to the Heyden Boat Works to be refitted with Packard Motors and a mastercruiser was made available to protect them. The addition of Rocco's fleet gave Hatch's Navy domination of the lakes.

If Sam Bronfman, president of Seagrams, wanted to ship booze on the Great Lakes in large quantities, he had to rely on Hatch's Navy. The independents were simply unable to guarantee delivery of large quantities. Moreover, Sam Bronfman, despite his reputation for a terrible temper, was somewhat in awe of the tough, hard-driving Harry Hatch, who made it clear that Bronfman could not operate in Ontario without his approval. Neither man had much love for the other, but neither was capable on his own of supplying the demand from the huge American market to the south. Consequently, a certain amount of cooperation was to the advantage of both.

As for the independents operating on eastern Lake Ontario, the Hatches seem to have had a grudging respect for their courage, if not their intelligence, in venturing out onto the lakes against odds that increasingly were stacked against them.

By 1923, whisky smuggling on the Great Lakes had dropped off dramatically. Whisky landed by ocean-going ships on the northeast seaboard was almost as cheap as the whisky delivered to the American side of the Great Lakes, and did not have to be trucked 300 or more miles to reach the major markets of Boston and New York City. To deliver booze to these markets via the lakes involved extra costs for trucks, drivers, and maintenance. There were also extra risks. Three hundred miles of trucking provided many opportunities for hijackers. To protect against them, the rum-runners hired gunmen to ride shotgun with the drivers and often sent an advance empty vehicle as a decoy. All of these stratagems added extra costs. If rival bootleggers got wind of the shipment, they would either attempt to hijack the load en route or they would alert the federal agents or border patrol and the whole load would be seized. These hazards contrasted to the relative ease, during the years when the three-mile limit was in effect, with which booze could be smuggled in from the sea. As a consequence, the market for lake-smuggled whisky was limited to centres close to the lakes, such as Rochester, Syracuse, Buffalo, Cleveland, and Detroit.

Enterprising rum-runners augmented the diminished trade in hard liquors by smuggling Canadian ale. The profit per case was less but the demand was greater, as the large ocean-going ships ignored ale in favour of the more profitable liquors, including champagne, rye whisky, and, especially, Scotch.

To make big money smuggling ale on the lakes required the use of larger boats. They had to be beamy and they usually offered a fairly high profile on the water. These characteristics, while enabling them to carry large loads, also slowed them down, made them easier to spot, and presented a larger target for coast guard guns.

After his release from the Rochester jail following his arrest in 1925, Ben Kerr did not rejoin the ale fleet, but instead returned to his earlier activity of smuggling whisky. His decision was timely. The coast guard's campaign against Rum Row and the extension of the three-mile limit had been successful; good whisky was once again in short supply. The mere announcement of the coast guard's expansion plans had caused an increase in prices, and the profits to the rum-runner had risen accordingly. The old mark-up of $3 a case had gone up to $7, and the pressure of demand threatened to push it still higher. In order to get their product to market, many Canadian breweries vied for the rum-runners' services by paying them a ten-cent-a-case bonus in addition to the mark-up of $2 to $3 paid by the American buyers. The inducement was not enough for Ben Kerr, who, henceforward, specialized in whisky and, for a brief period, pure alcohol.[1] Kerr was one of the smugglers who ordered a boat built to his specifications.

The *Pollywog* took a year to construct, but was ready by the fall of 1925. Powered by twin 180-horsepower Kermath engines, this sleek, black mahogany craft was capable of making thirty-five miles per hour while carrying a hundred cases of whisky. Although forty feet long, her carrying capacity was much less than the *Martimas*, due to a narrower beam and lower freeboard. The *Pollywog* sat low in the water, even her cabin's profile was low. Nevertheless, she was a fairly comfortable boat. There were bunks for Kerr and his two crew members, a galley for the cook, and a table used for eating or playing cards. There were even curtains on the cabin windows. Steel sheeting fastened to the hull enabled the *Pollywog* to travel the lake in all seasons.[2] When making deliveries in winter, Kerr would navigate his boat as close to shore as possible, ignoring the danger of being trapped in shore ice. When further progress was no longer possible, the load would be transferred to an ice punt constructed specifically for the purpose. Once the load was transferred, it became the American buyer's responsibility. Kerr himself never went ashore. As he told Jack Morris, "If they catch me again, I'll never get out of jail."

Why Ben Kerr continued in the dangerous game of rum-running, knowing his capture would result in a long prison term, is unclear. He had originally gotten into the business as a result of hard times following the war, but by 1925 that motivation was a good deal less compelling. Financially, he was in excellent shape with a large sum of money in the bank, rumoured at about $50,000, and a beautiful home on Bay Street North in Hamilton worth $40,000, roughly ten times the value of the average new home. As well, he owned three speedboats and a marina with thirty boat-houses, which provided a nice rental income. The post-war depression had lifted, so Kerr could have made a good living from plumbing or boat building. Of course, rum-running was far more profitable than either of these legitimate pursuits. But it was not only the lure of big money that kept him in the business. If money had been the only motive, he would have followed the example of Earl McQueen and other successful rum-runners and would have hired others to run his boats.

That way, he could have avoided the risk of a long prison sentence and the hardships and dangers of the lake in winter. Instead, he continued to captain the *Pollywog* personally, sometimes going alone. In doing so, he greatly increased the odds against himself. A crew member was essential in the event Kerr became ill, or the *Pollywog* suffered a mechanical breakdown.

Although he took a business-like approach to rum-running, this loner was clearly in it for more than the money. He needed to keep the adrenalin pumping, his nerves popping; ordinary living was just too dull. Like the Mario Andrettis and Bob Haywards of this world, he cooly calculated the risks, and then, supremely confident of his abilities, pushed his skill and luck to their outer limits.

In the year following his capture by Mason McCune, Ben Kerr made three or four deliveries almost every week.[3] He relied on secrecy, his own guile, and the speed of the *Pollywog* to elude the coast guard, and, for him, these tactics worked.

In contrast to Ben Kerr's success in evading the coast guard, Wild Bill Sheldon seemed to be constantly in their toils.[4] He was first captured on February 16, 1925, when he managed to get his boat, the *Dancer*, trapped in the ice off Braddock Point lighthouse, fourteen miles west of Rochester. A week earlier, the feds had been tipped off that a delivery of gin had been made to the same beach by Sheldon. They maintained a constant watch on the area and, when the *Dancer* got stuck, they crossed the ice on foot and arrested Wild Bill and his crew member, Ulrich Meade, who was the only recorded black rum-runner on Lake Ontario.

Wild Bill and Ulrich Meade posted the required $2,000 bail and returned immediately to the smuggling game. A few months later, Wild Bill was captured again. The arrest took place east of Rochester, which placed him within the jurisdiction of a different court. His previous capture had taken place within the jurisdiction of the Western District Court where he had given the name William Sheldon. Now he volunteered that he was William Sheridan. The presiding judge for the Northern District Court at Utica did not connect him with his pending trial at Rochester and, on October 2, 1925, he was freed on posting $5,000 bail. Later that same month, he was captured again, once again near his old stomping grounds off Braddock's Point lighthouse, west of Rochester. His boat and cargo of 100 cases of ale were seized. On posting $2,000 bail, Sheldon was released and ordered to appear for trial on May 18, 1926. The next month he appeared at Utica and was sentenced to pay a $750 fine.

During 1925, Wild Bill Sheldon, alias Bill Sheridan, had bungled himself into three arrests with no penalty beyond a relatively light fine, thanks to the confusion that had descended on the court system after the passage of the Prohibition Amendment. In a single day, one New York court processed no fewer than 144 cases. In a single year, upstate New York courts alone had to deal with 7,000 indictments under the Volstead Act. Moreover, many judges were so unsympathetic to Prohibition, they consistently handed down penalties that were less than the minimum prescribed by law. It would appear that Wild Bill was tried at Utica by one of those judges. The backlog of cases also meant that, once he had posted bail, a Volstead offender could anticipate a wait of a year or more before coming to trial. Sheldon and Meade, for example, were arrested in February 1925 but did not come before the court for sentencing until May 1926.

In the meantime, Sheldon carried on in fine style. Gerald Mouck, a farmer from South Bay, remembers Wild Bill and Ulrich Meade tooling around the gravel roads of Prince Edward County in a big touring Cadillac. They would stop in at Port Milford and visit with the fishermen and other rumrunners where Wild Bill would regale the habitués of the wharf with tales of his daring and narrow escapes, punctuating a good story with three fingers of bourbon which he knocked back neat. One such story involved Meade's and

Sheldon's escape from customs officers in a fusillade of bullets, one of which caught Wild Bill in the leg. "Hell," he would say, "they'll have to do better than that to stop me. They'll have to shoot me in the head." Puffing on his thick Cuban cigar and then lifting his three fingers of bourbon, he would toast the wharf rats: "Down the hatch, boys."[5]

Having lost his own boat, Wild Bill was now reduced to the status of "puller," that is, he drove boats owned by others. He was hired by George Hardy of Toronto to captain the *Jim Lulu*, one of the most handsome boats in the rum-running fleet. This forty-five-foot cabin cruiser had been hauling beer and whisky on Lake Ontario for at least two years. It contained conveniences not generally found on a black ship, including an electric-starting Peerless motor, built-in bunks, a stove, an ice box, a sink, and a complete toilet and lavatory. In spite of these conveniences, the *Jim Lulu* was no longer suited to rum-running. Her fifty horse-power engine was fine for pleasure-cruising, but gave the big boat a top speed of just eight knots.[6] With the arrival of the fast new picket boats, the *Jim Lulu* was obsolete.

Wild Bill was never one to worry about the odds. The *Jim Lulu* was easily the best equipped, most expensive rum boat he had ever commanded. He was at the helm in the early morning hours of May 18, 1926, when the crew of *CG-2330* spotted the *Jim Lulu* just off Watumak beach where Sheldon and Ulrich Meade had been captured twice before. Bo'sun A.L. Lindsey was in command of the picket boat, which quickly overtook the slower black ship. Lindsey ordered Wild Bill to "round 'er up there," but was ignored. Six rounds were then fired across the *Jim Lulu*'s bows with no effect. Finally, Lindsey ordered a crew member to use the Lewis machine gun to fire into the black ship's hull. With .30-calibre bullets ripping through his boat, Wild Bill finally surrendered. On board the *Jim Lulu*, the coastguardsmen found 150 sacks of Ecker Canadian ale. Another fifty sacks were discovered hidden in a garage at Watumak beach, suggesting the crew of the *Jim Lulu* had been unloading when they heard *CG-2330* approaching and had attempted to slip away undetected.

The capture at Watumak beach near Rochester took place on the same day Wild Bill and Ulrich Meade were scheduled to appear in Rochester for sentencing. Apparently, they had decided to make their trip to Rochester profitable. A third man, Frank Gordon, had been brought along to drive the *Jim Lulu* back to Toronto, while Wild Bill and Meade made their appearance in court. It was the third time the duo had been captured off Watumak beach near Braddock Point lighthouse and a stiff sentence could be expected.

Wild Bill was an arresting figure. His dark Mediterranean complexion had been blackened by years of exposure to the elements. Size-twelve boots were matched by hands, large and weathered, which contrasted starkly with the diamond rings that glinted on his tobacco-stained fingers. A mouthful of gold-capped teeth flashed a neon smile. All this was set off by a towering frame, covered by a massive sheepskin coat. When he strode into the courtroom, black and flashing, Ulrich Meade trailing behind, William Sheldon resembled some Turkish Pasha who had somehow strayed from the desert.

In keeping with Wild Bill's grand appearance, the judge fixed Sheldon's bail at the munificent sum of $10,000. Bail for the unlucky Ulrich Meade was set at $5,000, and for the hapless Frank Gordon, at a mere $2,500. None of the men were able to come up with the money and were held over in the local jail for sentencing.

Three weeks later, Sheldon and Meade were each sentenced by District Judge John Hazel to a $1,000 fine and six months in the Monroe County Penitentiary. It was a stiff enough sentence to send Ulrich Meade in search of other work. It did not, however, daunt Wild Bill.

The owner of the *Jim Lulu* also suffered a severe loss. Normally, captured rum ships were stored in the Rochester basin and then auctioned off. At these auctions, the former owners of the boats or someone acting as their agent would buy them for a fraction of their real worth. But Congress had recently passed legislation empowering the coast guard to impress captured rummies. The *Jim Lulu*, with an appraised value of $8,000 (more than the cost of a new picket boat), was inducted into the coast guard. As *CG-2380*, she spent her remaining days chasing rum-runners, finally ending a colourful career by accidentally catching fire and burning to the water line.

One particularly potent ally of the coast guard was Judge Frank Cooper. He presided over the Northern District Court of New York, which covered twenty-nine counties in the central and northern parts of the state. Court was held several times a year, usually in Syracuse or Albany, but occasionally in Binghampton or Auburn. Judge Cooper privately harboured doubts as to the wisdom of the Volstead Act, but was distressed by the volume of cases and the growing contempt for the law. As the roaring twenties progressed, violators flaunted their disdain for Prohibition more and more openly. Judge Cooper responded by severely increasing both fines and jail terms. In 1923, his court handed out fines totalling $448,747, the second highest of any court in the nation. The next year his court more than doubled its fines, to $938,350, 90 per cent of them for Volstead violations. In 1925, the judge initiated the drastic new plan of charging smugglers under both the Tariff Act of 1922 and the Volstead Act. By 1929, Judge Cooper estimated that his efforts at enforcing Prohibition had enriched the United States treasury by $5 million. Rum-runners dreaded being caught in his jurisdiction, and it is probable his presence had much to do with the greater volume of smuggling into the Rochester area, which lay outside his jurisdiction, compared to the Oswego and Syracuse areas.

One unfortunate soul who came before Judge Cooper was the former stunt pilot, Charlie Mills. Mills and his son, Bud

Mills, were captured in September 1925 and later released by the commissioner at Oswego on posting of $6,000 bail. By pleading not guilty, the two men were able to postpone their trials until the following summer. Edwin then opted to plead guilty and was fined $5,000 and sentenced to thirty days at Schenectady County Jail. Had he been charged only under the Volstead Act, he could not, as a first offender, have been fined more than $1,000.

The elder Mills, as owner and captain of the boat, could expect a somewhat stiffer sentence. Although he was living in Canada and could not be extradited, Charlie Mills nevertheless decided to take his chances and pleaded guilty. On October 12, 1926, he stood before Judge Frank Cooper. It was Mills's first offence, but Cooper had studied Commander Jackson's arrest report, which read in part:

> Mills Snr. stated it was his first load, but I have information that a man by that name has been operating at bootlegging for the past three or four years and every effort has been made to get him. If he is the same man, and I am sure he is, he is a Canadian...He is well informed and seems to know everyone that is connected with the bootlegging business in this section including the lawyer and the bondsman and I would not be surprised if they did not appear for a trial...I am sure it was an important capture...Mills is somewhat of a leader in the business.[7]

Judge Frank Cooper handed down a sentence that did nothing to diminish his reputation for toughness. Mills was fined $10,000 and sentenced to a serve a year and a day at the federal penitentiary in Atlanta, Georgia.[8] Had he been charged under the Volstead Act alone, the maximum sentence he could have received was six months. For the former stunt pilot and toast of Niagara Falls, it was a hard blow.

After forty-seven years of hard living, the slender physique of Charlie Mills was not equipped for the rigours of penitentiary life.

Another captured rum-runner was more lucky. Nick Vandeveer of Port Colborne argued vigorously that the coast guard had seized him in Canadian waters. The American judge at Buffalo agreed, dismissing the charges and ordering Vandeveer's forty-four-foot cruiser and cargo of 608 cases of ale returned to him. When Vandeveer went to collect, he found the cruiser badly damaged and 200 cases of ale missing.[9] The bespectacled, Dutch-Canadian made a bad enemy. His resolution to square accounts would lead to the famous "Battle of Point Abino," an engagement of considerable embarrassment to the coast guard.

12

THE BATTLE
OF POINT ABINO

There are no less than seventy-five of the liquor gangsters, smugglers, bootleggers and gunmen constantly on the job in Port Colborne these days....The bootleggers complained of the presence of a staff photographer and a correspondent for the NEWS to the Port Colborne customs authorities. The customs men arrested the reporters and ejected them from Canada.

> Buffalo *News*
> July 9, 1926

As the terminus for the Welland Canal on Lake Erie, Port Colborne was the natural port of exit for boats from Lake Ontario carrying whisky from Corby's, Wiser's, or Gooderham and Worts. From Port Colborne, these boats could clear for Cleveland, Toledo, or any number of ports on the American side of Lake Erie. The most popular destination was Buffalo, just thirteen short miles due east of Port Colborne, and most of that distance in Canadian waters. This posed an irksome problem for the coast guard as they could not legally seize or interfere in any way with a rum ship until it had crossed into American territory. But it was a boon to the rum-runners, who made Port Colborne the major centre for liquor exports on Lake Erie. In one twenty-five-day period in 1927, no less than 7,090 bags of ale, 86 cases of wine, 60 cases of gin, and 2,070 cases of whisky cleared from its docks for the short run to the U.S.A.[1]

A large number of rum-runners were based in the tiny city, particularly during the middle years of Prohibition from 1924 to 1927. But one family, the Vandeveers, remained dominant throughout the decade. The father, Aaron, was the organizing brains behind the team, but it was his son, Amos, known as Nick, whose escapades garnered all the publicity.[2] The two men operated several boats, hiring pullers for some but driving others themselves. Their success was due, at least in part, to their willingness to reduce their profit margin by buying off the coast guard, the customs border patrol, and any others who could upset their smooth-running operation. It was this businesslike approach that enabled Nick Vandeveer to build an impressive brick home, complete with bevelled glass windows and doors, and boasting the first electrically controlled central heating furnace to be installed in Port Colborne.[3]

As every businessman knows, there is always something you cannot anticipate or protect against. It was the unanticipated that caught Nick Vandeveer off guard, resulting in the so-called Battle of Point Abino.

On the warm summer's evening of June 28, 1926, Nick Vandeveer and his crew member, Davie Marr, were laying off Point Abino in an unmarked rum boat. On board their boat was a full load of Gooderham and Worts's Carstairs whisky, destined for delivery to the New York Central Railway's number one shed in Buffalo.[4] They were watching the red and purple slashes across the western sky, waiting for the sun to set. In their line of work, the less light the better. And so, relaxed, waiting for darkness, they did not notice *CG-2205* approaching from the east.

Vandeveer knew the dangers these speedy picket boats presented and had managed to put the bo'sun, who normally commanded the picket boat, on his pay-off list. What he did not know was that the man had gotten drunk that evening and had been replaced by Joe Hebert, a youthful twenty-one-year-old with only fourteen months' coast guard experience.[5] In going after Vandeveer, Hebert, a former housepainter, had the advantage of a faster boat armed with rifles, revolvers, and a machine-gun. They were not enough. For while he had no weapons, the thirty-two-year-old Vandeveer was already an old salt who knew the lake thoroughly and, more important, knew how to take sightings to determine whether he was in Canadian or American waters. The knowledge that he was in the former probably dulled his vigilance; neither he nor Davie Marr noticed the approaching picket boat.

When he spotted Vandeveer's boat, the inexperienced Hebert made a visual judgement that the black ship was in American waters and gave chase. When he was about five yards away Hebert's crew began firing at Vandeveer's boat. Hebert, who was at the helm, joined in with his .38-calibre service revolver. He also shouted for Vandeveer to "heave to" and "surrender." Finally alerted to the danger, Vandeveer put on full throttle and headed for the Canadian shore. At this point about fifteen rounds had been fired by the coast-guardsmen. The two boats raced across the lake for about two miles until *CG-2205* was slightly ahead of Vandeveer and on his starboard bow. Thinking to cut off the rum-runner, Hebert cut sharply to port. Vandeveer's big cruiser slammed into the picket boat amidships, stalling the smaller craft's engine with the force of the impact. At this point, engineer Lee Meston of the picket boat's crew elected to play the swashbuckling hero. Pistol in hand, he leaped onto the deck of the rum-runner's boat and demanded they surrender. But Vandeveer's boat was not immobilized; he simply ignored Meston's orders and resumed his course for shore.

At this point, there is a sharp divergence in the stories of what happened. Lee Meston claims he was disarmed by Vandeveer who came at him with a bottle. Vandeveer claims Meston first emptied his revolver at him and Marr before Vandeveer managed to get the revolver away from the coastguardsman.

Meanwhile, Hebert had been able to restart *CG-2205* and had resumed the chase, his crew occasionally firing at the fleeing Canadians with their two Springfield rifles. The young bo'sun realized he could not abandon his engineer and followed the rum boat well into Canadian waters. When Vandeveer beached his boat about a mile west of Point Abino, Hebert followed in close to shore and threw out his anchors. Hebert and a civilian, Hann, who had come along for the ride, then swam to shore and found Lee Meston alone and unharmed. In the meantime, the heavy sea had beached the picket boat and the Americans were unable to free it.

On reaching shore, Vandeveer ran to a nearby farmhouse and telephoned Canadian customs officer Catherwood. He then ran back to the beach, brandishing the revolver he had taken from Meston and demanded that the Americans surrender. A dozen angry farmers, carrying everything from pitchforks to rifles, had gathered at the scene. Two shots were fired over the picket boat and the Americans quickly capitulated. The mood of the mob was ugly, and Vandeveer was the angriest of them all. He had paid out large sums to certain coastguardsmen and felt he had been double-crossed. Even worse, they had chased him and shot up his boat when he was clearly in Canadian waters. Vandeveer went up to Bo'sun Hebert, pointed the revolver at his chest and demanded to know if he were the captain of the picket boat. If he was, Vandeveer stated, he would shoot him right there. Hebert denied he was in charge. At that point, Catherwood arrived and cooler heads prevailed.

Catherwood took the Americans to a nearby farmhouse where they were placed under an armed guard. While all this was going on, Vandeveer's boat was unloaded of its whisky, which was then hauled by horse and wagon to the farm of his brother-in-law, Lyle Minor. Carstairs whisky was being passed around by the monks, (men hired to load or unload the black boats), some of whom waded out to the beached picket boat to see what they could find. At about 4 a.m., Captain Daly, Commander of the Buffalo coast guard station, arrived. He discovered the picket boat had been looted and, among other things, was missing its two anchors, its two marine batteries (each weighing over 100 pounds), a compass, pistols, rifles, and the Lewis machine-gun. The looters had also cut the wiring and gas lines, and had badly damaged the engine. The red-faced crew of *CG-2205* were turned over to Captain Daly. The OPP placed their investigation under District Inspector Chris Airey. In a few days, Airey had recovered most of the lost equipment and conducted a thorough investigation.

Four months later, the trial of Nick Vandeveer and Davie Marr got underway. They were charged with theft relating to the coast guard equipment and with committing mischief to the engine of *CG-2205*. Magistrate Massie listened to the evidence against the two men for three hours. It was clear the Crown had no case against the rum-runners, but was merely going through the motions to satisfy the Americans. When all the evidence had been heard, Massie dismissed all charges.

It was sweet revenge for Nick Vandeveer. A year earlier, he and Davie Marr had been arrested and his forty-foot boat and 608 cartons of ale seized. A United States circuit judge had later ruled that the seizure had taken place in Canadian waters and had ordered the boat and ale returned to Vandeveer. When he had gone to the coast guard to claim his property, he had discovered 200 cases of ale were missing and the boat badly damaged. In settling accounts, he had rammed a coast guard vessel, kidnapped a crew member, seized the vessel, disarmed the crew, held them prisoner, threatened to shoot their captain, and probably instructed others to wreck the picket boat. If the coast guard was to get the better of Nick Vandeveer, they would have to send more capable and experienced officers.

When a determined rum-runner clashed with a capable and equally determined coast guard officer, the results could be quite different. Such was the case when Merle McCune and Leo Yott met in the early morning hours on Lake Ontario.[6] Yott, a long-time and highly successful bootlegger from Syracuse, had decided to go after the really big money by combining bootlegging with rum-running. He purchased the fifty-two-foot cruiser *Andy* for $8,000 and recruited James "Ching" Monahan and Pat Foley as crew – Monahan had previously served six months for bootlegging, and Foley was a dangerous underworld character with a long record.

The three men sailed out of Oswego on their first trip on July 2, 1926, arriving a few days later at Deseronto, which had a good natural harbour and, being a small town, did not have much law about. Beer or whisky could be shipped by train almost to the water's edge. In short, it was made to order as a liquor export centre. Mid "Shorty" Hunt operated a warehouse on the docks, where he stored large quantities of beer and ale for the O'Keefe Brewing Company. Leo Yott purchased 400 bags or 9,600 quarts and cleared customs with this load on July 10, 1926. Each of the 9,600 bottles cost Yott about twenty cents, but would sell in Syracuse for $1.25. If he could deliver the entire load of 9,600 quarts, his gross profit would be just over $10,000. As events were to prove, Leo Yott would go to considerable lengths to avoid losing such a profitable cargo.

To throw the coast guard off his track, Yott gave his destination as Rochester, not Oswego. This information, as well as his departure date of July 10, was phoned by Canadian customs to their American counterparts. Yott attempted to confuse the coast guard still further by not crossing the lake for several days after he had cleared from Deseronto. He and his crew laid over in Picton harbour for a few days before sailing out to Main Duck Island. Finally, six days after he had cleared from Deseronto, Leo Yott and his crew decided to chance a crossing. A little after midnight, with the lake shimmering in the moonlight, they left Main Duck and headed south for Fair Haven Bay, fourteen miles west of Oswego.

Another boat was running to Fair Haven Bay that night. Chief Bo'sun Merle McCune, commanding the *CG-2207*, had been keeping the area under surveillance for several days. As they approached a suspected landing place, McCune ordered engineer Bill Paeny to cut the engine. The picket boat barely moved on the glassy surface of the lake as each man strained to hear the muffled throb of a rum boat. They heard it almost at once. McCune started the engine and moved closer to the sound. Again he cut the engine and they drifted, the crew listening, the sound much closer. They repeated the procedure several times until, by the light of the full moon, they spotted the *Andy*'s wake. They followed it for about ten minutes, closing in on the black ship when it was about a mile and a half from shore.

Up to this point, both boats had been running without lights. Now, McCune flicked on his running lights, while surfman George Loomis trained the picket boat's powerful spotlight on the *Andy*, calling repeatedly over the hailer for the boat to stop. McCune brought *CG-2207* abeam of *Andy* and ordered Loomis and Paeny to fire warning shots into the air. Both a rifle and a pistol were emptied without effect. *Andy*'s crew did not slacken speed but continued for the American shore in the hope that the unloading party would come to their aid. McCune continued to shadow the rum boat and ordered bursts of machine-gun fire across her bow. In between bursts, Bill Paeny called on the hailer for the rum-runners to "round 'er up there." They responded by altering course and heading out onto the open lake. The picket boat had no difficulty in catching up to the heavily loaded *Andy* and, when the rum-runners continued to ignore his orders to halt, McCune finally ordered his crew to rake the rum ship with the Lewis machine-gun. A full pan of .30-calibre machine-gun bullets was fired into the bows and port side without effect. A second pan of forty-eight bullets was inserted, and McCune ordered his gunner to fire at the pilot house. *Andy* suddenly swerved and came to a stop. McCune and his crew waited. After about five minutes, two men emerged from the pilot house and surrendered. Leo Yott, aged thirty-three, was inside bleeding profusely from a fatal wound in the shoulder. The prisoners were taken to the Oswego coast guard station, arriving at about 4 a.m. Leo Yott died that night – the first rum-runner on the Great Lakes to be killed by the coast guard.

In his detailed report on the incident, Commander George Jackson noted that, in all, the crew of *CG-2207* had fired eight revolver, six rifle, and ninety-three machine-gun shots before the *Andy* had stopped. He concluded by noting, "It is regretted that it was necessary to use extreme measures to make seizure but it was evident that he did not intend to be taken and his death has made a lasting impression on others that have taken the Coast Guard lightly, thinking and saying, we would not use the guns if they would not surrender."

Following the death of Leo Yott, hostilities between the coast guard and the bootlegging community intensified. A Syracuse gang made threats against the three crew members of *CG-2207*. The McCune brothers, in particular, received many threats. At Erie, Pennsylvania, Maurice McCune was offered a cigar wrapped in a $500 bill. He dropped the cigar into the water, which caused some consternation among the men who had proffered it. Later, they would shoot his teen-age daughter's dog and, when that failed to work, they threatened to kidnap the daughter.[7] But the McCune brothers, and, indeed, most members of the coast guard, could not be bought. As a consequence, the conflict between the two factions increased. Many rum-runners who had formerly eschewed violence began carrying arms and some, including Wild Bill Sheldon, even carried sticks of dynamite with which to blow the pursuing cutters out of the water.

For those with no stomach for violence or who simply felt the risks posed by the coast guard were too great, there were two forms of smuggling open to them. They could short-circuit their loads back into Canada, or they could make even bigger profits by smuggling pure alcohol from the States into Canada, where they could sell it to the major distilleries. Always alert to profit potentials, Ben Kerr was heavily engaged in the smuggling of pure alcohol by the fall of 1925.

13

SMUGGLING INTO CANADA

"Dry America is now bootlegging to Wet Canada, the rum runner on his way north carries raw alcohol, purchased in New York or Syracuse. On his return journey, he carries whiskey and beer."

Quoted in the
Daily-Intelligencer,
July 14, 1925

Lieutenant Gorenflo of the New York State Police made this statement to the press after the police had made a thorough investigation of the burgeoning trade in pure alcohol. When the border patrol first discovered alcohol hidden in five-gallon tins in cars headed north, they were at a loss to explain their findings. The smugglers, of course, weren't talking. The investigation revealed a large-scale operation involving American bootleg operators who set up front companies in order to purchase industrial alcohol. This product was manufactured under licence from the federal government to be sold to perfume companies and other legitimate users. Initially, the bootleggers "cooked" the alcohol to remove the denaturants, thereby making it reasonably safe for human consumption. Most of this raw alcohol was then flavoured and coloured to simulate good whisky and, as such, was sold to a thirsty and gullible American public. But some of the alcohol was sold to rum-runners for $7 a gallon and then smuggled into Canada where, according to Lieutenant Gorenflo, it was being sold to Canadian distillers for $17 a gallon. It was a nice arrangement for the rum-runners, who were making profits on both legs of their trip across the lake.

In 1923, the OPP made its first seizure of smuggled raw alcohol.[1] Gradually, the number of arrests and seizures increased as the volume of alcohol flowing northward grew, reaching a peak in 1925. By that time several groups were operating on Lake Ontario and at border points from Niagara Falls eastward to Lake Champlain on the New York-Vermont border. Curiously, there was no evidence of any traffic on Lake Erie. At Niagara Falls, a fleet of eight cars operated daily, each car carrying from fifty to eighty-five gallons. They managed this by removing the back seat and loading both this area and the tonneau with either one- or five-gallon tins. The customs officers at Niagara Falls were paid not to look too closely when these cars cleared the border.[2]

The OPP and the U.S. customs border patrol were able to intercept several of these vehicles and seize a few cargoes, but they were never seriously able to impede the traffic. District Nine of the border patrol had only nineteen men to cover the area from the Pennsylvania state line east to Niagara County on Lake Ontario. The OPP was spread even more thinly, with fewer than 200 officers for the entire province. The force had no patrol boats, and their patrol cars were not yet equipped with radio. Not surprisingly, the OPP was never able to capture any of the boats smuggling raw alcohol into the province.

Only one such capture was ever made on Lake Ontario. This was accomplished by G.H. Cothran, a particularly resourceful deputy sheriff from Youngstown, New York, who staked out the lakeshore east of the Niagara River. On the evening of June 5, 1926, Cothran, together with Constable Ed Bedell, watched from the bushes as a large launch, operated by Clarence Smith, pulled in close to shore. There it was met by four men with a horse-drawn wagon loaded with five-gallon cans of alcohol. Sheriff Cothran waited until part of the load had been transferred to the launch before drawing his weapon and rushing the smugglers. He met with no resistance, but the smuggler, Smith, took Cothran aside and offered the officer a large bribe, which he turned down. Although Smith refused to give the name of his employer, the statements he and the others made point in an interesting direction.

The four monks who had been loading the boat were all neighbourhood farmers, who testified that they had loaded the craft with cans of alcohol on several different occasions. Earl Fletcher, on whose farm the arrests had taken place, stated Smith had told him it took fifty-eight minutes to cross the lake to Toronto, where he delivered the loads. The large cruiser seized by Deputy Sheriff Cothran was named *Spray Z900*.[3] When Smith pulled Cothran aside and offered him the bribe, he stated that the operation was a "big deal and going to big people in Canada."[4]

Other evidence linked Rocco Perri to the operation. A man in Whitby told the OPP he had observed the *Spray* in the harbour at various times over the previous two years and had heard that the launch belonged to the dapper little Italian.

The traffic in raw alcohol, while a problem, was not nearly as great as the traffic in liquors, which were loaded daily at scores of export docks along the Great Lakes and, while ostensibly destined for a foreign port, were, in fact, smuggled back into the province under cover of darkness. As the risks were not as great as those taken by rum-runners crossing the lake, the boat operators involved in short-circuiting were paid much less, usually only $25 to $50 a trip.

Joe Burke of Port Credit was a fairly typical operator. At

one time, he had been the Canadian amateur heavyweight boxing champion, but tuberculosis had reduced him to a shambling hulk. Burke owned the Lakeview Inn, but he directed his bootlegging operation from Martin Murray's shoe repair shop, where he had an office on the second floor overlooking Port Credit harbour.[5] The ex-pugilist was a cautious operator and, unlike the Perris, never phoned his orders to Gooderham and Worts from either his hotel or his office. How he got his orders to the distillery is not known, but it is likely he used the phone of one of his Toronto cronies. As a call within Toronto was not long distance, it could not be traced. The order would be for delivery to a ficticious buyer in the United States, and Joe Burke would be named as carrier. Burke himself never touched the cargo, drove a truck, or piloted a boat. Like Rocco Perri, he hired others for these jobs. As a consequence, the police found it very difficult to nail him.

Nels Anderson was a young fisherman when Burke hired him to accompany Al Smith in one of Burke's two large open fish boats. On a typical job, they travelled the twelve miles from Port Credit to Toronto, where they tied up at the Gooderham and Worts export dock at the foot of Parliament Street. The load of whisky, which Burke had earlier ordered by telephone, was delivered to the dock by a Gooderham and Worts truck. All the export papers were made out at the distillery. The outside customs inspector checked them and saw that the load went into the boat. Anderson and Smith then took the fish boat out through the western gap and onto the open lake. They cruised westward about a mile off shore until they spotted the tall stack of Port Credit's abandoned brick factory. Their unloading point was usually close by.

On shore, a number of automobiles were parked between the brick factory and the shoreline. One of the drivers was Vince Doyle, a high school student who had been recruited by the gang at the age of sixteen. At first, Vince had been "tried out" in the job of lookout for which he received five dollars a night; his job was to alert the group on shore if anyone approached. The town constable, and there was only one, was an early-to-bed man equipped with a horse and buggy. He did not pose much of a threat, but hijackers did. If they got wind that a load was being delivered, they would swoop down with guns blazing and try to steal the load. Secrecy was the best defence against them, which was why young Doyle was first "tried out." If he could keep his mouth shut, he would get other jobs. Eventually, he graduated from lookout to driver. He quickly learned the various signals used by the drivers on shore to alert the men on the boat. These were varied from time to time to confuse any watchers. One night, for example, the all-clear signal would require that three of the waiting cars turn on their spotlights. (Each car had two spotlights below its headlights.) Another night, the all-clear signal would require all the cars except for one to douse their lights. Lights blazing on all three cars was the signal for the crew to sail off to a hideout.

After Nels Anderson and Al Smith had unloaded their whisky, it was delivered by the drivers to various bootleggers in the area. Vince Doyle's first job as driver was to deliver a load to Mimico. The gang supplied bootleggers in a number of towns including Brampton, Bronte, and Cooksville. These local bootleggers sold directly to the public and, depending on the number and thirst of their clientele, would purchase anywhere from ten to fifty cases at a time.

Vince Doyle, like all whisky drivers, had to memorize the back roads, which were not well signed, if at all. In the dark it was easy to make a wrong turn and end up in some farmer's lane, hopelessly lost. Also, there was more risk of arrest if the driver was unfamiliar with his route. The OPP had no boats, but it did have squad cars and, after 1922, motorcycles. In the larger centres, the police usually had at least one car and were likely to have all-night patrols. To elude them the rum-runners used "whisky sixes." Hudsons,

Packards, and Chryslers were preferred because their powerful six-cylinder engines enabled them to accelerate quickly
after negotiating one of the many ninety-degree turns. The
"whisky sixes" could exceed sixty miles an hour but seldom
went that fast. Most of the province's roads were unpaved
and far too narrow for speeds much in excess of the provincial limit of twenty-five miles per hour.

It was on these roads that the OPP managed most of its
seizures. The force had been established in 1909 and had
consisted for many years of no more than fifty officers in all
ranks. In the municipalities of rural southern Ontario, local
politicians preferred to appoint their own constables. Crime
was not a problem in those simpler times, especially in the
settled rural areas where everyone knew his neighbour. The
county constable invariably had no professional training but
could rely on neighbourhood gossip to help him solve what
few serious crimes did occur.

By 1920 this peaceable life had altered considerably. The
development of a provincial highway system and the great
increase in the use of the automobile made possible a new
type of crime. Small towns and villages were suddenly
vulnerable to armed robberies, committed by men from outside the community who made their getaways in fast cars.
Bank hold-ups increased dramatically. Local constables were
totally unprepared to deal with this type of professional
crime.

The United Farm government of Premier Drury decided
to reorganize and enlarge the OPP, so that it could deal with
the new, more mobile criminal and also enforce more rigor-
ously the Ontario Temperance Act. In 1921, the OPP began a
reorganization that took two years to complete. New men
were brought in, including Major-General Victor Williams
who was recruited for the top post of Police Commissioner.
Williams was a proven administrator. During the war, he
had held the position of Adjutant-General, the army's top
administrative post. He also saw action on the front lines,

where he was wounded and taken prisoner by the Germans.

The new commissioner divided the force into two divisions. The Criminal Investigation Branch was headed up by Superintendent Joe Rogers, an old-style policeman who believed you had to use criminals to catch criminals. To head up the new OTA division, Williams recruited Alfred Cuddy from the Alberta Provincial Police, where Cuddy had been serving as commissioner. The liquor licence inspectors, charged with enforcing the OTA, were then transferred by Attorney General Raney from the Board of License Commissioners to the OPP and placed directly under the command of the new Assistant Commissioner. The addition of these licence inspectors increased the force to 105 constables from its former sixty-five. These numbers seem ridiculously small by today's standards, but it must be remembered that the population was much smaller and there were still a great many county, village, and town police forces doing work that to-day is done by the OPP.

The increase in the size of the force was less important than its modernization and improved efficiency. Williams moved quickly to bring the OPP into the twentieth century. He set up a central bureau for the filing of criminal records, hired an expert to travel to each division and train the officers in the taking of fingerprints, and organized a motorcycle squad for patrolling the provincial highways. He also pushed the government for funds to set up a police radio network. In this, he was far ahead of his time. He succeeded in creating a truly province-wide police force, one which saw the inspectors of each division cooperating with neighbouring inspectors via the telephone to apprehend law breakers.

This reorganization had an immediate impact on bootleggers and their business. In his 1925 annual report, Commissioner Williams was able to report that the force was responsible for fines under the OTA totalling $378,298.20, and that no fewer than 4,215 charges had been laid. The officers had further enriched the provincial treasury by seizing

11,371 cases and 1,510 gallons of beer, 1,945 gallons and 1,588 cases of liquor, and 3,764 gallons of pure alcohol. Much of this liquor was turned over to the government dispensary, where it was sold only to those bearing a doctor's prescription. Over $5 million worth of "prescription liquor" was sold to Ontario residents in 1924.

In his report, Williams also noted that the OTA had been amended in 1924 to allow for the seizure and confiscation of motor vehicles found transporting liquor illegally. This amendment had enabled the OPP to confiscate eighty-three vehicles from rum-runners. One of these was a touring car seized near Hamilton on November 5, 1924, and found to be loaded with beer. The vehicle was registered in the name of Joe Burke of Port Credit. The ex-fighter was not in the car and claimed he had no idea it was being used for illegal purposes.[6]

Under the OTA, the maximum fine that could be levied was $2,000, which was not too damaging in comparison with the enormous profits to be made. Frequently, judges assessed fines well below the maximum so that bootleggers came to regard the fines as part of the cost of doing business. The loss of their cargoes and vehicles was yet another cost that, providing it didn't occur too often, could be written off as an operating expense. For the large-scale bootleggers, these seizures didn't occur often enough to hinder seriously their operations. Rocco Perri, for example, kept forty souped-up Reo trucks delivering booze to a network of bootleggers, stretching from Niagara Falls through to Kitchener. Only rarely were these trucks intercepted by the police, and when they were, they could not be traced back to Perri.

As the largest bootleggers in the province, Bessie and Rocco Perri were in a unique position. Not only were they able to buy local protection, they also had influence in the highest levels of government. It was common knowledge that they entertained lavishly in their nineteen-room mansion, which, with its grand piano, oriental rugs, billiard room, (and secret subterranean distillery) was the envy of the neighbourhood. Here cabinet ministers, magistrates, top civic brass, and visiting socialites would rub shoulders with U.S. and Canadian mobsters, no doubt enjoying a vicarious thrill from their contact with these underworld kings. For underneath their patina of good grammar and expensive tastes, that is what Rocco and Bessie were. Rocco mixed with some of the highest in the land, but he never ventured out without his two bodyguards, Bill "The Butcher" Leuchter and John "Mad Gunman" Brown. These two hoods were later murdered in gangland wars.

In spite of their high connections and hired guns, Rocco and Bessie were never able to obtain total protection. At the time of the Gogo shooting in 1923, Toronto police seized two trucks and two touring cars, as well as 210 cases of Corby's whisky, all of which were probably owned by Rocco and Bessie. The booze alone had cost $8,400.

Less than a year later, they suffered another set back. The OPP received a tip that a boat would be delivering a load of Gooderham and Worts whisky to a secluded country dock near Burlington. In a cooperative effort involving Inspector Elliott of Toronto and licence inspectors McCready, Griffiths, and Williamson, the OPP staked out the location and was able to capture the truck driver and seize his truck and load. The men aboard the boat escaped. The officers then searched an abandoned farmhouse nearby and found a cache of seventy-eight cases of whisky. Altogether they seized a total of 233 cases with an estimated value of $12,000. At bootleg prices, it would be worth a lot more.[7] After the seizures, the police encountered Rocco Perri, who just happened to be in the neighbourhood at 3 a.m.

Over the years, many seizures of liquor were made that, on the surface, were not connected to Perri when, in fact, he and Bessie were the real owners. For example, Frank Di Petro was arrested on several different occasions transporting liquor in trucks registered in his own name. He was one of those arrested at the scene of the Gogo shooting and, as the registered owner of the trucks, was fined $1,000. As late as 1927, he was captured driving a load on the highway between Hamilton and Kitchener. In his possession were B-13s made out to a J. Penna of Wilson, New York. Penna was the ficticious name Perri used when ordering booze from Gooderham and Worts.[8]

These seizures, while costly to Ontario's bootleg king, were never sufficient to put him out of business. During his interview with the *Toronto Star* he stated he sometimes sold as many as 1,000 cases of whisky a day. The 1927 Royal Commission estimated the Perris grossed close to a million dollars a year.

In eastern Ontario there were no bootleggers whose operations even remotely approached the scale of Rocco Perri and Bessie Starkman's. But some were equally colourful. "Dollar Bill" Allen from Kingston was certainly the most eccentric. Residents of the limestone city still recall the pudgy bachelor sporting a three-piece suit and riding his bicycle about town, a fat cigar stuck in the middle of his round face, a red hunter's cap jammed firmly to his ears, and both pant legs circled by metal bicycle clips. He was invariably accompanied by his little dog who parked himself contentedly in the basket attached to the rear of the seat.

Dollar Bill rented the old Curtis-Reid airport hangar located at the mouth of the Cataraqui River. Here he lived, sold illegal drinks, and held court with the city's finest citizens, including a judge who enjoyed the nightly poker games. Dollar Bill frequently joined in these all-night marathons and, if he did well, dispensed silver dollars to any youngsters who showed up the next day. This was the origin of his nickname. Regardless of his gambling luck, he always provided free soft drinks to those youngsters from the less prosperous parts of town. In fact, Kingstonians remember Dollar Bill more for his charitable activities than for his bootlegging. Russell Purtell recalls playing hockey on the ice in front of the hangar and Dollar Bill bringing out sandwiches and soft drinks for the players. "We thought of him as a sort of Santa Claus," Purtell said. As he got older, Purtell would become part of Dollar Bill's clientele and get to see the seamy inside of the hangar from where drinks and food were dispensed, but his status was never sufficiently elevated to allow him entrance to the curtained-off section where the famous card games were held.

Purtell remembers that the bootlegger's speech was as arresting as his appearance. He spoke rapidly and polysyllabically. Many thought he had been a university professor but Purtell deduced, probably correctly, that the Santa Claus bootlegger didn't understand half of the words he used.[9] His real name was Bill Allen and he had been at university, but not as a professor. For three years he had worked at Queen's University taking care of the football team's equipment. This is probably where he picked up his flatulent speech habits.

Dollar Bill's eccentricity was nowhere more evident than in the prices he charged. During the 1920s, bootleggers were notorious for providing liquor of questionable authenticity at outrageous prices. But Bill Allen sold mickeys, which cost him eighty cents, for only a dollar. His generosity and colourful eccentricities made him a popular figure around Kingston, and the law generally left him alone.

One the one occasion he was arrested, Dollar Bill provided the court with one of its lighter days.[10] He decided to conduct his own defence and spoke so rapidly for over an hour that the experienced court stenographer had to keep interrupting with requests that he slow down. When she asked him to repeat what he had just said, he had already totally forgotten it. When the Crown prosecutor interrupted his machine-gun delivery with a question, Dollar Bill replied, "Please do not interrupt me in this continuity. I am a great man on continuity." He then went on to tell the court his life story and a great many other things largely irrelevant to the charges brought against him. Eventually, the monologue ended and the Crown attorney was able to ask a few questions. "How..., are you able to pay the rent if you don't charge people for the drinks and food that you serve?"

"Do you see my little dog," responded Dollar Bill, "I can get a thousand dollars for him. I have been offered nine hundred and ninety-nine dollars already. I have also ducks and chickens. My friends come to my place and find there a man who is clean mentally, morally, and physically." And so it continued for the rest of the morning. When the show was finally over, Magistrate J.W. Bradshaw found Dollar Bill guilty of keeping liquor for sale and, albeit somewhat reluctantly, fined him $100.

Norm Conley of Wolfe Island was a more typical bootlegger.[11] At the age of sixteen, he was hired by an American, known only as Sinbad the Sailor, to drive to Quebec, pick up loads of whisky, and then take the loads across to Oswego by boat. After two years of this, Sinbad got bored with Kingston and went back to Chicago. Norm Conley, alias Leo Gauger, was then free to go into business for himself. He joined forces with two Americans, Howard Bidwell, a real estate salesman, and Len Cramer, an airplane pilot. They purchased an old Stinson Detroiter and began flying loads to an outfit in Syracuse. After some months at this, the three men convinced a Miss Grey, who owned three banks in Syracuse, to lend them $15,000 to buy a larger aircraft as the Detroiter could carry only ten cases at a time. With the new plane, they were able to carry twenty to thirty cases each trip. Conley stayed at this for eight months and left with $17,000 in his pocket. But, like most young men in the business, the money was quickly spent, much of it in the same speakeasies that Conley and his friends were supplying.

Later Conley combined his rum-running activities with bootlegging. As well as taking loads across the St. Lawrence River between Cape Vincent, New York, and Wolfe Island, he also supplied beer to Mike Johnson, owner of the Wolfe

Island Hotel. Johnson bought fifty bags every two weeks and sold these in the hotel when the law wasn't around.

The Kingston Ale Company sold their Old Tower beer "for export" at $4.50 a bag. Each bag contained twenty-four quarts. Conley had certain customers in Cape Vincent, including Claude Cole and a judge, to whom he sold direct for their own consumption. Each quart of beer cost Conley less than twenty cents and was worth between $1 and $1.50 to his U.S. customers.

In his career as a rum-runner and bootlegger, which covered the years from 1923 to 1933, Norm Conley smuggled by car, by rowboat, by motor launch, by steamboat, and by airplane. He lost quite a few loads, but he was never in jail. His closest call came while taking a load to New York by car. Unexpectedly, he ran into a roadblock put up by the border patrol. He ditched the car and headed for the fence, only to find himself hung up on the barbed wire. By this time, the border patrol were firing at him for trying to escape. One bullet nicked him in the leg and, at that point, he found the extra energy needed to jerk himself free of the barbed wire and take off into the woods.

During his years in the business, Norm Conley knew many men who met violent ends. Some, such as Len Cramer, the airplane pilot, were killed accidentally, in Cramer's case in a plane crash. Others who dealt with American criminals, expired from what Conley describes as "lead poison." When Prohibition ended, Norm Conley had a lot of stories but had saved not a dime. He headed north to the gold mines to find work.

Combining the activities of rum-runner and bootlegger was a fairly common practice in eastern Ontario. At Belleville, for example, there were three major bootleggers, Doc Welbanks, Harry Ketcheson, and Harry Yanover. Both Welbanks and Ketcheson were also rum-runners.

Yanover might have done better if he had gone through with his original intention to be a rabbi. As a bootlegger, he was constantly raided by Licence Inspector Frank Naphan, one of the most persistent and successful operatives on the force. The local police suspected that Harry Yanover was buying his whisky from boats operated by J. Earl McQueen. Naphan's superiors attempted to suppress McQueen's liquor export business by ordering Naphan to seize the rum-runner's boat and load while he was carrying on his regular business. On October 16, 1922, Naphan seized the *Sonora* while she was being loaded with 200 cases of Corby's whisky at the Belleville government dock. McQueen was charged with having liquor in a public place contrary to the provisions of the OTA.[12] James Boyle, a shipper at Corby's, was also arrested when, on instructions from the plant manager, he drove to the docks with a case of samples left at the plant by mistake. Boyle was charged under the Carriage of Liquor Act, which prohibited the transportation of liquor over provincial highways. Harry Hatch testified in McQueen's and Boyles's defence. The government sent Inspector Frank Elliott of Toronto and also called on OPP District Inspector Reg Bumpstead to testify. The case was thrown out by Magistrate Masson who ruled that McQueen was a bona fide carrier as defined under the act, and that the Carriage of Liquor Act was beyond the powers of the legislature of the province. These decisions were appealed to a higher court where they were upheld by Judge Deroche. Unable to stop McQueen's liquor export operation, Inspector Naphan concentrated his energies on bootleggers; Harry Ketcheson and Harry Yanover were his prime targets.

Ketcheson owned a farm on the north side of the Belleville-Trenton road. This posed a problem as the Bay Bridge was located between the government dock, where Ketcheson picked up his load of Corby's whisky, and the shoreline in front of Ketcheson's farm where the whisky was unloaded. Most cruisers were too large to pass under the bridge. Eventually, Ketcheson found a boat with a low enough freeboard to pass safely under the bridge when fully loaded. The booze so transported was then stored in a specially constructed barn and later distributed to smaller bootleggers throughout Prince Edward and Hastings counties. The OPP and, in particular, Naphan made many searches but were never able to locate the Trent Road farmer's secret cache. But eventually, Ketcheson slipped up. He was driving along a lonely country road about midnight on June 25, 1924. In the back seat of his big sedan were three cases of Gooderham and Worts whisky, which he was taking to one of his small bootlegging customers. When Inspector Naphan spotted Ketcheson's car, the bootlegger took off at top speed. In the ensuing chase, Naphan got alongside Ketcheson who refused to pull over. As the two vehicles careened along the narrow country road, the 280-pound Naphan turned the wheel over to Trenton Police Chief William Bain and leaped onto the running board of the speeding sedan. Not surprisingly, the bulky policeman sprained his ankle, and probably dented the running board. But he succeeded in his purpose: Ketcheson was caught with the goods in his car.[13]

In contrast to the wily Ketcheson, Harry Yanover was relatively easy to catch. During the years from 1923 to 1927, the police laid eight charges against the stubby merchant, who gave his occupation as fur-buyer. Of these eight charges, one was for violation of the game laws, the other seven were for infractions of the OTA. Frank Naphan was responsible for all but one of these charges.[14]

In pursuing these bootleggers, Naphan came close to breaking the system. By checking over whisky case numbers obtained from B-13s provided by the customs officers, he was able to ascertain that liquor found in Yanover's basement had been shipped on Earl McQueen's boat, the *Ullacalula*, ostensibly to a G.W. Smith in New York State.[15] Naphan made similar connections when he raided a bootlegger in Madoc and found several cases of Corby's whisky, which, according to custom's records, had been exported to Mexico. Numerous seizures of a similar nature proved that short-circuiting was taking place on a large scale. Nevertheless, the evidence was considered too circumstantial for charges to be laid against the "exporters." Naphan and his associates would actually have to catch them in the act of bringing the booze back into Ontario.

The location of the Corby plant, just a few miles north of Belleville, helped make that city one of the busiest "export" centres on the lakes. In the 1920s, the Corbyville distillery was the largest in the British Empire, capable of producing 10,000 gallons a day.[16] Much of this production was shipped out by freight cars to Windsor and other cities, but a substantial amount was exported by boat directly from the Belleville government dock. On average, between 350 and 500 boats cleared the local customs house each year, most of which were carrying booze.[17] With so many vessels clearing each week, it was relatively easy for a few of these to come back in and unload their cargoes without being detected.

To facilitate this process, Herb Hatch had purchased Cedar Island in 1922 while he and Harry were still connected with Corby's.[18] If McQueen was scheduled to bring a load back into the region, he would simply sail east from the government dock in the direction of the gap leading into Big Bay. Before reaching the gap, he would pass Cedar Island, which lies close to the north shore of Prince Edward County. Normally, he would continue on, past the island and out through the gap on his trip to the States. But, if he was short-circuiting a load, he would simply pull in behind the island, out of sight of anyone on the government dock two and a half miles away. There, he would throw out an anchor, sit back, and relax until dark.

One of the favourite landing spots for short-circuiters was a mile or so east of Cedar Island, near Point Anne. A little further east along the shore was another, near Shannonville. At both these locations, local bootleggers purchased the loads and then resold them to smaller operators. Some of the loads were actually brought right back into Belleville. In a half-mile stretch along the main street, there were no fewer than nineteen places where a thirsty patron could buy an illegal drink.[19] This number did not include the city's many private clubs. One of these, the Belleville Club, counted many of the city's most distinguished citizens as its members. Earl McQueen kept them supplied with the best brands of Scotch and rye. Major E.A. Geen, whose father, Reverend A.L. Geen, founded the drugstore which still bears the family name, often savoured a glass of his favourite rye while enjoying the fellowship of the club. The Major was for many years the chief excise officer at the local customs office.

Another prominent citizen who, like McQueen, engaged in both exporting and short-circuiting was Doctor Hedley Welbanks. The son of a Milford farmer in Prince Edward County, the doctor had served in the veterinary section of the British Army during the war, where he saw action at Salonika in Greece. For some months Captain Welbanks was posted to England where he met and married an English girl. At the end of the conflict, the doctor left his war bride and slipped away quietly to Canada where he already had a wife and family. Doc Welbanks, it appeared, liked women almost as much as he liked horses and good whisky. His marital indiscretion might suggest otherwise, but those who knew him best maintain that the doctor's first love was his horses. Accompanied by his driver, Little Billy Smith, he was a regular competitor around the sulky tracks of Eastern Ontario. His great delight was to join his friends in the tack room and swap tales about racing and the breeding of horses. Little Billy was not only his driver, he also assisted the doctor in his rounds throughout the countryside. When Welbanks decided to go into the liquor export business, it was Billy who went along with him in the boat. They were a Mutt and Jeff combination. Little Billy was barely five feet tall, whereas the burly, thick-shouldered doctor stood a foot taller and was more than double Billy's weight.[20]

When he first got into the business, the doctor would take

along the Webley service revolver he had carried as a captain in the army. He was a tough, blunt man and there is not much doubt he would have used it on any would-be hi-jackers. In the early days of Prohibition the coast guard was not a problem, and the doctor soon had enough profits to expand his operation. By 1925 he had three boats and was no longer taking loads across the lake himself. He acted as a contact man for Corby's, working closely with Wes Kaiser, who ran a fleet of fishing boats smuggling Corby's whisky across to Rochester.[21] The hard working veterinarian also carried on an active bootlegging trade. Certain provisions of the OTA made it particularly easy for him to do this. Whisky was still regarded as a medicine, and the act allowed a vet to carry as much as a quart to administer to sick horses. Doc Welbanks saw a lot of sick horses on his rounds.

An even larger profit was available to him, and indeed to veterinarians across the province, through the provisions in the act allowing them to buy raw alcohol for use in making medicines. As veterinarians were exempt from the usual government taxes, they were able to buy raw alcohol by the barrel for $2.60 a gallon. To each gallon they would add two gallons of water to make a regular strength whisky. It didn't taste like properly aged whisky, but it was safe and it packed a wallop. Doc Welbanks sold it in quart bottles for $5 a bottle. The bottles bore a blue label emblazoned with a black horse and the title, *Doctor Welbanks' White Liniment*. The alcohol itself, after dilution, cost the doctor twenty-two cents a quart, the bottle and label cost slightly more.[22]

The local police obtained warrants to search the Welbanks home on several occasions, but were unable to find anything incriminating. Naphan then gathered evidence showing that three of the local vets had been purchasing more than the quart of whisky a day allowed them under the OTA. This was fairly easy for Naphan to do because the only source of supply in the city were the local druggists, who were required to keep a record of all transactions. The Crown attorney decided to bring charges against Dr Harkworth Honeywell, a well-known boozer who had abused his position as a veterinarian to buy liquor so frequently one Belleville druggist refused to sell to him.

At his trial, all four local druggists testified to the large and frequent purchases made by the accused, who sometimes returned to a drug store as often as three times in a single day. Usually the good doctor purchased at least a quart but, on one occasion, ordered a mere three ounces. This moved the bench to remark that perhaps he was treating a canary bird.

The evidence left no doubt that Dr Honeywell was in breach of the OTA regulations governing the amount of liquor a veterinarian could purchase. But Magistrate Masson held that the prosecution had not proven he was guilty of actually selling any of it. He dismissed all charges.[23]

An often unfriendly court added to the many difficulties the police faced in trying to enforce the OTA. Setbacks such as this did not seem to bother Inspector Naphan, who appeared to operate on the premise that the more charges you laid, the more lawbreakers you would eventually put in jail. His most successful effort came about as a result of a fiasco at Cressy Flats. This series of events resulted from spring mud, talkative farm lads, thieving neighbours, and good detective work.

In April 1925, the rum-runner Charlie Mills delivered a boat load of Corby's whisky to Prinyer Cove on the flats near the hamlet of Cressy at the southeast tip of Prince Edward County. The load was transferred to two waiting automobiles by Bain Hurlburt, a local farmer, who hauled the booze up the embankment using a team of horses hitched to a Finnegan lumber wagon. During the transfer, one of the automobiles got stuck in the muddy goo of the township road. Harry Yanover called on several of the local lads to help push the car onto drier land. As Yanover was originally from Picton, a number of them recognized him. While this was going on, three of the more astute farm boys noticed that, during the confusion, the whisky on the Finnegan wagon had been left unguarded. Stewart Powers, Ross Hicks, and his brother, Earl, tucked a case of whisky under each arm and made off into the bushes. In the darkness of the early evening and the confusion surrounding the mired automobile, no one noticed that six cases were missing.

In those days a farm worker earned a $1.50 a day. A case of good whisky sold for about $60 and had a bootleg value at least double that amount. To protect their liquid gold, the three young farmers went to considerable, if unimaginative, efforts to hide it. Unfortunately, the temptation to brag about their good fortune was too great. At least it was for Earl Hicks who, the next day, foolishly divulged their secret to a number of his neighbours lounging about the Cressy general store. Earl had never had so attentive an audience. One rapt listener inquired as to how he could be sure it was hidden safely. Basking in his new-found importance, the young farmer babbled on, dropping hints as to how cleverly the booze had been stashed in a neighbour's barn.

Earl Hick's indiscretion touched off a series of midnight raids which saw the whisky moved from barn to barn as one group stole it, another group stole it back, and so on, until the whisky had been into more barns than a prize bull.

Word of these nocturnal raids soon reached the police. District Inspector Reg Bumpstead provided three officers to assist Inspector Frank Naphan, and the investigation got underway. When the OPP squad car and the four officers arrived at Cressy, they stopped a local farmer at the general store and asked for directions to the homes of the various suspects. The farmer obliged the officers with detailed directions, then, after they had departed, took off for Kingston to spend two weeks with his sister. One of the farms he had directed them to was his own.

The next two weeks were among the most eventful in the entire history of the hamlet of Cressy, as first one farmer and then another was subjected to lengthy police interrogation. If a man's story didn't tally with his neighbour's, he was questioned all over again. For the tiny community, it was great drama. There was no television to watch, no radio to listen to, even the Picton Theatre would not be open for another year.

At the end of two weeks of investigation, Inspector Naphan had his case. Seven men were charged and all but one were convicted. Bain Hurlburt, who hauled the whisky from the boat in his wagon, was fined $200 for illegally transporting whisky. Stewart Powers and Nathan Hicks were each fined $200 on a similar charge. Two other men were fined $100 and court costs for drinking in a public place. Ross Hicks, who was charged with illegal transportation of liquor, was acquitted when he claimed not to have known what was in the cases. But the biggest fish in the police net was Harry Yanover. The George Street fur merchant was fined $1,000 and costs.[24]

Years later, a Cressy resident, Dick Slater, went to see Picton Police Chief Bert Biddle and presented him with two bottles of Corby's whisky. It seemed that Stewart Powers had given these to Slater and told him to hide them "until things blow over." The stolen whisky had caused such a stir, Slater had been afraid to drink them. In fact, whenever he thought of the two bottles of contraband, he got uncomfortable. Even his wife didn't know he had them, so he was easing his conscience. He hoped the Chief would treat him leniently. Slater left.

What was the Chief to do? Prohibition was over. Possession of liquor was in itself not a crime. He could charge Richard Slater with possession of stolen property, but that seemed unnecessarily harsh. Slater was a family man; a hard-working farmer, and more honest than most.

It took a man quite a few steps to walk around the Chief. His circumference was nearly equal to his height. The big man sat there and stared at the two bottles of amber coloured liquid for a long time. The Chief sat and stared some more.

What happened to the two bottles of whisky will never be known.

In the fiasco at Cressy flats, the work of Inspector Naphan and the OPP had several positive results in the war against bootlegging. In the first place, Harry Yanover suffered a substantial financial setback. Moreover, his conviction made him more vulnerable. Within six months Naphan would catch him again, resulting in yet another $1,000 fine plus four months in jail. Finally, the farmers in Prince Edward County, having observed the relatively heavy penalty handed out to Bain Hurlburt, were less willing to assist rum-runners in short-circuiting their loads into the county. In only one respect did Naphan fail. No charges were brought against the rum-runner Charlie Mills, possibly because the local farmers could not or would not identify him. Both Earl Hicks and Stewart Powers knew who he was. A few months later, the U.S. coast guard managed what the OPP could not when Merle McCune captured Mills and his son near Oswego. Charlie Mills was subsequently sentenced to a year and a day in the federal prison in Atlanta, Georgia.

Inspector Frank Naphan's lack of success against lake smuggling was typical of the force generally. They had much better luck against smugglers on land. Naphan himself had a great deal of success in catching smugglers from Quebec. In one case he seized 12,600 pints of Dow Ale, which had been shipped from Côte St Paul in a CN freight car hidden behind two-by-four scattling lumber. The waybill described the cargo as birch lumber. This seizure took place within two weeks following the investigation at Cressy flats. Naphan, who seemed to be always on the job, made the seizure on a Saturday afternoon.[25]

A few months later, the vigilant Inspector found himself involved in the most exciting pursuit of his career. Provincial Police headquarters in Toronto phoned all detachments east to Kingston to be on the look-out for a McLaughlin Buick thought to be carrying a load of contraband liquor. At 3 a.m. that Sunday morning, Naphan, accompanied by Sergeant Rae and Constable Kenny, spotted the car east of Belleville and chased it into the city. The squad car, a Paige, was not fast enough to overtake the larger, more powerful Buick, but when they got into the city, the police, being more familiar with the streets, managed to draw even, and the two vehicles roared up Front Street at speeds in excess of sixty miles an hour. The bootleggers then forced the lighter squad car up onto the curb and shot off over Church Street hill. A few minutes later, Inspector Naphan and his men located the big Buick, abandoned at the foot of Church Street. In the back seat section of the car, the rum-runners had stashed 400 bottles, including champagne, crème de menthe, and other fine liqueurs. The alcohol was seized and sent to the provincial dispensary in Toronto. The car was traced to a man in Niagara Falls who was subsequently charged. At a hearing a few days later, Magistrate Mason ordered that the car, worth $1,800, be confiscated and sold at public auction.[26]

Captures similar to these occurred fairly regularly across the province, partly because many officers were extremely dedicated, but also because the sheer volume of smuggling made it inevitable that some of it would be uncovered. Brewers and distilleries shipped out their products by freight car and, with the connivance of corrupt railroad employees, described the booze in their waybills as formaldehyde, or soda, or flour, or as any number of things other than the real substance. The freight car would get shunted off to a siding, usually in a major centre such as Toronto, and the booze would be unloaded and distributed to local bootleggers in the area. Other smugglers would travel to Quebec by train and return with two or three innocent-looking suitcases filled with liquor. Others brought it in by truck or car, and some even flew it in. On the province's western border, booze was smuggled in from Manitoba.

To stem the flow of illegal booze into the province would

have required many times the number of police officers available. The difficulties faced by the police were outlined by Commissioner Victor Williams in his annual report of 1923, in which he wrote:

> From information in our possession, we learn that the chief source from which the liquor percolates to the consumer are to-day administered in a very highly organized and systemized manner by men who finance the undertaking, and who...have developed such a smooth working system...that they themselves are practically immune, in fact, often unknown; further, the work of delivering the supplies is carried out in a way so apparently respectable and innocent that detection is often more by chance than by design.

Commissioner Williams, in his references to those at the top, was probably alluding to men like Rocco Perri but, as the 1927 Royal Commission would later reveal, it was the presidents and owners of the breweries and distilleries who were organizing the illegal trade. Turning his attention to the various sources of contraband, the Commissioner noted that:

> A considerable quantity of liquor has come in...from Quebec by road, rail and water, and many (almost unbelievable) have been the devices employed to camouflage the transportation so that it would escape the notices of officers...There is another, perhaps the most difficult source of supply to check, liquor ostensibly shipped from the distilleries and breweries for export, a considerable quantity of which must...find its way...into the stock of the bootleggers of this Province.

The Commissioner went on to list the problems of dealing

with home-brew stills, the fraudulent printing of counterfeit labels, and a new phenomenon, the bootleg druggist. To cope with all this, and the regular enforcement of the Criminal Code, Commissioner Williams had a total force of 105 men or, to put it in military terms, a company. To do the job, he needed at least a division.

Even with that many men, it is doubtful the OTA could have been enforced. In a democracy, if a law is to succeed and be observed, it must have the support of the vast majority of the population. On matters that deeply affect people in their private lives, a simple majority is not enough. The plebiscite held in 1924 revealed that the province was deeply split on the issue. The United, Baptist, and Methodist churches were committed to Prohibition on moral grounds. Farmers and residents of small towns generally favoured it. Roman Catholics, Anglicans, and members of labour groups were generally opposed to it, as were a majority of city dwellers. The plebiscite put these divisions in stark relief. To oversimplify, Methodist farmers were forcing Anglican and Roman Catholic city dwellers to adhere to a social code in which they did not believe.

When he called for the plebiscite, Premier Howard Ferguson, elected in 1923, had obviously expected that the wets would win and he could then do what he wanted to do all along, end Prohibition and call it the will of the people. When the drys squeezed by with a narrow 33,000 plurality, the Premier was put in a political quandary. Some city councillors and mayors were so angry they spoke of ignoring the law. In Sturgeon Falls, the town council passed a resolution advising that, "the Chief of Police be instructed not to enforce the...Act." Only 109 locals had voted in favour of retaining the OTA: 1,040 had voted against it.[27]

Premier Ferguson took a tentative step to appease the wets and, in particular, the labour vote, by legalizing a 4.4 per cent beer, which was quickly dubbed "Fergie's Foam." There was some initial enthusiasm and many Americans crossed the border to try the new beverage. But the new suds compared unfavourably to the pre-prohibition 9 per cent beer and was soon scorned as having no kick. The *Toronto Star* offered a $100 prize to the first person who could get drunk on the stuff. Two months later, the prize was still unclaimed when one Moe Kelly was brought before Magistrate Cohen, charged with being drunk in a public place. Kelly explained that he had got into such a state while drinking Fergie's Foam. "What's that!" exclaimed the Magistrate. "Did I hear you say you got drunk on the four point four?" Kelly allowed that he had indeed, and a *Star* reporter, sitting in the audience, perked up his ears. Not knowing about the $100 prize, Kelly went on to explain that he had had just one drink of alky. Unfortunately for the hapless Kelly, his admission disqualified him. The prize went unclaimed.[28]

The incident points up the increasing lack of seriousness accorded the act by members of the judiciary and also by the newspapers of the time, many of which poked fun at the OTA. This levity contrasted with the sternness of the Methodist and fundamentalist churches, the Women's Christian Temperance Movement, and many farm organizations, all of which equated liquor with original sin and were determined to enforce their narrow victory of 1924. With public opinion deeply divided, the Premier looked for a way to please both sides.

The events that helped push Ferguson into abandoning Prohibition were both ironic and tragic. They involved a number of big guns in the liquor trade, including Ben Kerr and Rocco Perri. They also involved a shipment of poison liquors, a number of civilian deaths, and a province-wide police investigation.

14

POISON LIQUOR

With the knowledge that this alcohol was deadly, Voelker and his partners dispensed the poison alcohol as a beverage to the unsuspecting public. Analysis...of the Voelker shipment shows it to contain: Wood Alcohol, 93.09%; Acetones, .49%; Acetic Acid, 1.13%; Water, 3.00%. The rest of the liquid was composed of traces of ethyl alcohol, formaldehyde, and formic acid. Three of the ingredients, wood alcohol, formic acid, and formaldehyde, are deadly poisons.[1]

In a period of eighteen days in the spring of 1926, twenty-one Ontario residents died from drinking the "alcohol" sold by James Voelker, a millionaire Buffalo booze baron. Another twenty-six people died on the American side of the border. Several others recovered but were left blind. All of these poisonings took place within the narrow hundred-mile band of towns and cities running between Toronto and Buffalo.[2] Although Americans and, to a lesser degree, Canadians had become inured to deaths from alcohol poisoning, they were shocked and frightened by such a large number of fatalities concentrated in so small an area. The deaths touched off a massive cooperative effort between several police forces. In Ontario, Deputy Commissioner Alfred Cuddy directed the OPP's investigation, which enlisted the aid of police forces in Toronto, Hamilton, Oakville, and St. Catharines. The RCMP, U.S. federal agents, and New York State Police lent their assistance. Even Scotland Yard was eventually involved.

In May 1926, federal agents raided the Third Ward Political Club in Niagara Falls, New York, uncovering a secret tunnel and a complete redistilling plant. Books and records seized on the premises revealed that the club had been buying denatured alcohol from the Jopp Drug Company and the Falls Tonic Manufacturing Company. Arthur Jopp and two directors of the company were arrested. Jopp was considered to be the "arch conspirator" who master-minded an organization that boasted its own legal bureau, a flotilla of sea-going and river-going boats, a fleet of automobiles, and a vast network of warehouses and vats where the alcohol was stored after its denaturants had been removed.[3]

The Third Ward Political Club was just one of the many organizations that bought this alcohol and distributed it to smaller bootleggers. It was headed by Joseph Sottile, a wealthy and well-educated Italian-American, who had fled the United States and was under indictment for manslaughter in both Canada and the U.S.A. Believing he might be in Canada, the government of Ontario offered a $2,000 reward for information leading to his arrest. Posing as a commercial traveller, Sottile went to Montreal where he was able to obtain a Canadian passport under an assumed name. He then boarded a ship for Liverpool, England. Scotland Yard was notified, but Sottile somehow managed to elude them and, it is presumed, made his way to Italy.

A number of Canadians were also implicated in the distribution and transportation of the Jopp Company's alcohol. Records found in the raid on the Third Ward Political Club revealed that the largest Canadian buyer was a well-known bootlegger from Toronto, Max Wortzman. During the month of December 1925, Wortzman bought 4,004 gallons from the Jopp Company, paying $5.50 a gallon, and reselling it at $5 a quart. His December purchases yielded him a profit of $58,058. Other buyers of the Jopp alcohol included Harry Goldstein of Toronto, John McRae, William Herbert, and James Sacco of Niagara Falls; Frank Secord of Lincoln County; John Tyminsky of St. Catharines; and Rocco Perri and Ben Kerr of Hamilton. Other names were illegible, but phone calls were traced to Nick Vandeveer of Port Colborne, and Louis Sylvester, alleged to be an agent for Rocco Perri. All of the above, with the exception of Vandeveer, were arrested on charges of manslaughter and held without bail. The Hamilton *Spectator* observed sarcastically that police officers were somewhat bemused at the luxuries being provided the men (meaning Perri and Kerr) held at the local headquarters, which included downy pillows, white sheets, fine blankets, and T-bone steaks.[4] Even in jail, Rocco Perri's wealth had reach and power.

The generous treatment accorded Ben Kerr was probably due to other considerations. He was prosperous but certainly not enormously rich like Perri was. Perri had emigrated to Canada in 1912 from Regio Calabria, Italy, in a state of dire poverty. Ben Kerr, on the other hand, came from a solid middle-class background. His father was known and respected as the fish and game inspector for Wentworth County, a post he held for thirty years. His brother was a well-respected businessman. The entire family, other than Ben, were active participants in Christ Church. The Hamilton *Spectator* appears to have shielded them when covering the errant behaviour of the family's black sheep. For example, when Kerr was captured at Rochester on the *Martimas*, the *Spectator* wrote about the incident but gave his address as Toronto. During the poison liquor investigation, the newspaper continued to refer to him as a boat builder, which he no longer was, while other papers described him as a rum-runner.

A week after Perri, Kerr, Wortzman, and the others had been arrested, the federal government appointed a special prosecutor to deal with the smuggling aspect of the case. He quickly concluded that the shipment of poison alcohol that was causing all the deaths – they were still occurring – had been shipped under loads of coal by a fuel company in Niagara Falls.[5] Meanwhile, Assistant Commissioner Alfred Cuddy of the OPP and the attorney general's office directed a province-wide investigation that had the smuggling and bootlegging community running for cover.

As the bootlegging business in the Niagara Peninsula was largely controlled by Italians or Canadians of Italian descent, the OPP sent an undercover operative into the area who was fluent in that language. Known only as J.C.S., he quickly discovered that the bootleggers were furious with the Americans for sending them the poisonous booze and jeopardizing everyone's business.

On the evening of September 1, 1926, J.C.S. met a night-club owner in Niagara Falls who called himself James Briand, but whose real name was Vicenzo Brindano. The men spoke in Italian, and J.C.S. translated Brindano's comments as follows:

> That dirty...on the other side is the guy who is responsible for the whole works. Yes Voelker: he was told by his own chemist not to go ahead with that stuff because it was rank poison...The alcohol was shipped to a distillery near the Falls in sixty-gallon drums...It was redistilled into one- and five-gallon cans, and again the analysis proved poison. But they have been getting away with stuff like that for two years, and Voelker told me he only wanted a couple more years of it and he was going to quit...The biggest part of it was shipped from Port

Claude "King" Cole (left) and Mac Howell on Main Duck Island, circa 1925.

Part of the cache of Corby's liquor seized by the police from Cole's cellar on Main Duck in 1921.

The *C.W. Cole* in dock at Cape Vincent, New York. Cole used this boat to haul fish and booze from Main Duck to Cape Vincent.

Fishermen and their families on Main Duck Island in 1916. Bruce Lowery stands rear, second from left.

Toronto detectives on board the *Hattie C* after its capture during the Gogo shooting in 1923. Bullet holes have been marked in white for the benefit of the jury in the trial of the four Toronto police officers.

Harry Clifford Hatch, circa 1925.

Herbert E. Hatch, circa 1950.

Sir Mortimer Davis, owner of Canadian
Industrial Alcohol.

Who's who in Canada, 1922

Sir Albert Edward Gooderham.   William George Gooderham.

C.W. Hunt

The oldest distillery in Canada – Gooderham and Worts in Toronto.

The Globe Hotel in Picton, circa 1915. Mac Howell is seated in the sulky (right).

Jim Hutchinson, circa 1935.

Doc Welbanks, veterinarian and rum-runner, circa 1916.

Rocco Perri (right) with Acting Police Chief Joe Crocker after Perri's car was bombed in 1938.

Jack Morris, Jr.

Chris Goyer

Jack Morris, Jr., circa 1935.

Lawrence "Gilly" Goyer, a hockey
player like his brothers, circa 1931.

The Goyer brothers and their father in 1920. Archie Goyer stands far left, back
row, and Lawrence "Gilly" Goyer is seated, front right.

Captain Don McCune (retired).

Coastguardsmen Maurice (left) and Merle McCune, circa 1938.

CC-SSD1

C.J. Williams

The coast guard picket boat *CG-2207* in 1927. The boat was used during the seizure of many "black" boats.

Ben Kerr's boat, the *Martimas*, under seizure at the Charlotte coast guard station near Rochester in 1925.

Mason McCune sighting down the Lewis machine-gun used to capture Ben Kerr.

Len Duetta

Hazel Dodds

Bruce Lowery with
his younger brother,
Jimmy, and girlfriend
Letty Hicks, circa
1924.

Lowery looking
dapper during the
heyday of the
rum-running
years, (circa 1929).

Norman Sudds

Victor Sudds and his wife, Eva, circa 1925.

Hazel Dodds

Claude "King" Cole, outside his Cape Vincent farmhouse, circa 1925.

Bob Humphries

Slim Humphries and family at Whitby, circa 1933.

F.J. Taylor

Trenton Police Chief Bill Bain (left), circa 1936. Bain assisted in the capture of the bootlegger Harry Ketcheson.

Nancy Thomas

Harry Ketcheson (second from right) and friends celebrate the end of Prohibition in Ontario in 1927.

Sam Yanover

Belleville fur merchant and bootlegger Harry Yanover, circa 1940.

"Gentleman" Charlie Mills with his girlfriend, Jennie Batley, in 1929.

Amos "Nick" Vanderveer with his wife, Carrie, and daughter, circa 1920.

Harry Ketcheson hoists a beer in the company of two armed friends.

Commander J. Earl McQueen in 1942. During prohibition he organized the rum-runners who worked out of Belleville.

Heavily armed police keep a close watch while 4,000 cases of Canadian beer are unloaded after the *Amherstburg 18* was captured in 1930.

Colborne where they had a bunch of crooked customs officers.[6]

J.C.S. continued his undercover investigation for several weeks under the most dangerous conditions. After spending the evening with his new-found underworld buddies, he would return to his room and write out his reports in the dark, fearing to switch on his room light in case he aroused the suspicions of the men tailing him. Mildred Sterling, an underworld gun moll who took a liking to J.C.S. and spent at least one night in bed with him, spoke of the fears in Hamilton's underworld. "Rocco Perri and his strong-arm men have the town scared to death and those fellows [poison liquor survivors], who narrowly escaped death are afraid, more now [since Perri is held] than ever before." She went on to state a view that was common in Hamilton at that time. "The law has nothing on Perri, but he has plenty on the big fellows in this town." Shortly after this conversation, the court released Rocco Perri, Ben Kerr, and the other defendants on posting $20,000 bail each.

Despite an extensive investigation, the police were unable to connect Perri or Kerr to the poisonings. The evidence that they were smuggling alcohol into Canada, while strong, was not conclusive. Kerr argued that his payments to Voelker was part of his export liquor operations. Eventually four small fry, men who sold the poison liquor directly to the victims, were tried and convicted.[7] After numerous postponements the case against the other defendants was dropped. The investigation had uncovered a large-scale smuggling operation, but no evidence could be unearthed to tie Max Wortzman, Rocco Perri, or any other big guns to the poisonings. These big operators did not sell directly to the consumer, and the bootleggers they did sell to were afraid to testify against them.

How much influence the poison liquor deaths had on Premier Howard Ferguson's decision to end Prohibition in Ontario is not known. The Premier had been convinced for some time that the OTA could not be effectively enforced. The annual reports of OPP Commissioner Victor Williams stated this fact, year after year.[8] The poison deaths and the inability to indict the big operators underlined the risks to the public inherent in the OTA, and also the inability to really enforce the act. In the United States, deaths from alcohol poisoning had almost quadrupled, from 1,064 in 1920 to 4,154 in 1925. The investigation made clear that organized crime, enticed by the profits from illegal booze, was spreading its greedy, amoral tentacles into Ontario.[9]

There were many factors influencing Ferguson's decision. He was not, personally, an abstainer. Indeed, his college days had been marked by high spirits and by the friendship of Canada's best known humourist and opponent of Prohibition, Stephen Leacock. Still, the Premier was too much the consummate politician to let his personal predilections determine so crucial a decision. Undoubtedly, he was influenced by the positive effect that government regulation and sale of liquor would have on the provincial treasury. He seemed also to believe sincerely that this government regulation would lessen, if not eliminate, bootlegging in the province.

As a lawyer from the little town of Kemptville, the Premier was acutely aware of the depth of prohibition sentiment in rural and small-town Ontario. He knew also that in every plebiscite held since 1894, the province had voted in favour of Prohibition. In the 1924 plebiscite, the prohibitionist majority had been reduced to 33,000, the lowest ever, indicating that more and more respectable middle class people were concluding the OTA was a noble experiment that had failed. The poison liquor deaths were further evidence of this and might change the minds of those 'drys' whose support for Prohibition was wavering.

Across the nation, province after province had repudiated Prohibition in favour of a system of government regulation and control of the sale of liquor. Quebec, the Yukon, and Western Canada had all gone this route, but only after first holding a plebiscite in which the public had had an opportunity to express its will. The Premier of Ontario was the first to decide to end Prohibition without first having that decision approved by voters.

On the 19th October, 1926, Ferguson announced that a provincial general election would be held on December 1. He outlined several planks in the government's quest for re-election, but only one really mattered. Despite Ferguson's wish to the contrary, it would be a one-issue election, and that issue was Prohibition. Ferguson pledged to bring in government control of the sale and consumption of alcohol through government liquor stores, which would only be established in communities that voted in favour of them, a system known as local option.

In his statement outlining the reasons his government had decided on this policy, Ferguson noted, "The numerous deaths from poison alcohol over a considerable period, culminating last summer in the deaths of about fifty people in various parts of the province, have filled the public, as well as the Government, with horror and alarm." He described the OTA as a failure and as a law that could not, in fact, succeed. "Despite the vigilance and best efforts of the law enforcement officers, bootlegging flourishes, and those engaged in supplying the demand for liquor are growing rich in the traffic. Experience has shown the difficulty, if not impossibility of suppressing this traffic. Would it not be better that this demand be supplied through properly controlled channels, and the profits, instead of enriching the few, be available for the extension and improvement of hospitals, education, highways, and other public services?"[10]

Ferguson's election platform also dealt with the reorganization and improvement of the highway system, the opening-up of Northern Ontario, and other matters of great import to the people of the province. All these vital issues were ignored. Whenever Ferguson spoke on any of these topics, his audience would drift off, or interject with questions on the prohibition issue. Prohibition involved the voters' perception of the kind of society Ontario would become. Many viewed it as a moral issue and, therefore, the most difficult on which to compromise. It cut deeply, often dividing and embittering members of the same family. It also divided members of the same political parties. On the day he announced the election and his party's stand on Prohibition, Ferguson had to contend with the announcement that William Nickle, his attorney general, was resigning over the government's stand. Nickle, the prominent and talented MPP for Kingston, was also a deeply committed supporter of Prohibition.

Fortunately for the Conservatives, the Liberal Party was even more divided over the issue. William Sinclair had to contend with a revolt from his Franco-Ontarian members, four of whom rejected the party's support of the Ontario Temperance Act and resigned from the party caucus to run in the election as independents.

The Progressive Party, which had sprung up as the replacement for the United Farmers of Ontario, was led by William E. Raney. Raney had fought strenuously against the liquor interests when he had been attorney general in the United Farm government of Premier Drury. He was, if anything, now even more committed to Prohibition and led a united party into the fray.

At the local level, Prohibition was making for some strange bedfellows. Rocco Perri was rumoured to have contributed $30,000 in support of the prohibitionist parties.[11] In Belleville, Ralph Boulter, a local liquor exporter, threw himself behind the prohibitionist cause, even going so far as to hold an organizing meeting in his home.[12]

Various churches involved themselves in a manner not seen before in Ontario politics. The United Church, the Baptists, most evangelical churches, and the Methodists, came down firmly on the side of Prohibition. Of these, the United

Church had the most adherents and was particularly bitter in its denunciation of Ferguson, calling him a traitor to his own party. The Toronto Conference of the United Church called on its members "to support for Parliament and public life, only those, irrespective of party, who will give their strength and influence to defend and maintain temperance legislation."[13]

Spokespersons for Prohibition sometimes took positions so extreme they must have driven many moderates into Ferguson's camp. Speaking to a well-attended meeting in Belleville's city hall, Mrs. Gordon Wright, Dominion organizer for the Women's Christian Temperance Union, equated the exodus of young people to the United States with the much greater prosperity existing in that country, a prosperity due solely, she insisted, to the existence of total prohibition in the United States. She averred that the liquor traffic was akin to such horrors as the opium and white-slave traffic. "It is," she declared, "a serpent which has left a dark, gruesome trail across the Dominion."[14] She beseeched her audience to vote for candidates solely on their position on the liquor question.

Not all churches supported the prohibitionist position. The Anglican and Roman Catholic churches had, at best, been lukewarm in their support of the OTA. The Anglicans were inclined to view government by plebiscite as a sort of tyranny of the masses that contradicted the ideals of British liberty.

One highly respected Catholic priest, Reverend John Burke, came out with a strongly reasoned defence of Ferguson's position. Noting that he had earlier been a strong supporter of the OTA, Burke denounced it as "a ghastly failure," whose effect upon the youth of the province had been the reverse of that intended.[15]

Rumours circulated that Ferguson had been bought off by the liquor interests. More specifically, it was claimed, he held extensive stock in Gooderham and Worts.[16] The rumours may well have been true. Ferguson had allowed some of his wealthy friends to invest on his behalf in the stock market. Gooderham and Worts was, at that time, a very hot stock, having risen in value by 350 per cent in just three years. But Premier Ferguson's decision to end Prohibition was clearly not based on personal profit. His entire life had been, and would remain, committed to politics. The opportunities for profit were much greater in the private sector, but he remained in public life, often at great cost to himself. Moreover, his decision on Prohibition was consistent with his earlier views, and had been anticipated by his political enemies since he first became premier in 1923.

Despite the rumours, innuendoes, and clergy-inspired attacks, Howard Ferguson was able to wage a masterful campaign, putting himself above the mud slinging and cleverly exploiting his opponent's weaknesses. When the ballots were counted on election day, Premier Ferguson and the Conservative Party found themselves swept back into power with seventy-five seats: the Liberals managed only twenty-one, the Progressives thirteen, and the remnants of the United Farmers only three. The Premier had, once again, justified his nickname, "Foxy Fergy."

The election spelled the end of the eleven-year prohibition experiment in Ontario. It would take some time for the new legislation to be drawn up and put into effect, but on June 1, 1927, the Ontario Temperance Act passed into history. Under the new legislation, all residents of the province "of good character" over the age of twenty-one could obtain liquor permits authorizing them to purchase spirituous beverages at the new Liquor Control Board of Ontario stores. Each purchase was written into the buyer's permit book by an LCBO clerk, and the purchaser was then legally required to take the treasure directly home. There was no return to the wild and woolly saloon, nor, indeed, to public drinking of any kind. Each citizen could buy a supply and drink it, just so long as he or she did it in private. L.A. Mackay captured the prevailing attitude to booze in his poem "Frankie Went Down To The Corner," when he wrote:

Ontario's such a respectable place
Drinking's no crime, but it's still a disgrace,
So hide us away behind curtain and screen
While we stealthily go through the motions,
obscene.

Ontario's attitude to drinking suffered from a split personality. On the one hand, a resident of the province could have his or her application for a liquor permit rejected if found to be not "of good character." But the good burghers of the province were still shrewd businessmen and made provision in the act for permits to be issued to tourists entering Ontario. They were required to spend twenty-four hours in the province, but there were few restrictions. Needless to say, residents of American border cities made up the bulk of the sudden influx of tourists into Ontario. The province, which had been trailing wet Quebec in tourist popularity, now leaped into the lead. Attorney General Price, in his annual report for 1928, explained that the increase in liquor revenues was due primarily to the great increase in the number of tourists visiting the province; 500,000 more automobiles entered the province in 1928 than had in 1927.[17] This led to a spate of editorials defending Ontario's virtue and enunciating its many attractions to American visitors. One such editorial ran under the headline, TOURISTS DO NOT ALL COME FOR LIQUOR.[18]

The tourist permit system did affect relations with our neighbours to the south, sometimes in surprising ways. At Cobourg, the ferry arrived from Rochester at 2 p.m., and departed for Rochester an hour later. Residents of the town were soon complaining that hordes of Americans were riding over on the ferry and loading up, both internally and externally, with booze from the LCBO store. The behaviour of these noisy visitors so upset the residents, they took up a petition. In response, the LCBO agreed to close the Cobourg liquor store during the hours the ferry was laying over. At Erie, Pennsylvania, the sheriffs of that state were holding their annual banquet when it was unexpectedly raided by prohibition agents. At first the sheriffs thought it was a joke, but when they realized it was not, fisticuffs ensued. After the federal agents departed, the assembled sheriffs voted unanimously to hold their next annual meeting across the lake at Port Dover, in wet Ontario.[19]

Equally important was the effect on organized crime. The huge profit it had gained was now diverted into the treasury of the province, where it could be spent on socially useful projects. Bootlegging did not end, but its enormous profit was gone. Unfortunately, large-scale, organized crime did not leave the province. Having grown fat and prosperous on booze, it now turned its attention to other activities, such as gambling, prostitution, and narcotics.[20] For liquor exporters, such as Rocco Perri, there were still several boom years left in the booze business.

Shortly after the election of December 1, 1926, the liquor business was again very much in the news. There was to be massive probe of the industry. Known as the Royal Commission on Customs and Excise, it would strike fear into the hearts of captains of industry, who for years had been running their liquor fiefdoms with contemptuous disregard for the laws of the land. The commissioners could compel witnesses to attend and testify. They could oblige distilleries and breweries to turn their records over to the commission. They could force into the open certain practices that might discredit some very wealthy and powerful men. Investigations undertaken by the Smuggling Committee, earlier in the year, had already caused some of these booze barons to run for cover. The prospect of being subpoenaed and forced to testify, under oath, before the Royal Commission sent shock waves of apprehension through the ranks of Canada's liquor barons.

When the species itself is threatened, the bold and avaricious will often devour their more timid and cautious members. Neither Harry Hatch nor Sam Bronfman was timid or cautious. By the end of 1926, one of them would emerge as the whisky king of Canada.

15

HARRY HATCH
BUILDS AN EMPIRE

> He became a great expert at selling liquor under
> any circumstances: people like to buy from this gay
> gentleman...By 1923 he was a millionaire.
>
> *Fortune*,
> November 1933

During the first six months of 1926, a Special Committee of
the House of Commons, dubbed the "Smuggling Committee" by the press and chaired by the Honourable Harry Stevens, delved deeply into the operations of the Customs and
Excise Department. In the course of a few days, the probe
revealed a network of corruption extending to the highest
ranks of the Civil Service and even into the ranks of the
House of Commons. The Smuggling Committee was able to
prove that the Honourable Jacques Bureau, minister of customs, had ordered the chief customs inspector at Montreal to
ship him case after case of illegal samples.[1] In so doing, both
Jacques Bureau and his inspector were breaking the regulations of the government department in which they both held
high office. As well, by having the inspector ship the liquor to
Bureau's home in Ottawa, the cabinet minister was himself

violating the law of Ontario, which prohibited the importation of alcohol from outside the province. Prime Minister Mackenzie King moved to protect his government's reputation by removing Bureau from the cabinet. In return for his resignation, the corrupt minister of customs was "kicked upstairs" to the Senate.

Several top civil servants in the department were also forced to resign. One of these, Inspector J.A. Bisaillon of Montreal, was clearly in collusion with the smugglers in the area. Bisaillon's salary was in the range of $2,500 yearly, yet he somehow managed to accumulate $68,000 in one bank account and was suspected of having others.[2] Although Bisaillon's corruption was widely known, Bureau had nevertheless promoted him to chief preventative officer for the Province of Quebec, which meant Bisaillon was responsible for preventing smuggling into the province. The promotion was comparable to hiring the town dipsomaniac to guard your wine cellar.

The corruption of Bisaillon and dozens of others was unearthed by Walter Duncan, a special undercover operative employed by the Justice and Finance departments. During an eighteen-month undercover operation, the diligent detective unearthed so much corruption and dishonesty, his report to the Smuggling Committee ran to several hundred typewritten pages.

The committee began examining witnesses on St. Patrick's Day, 1926, and was soon ordering representatives of the distilleries and breweries to turn in their books for examination. These companies were required to pay a sales tax on alcoholic beverages sold in Canada, as well as an excise tax on beverages sold to the United States. It soon became apparent that the federal government had been defrauded out of hundreds of thousands, perhaps even millions of dollars.[3]

A gallon of whisky, when sold within the country, required the payment of a $10 sales tax. The Smuggling Committee dug up evidence indicating that hundreds of thousands of gallons, ostensibly exported to the U.S.A. and other countries and therefore exempt from sales tax, had been short-circuited back into Canada. The committee also found hard evidence that the distillers had adopted devious practices to avoid the $9 a gallon excise tax. The law provided that when a landing certificate could be obtained from a customs or other official, confirming that a load of whisky had been delivered to a foreign port, the excise tax did not apply. No American officials could give such a certificate. This is why vessels left Canadian ports ostensibly bound for Cuba or other countries where importing liquor was legal. Corrupt officials in these countries would sign the necessary papers and return them to the distillery. The usual charge to the distillery for this service was fifty cents a document. The cargo itself would be delivered somewhere along the United States coastline.[4]

The corruption unearthed by the Smuggling Committee was headline news all during the winter and spring of 1926. The media railed at the government, blaming the cabinet and the Prime Minister for allowing the mess to develop. *Maclean's* ran several articles, one of which described the customs department as "not only inefficient, but corrupt and debauched as well."[5] The *Financial Post* went even further and declared in one headline WEAK MEN IN CABINET ALLOWED SORRY MESS TO FESTER – PRIME MINISTER'S RESPONSIBILITY FOR SMUGGLING GROWTH NOT TO BE DENIED.[6]

Mackenzie King led a minority Liberal government now weakened by charges of graft and corruption. It was obvious to the most obtuse businessman that the government had to take action against the brewing and distilling companies to recover the sales and excise taxes they had previously avoided. The total amount probably ran into the millions and might bankrupt some of the weaker firms. Moreover, the recommendations the committee made when it presented its report to the House of Commons on June 18, were all hostile to the booze industry.[7] The committee recommended reinstituting the two-year maturity period before whisky could be released from bond and sold. This would have severely limited the industry's ability to supply the huge U.S. market. Aged whisky was in short supply, particularly at Gooderham and Worts.

The report of the committee was followed by the setting up of a Royal Commission to carry on the committee's investigation. A Royal Commission has powers a Commons committee does not possess, including the power to subpoena witnesses and compel them to testify. It can also issue orders to seize documents. This posed a unique problem for the two Walker brothers who controlled Hiram Walker. The company's head office and plant were located in Walkerville – now part of Windsor – but the Walkers were American citizens residing in Detroit. If they retained ownership of the distillery, they could be compelled to appear before the Royal Commission and forced to testify. That testimony would reveal that Hiram Walker and Sons was soliciting orders for its product in the United States. To admit this fact, under oath, to a Canadian Royal Commission, would inevitably lead to their being charged in the U.S.A. under the Volstead Act. The penalties under the act were not that severe, but the family name would be impugned.

The Walker distillery had been established in 1858. The Walkers were an old and highly respected family noted for their philanthropic pursuits. The town of Walkerville had been named in their honour, and had received as a gift the company's original head office building to be used as the Town Hall. Old money is generally more scrupulous than new, and the Walkers were increasingly uncomfortable about the deceptions necessary to survive in the Canadian whisky business. They began looking around for a buyer.[8]

The Bronfmans had completed their first major distillery, located in Montreal, in the spring of 1925. The volatile Sam Bronfman was soon looking to expand and in 1926 began negotiations with DCL of Edinburgh and London. DCL or

Distillers Company Limited, controlled more than half of the world's Scotch production. Its directors, who included Field Marshal Earl Haig, Lord Dewar, Sir Alexander Walker, and other Empire heavies, regarded the Bronfmans as upstart colonials, but recognized that the fast-rising Canadians could sell and deliver large quantities of their products to the huge but illegal American market. These upper-class merchants had been forced to deal with the underworld thugs who dominated the American booze business and were happy to leave such unpleasant activities to the brash Bronfmans. After some tough negotiations, Sam Bronfman obtained his goal, namely the exclusive right to distribute the prestigious DCL Scotch brands throughout North America. In return, the canny Scots paid the Bronfmans $1 million for a 50 per cent interest in the family liquor business, which the Bronfmans were loath to surrender as it gave their new partners a veto power. Later that year, the new company moved to acquire the Seagram distillery in Waterloo, and in the resulting corporate reorganization, it was the Scottish chairman of DCL, W.H. Ross, who became president. Sam Bronfman was appointed vice-president. The preoccupation of the Bronfman family with these corporate activities could explain why they were not among those bidding to acquire Hiram Walker.

The most likely buyer appeared to be Sir Mortimer Davis, chairman of the Industrial Alcohol Company, the largest distilling company in the British Empire and one of the largest in the world. For two months, in the fall of 1926, his accountants had scrutinized the books of the privately owned Hiram Walker Company. Then, in early December, Sir Mortimer Davis returned to Canada from the French Riveria in order to take part in the final negotiations. The Walker brothers were prepared to sell for less than $15 million, a figure well below the book value of the company's assets.

One of Canada's wealthiest citizens, Sir Mortimer had

made his first fortune by creating the Imperial Tobacco Company, which he subsequently augmented with the profits from the Canadian Industrial Alcohol Company. In 1923, he converted Industrial Alcohol from his own private company into a public corporation. As Sir Mortimer held all, or nearly all, the shares in the private company, he almost certainly retained at least 51 per cent of the issued shares in the new public company. These shares subsequently rose dramatically and, by 1926, were trading at 500 per cent of the original issued price, no doubt as a result of a doubling of profits since 1923 and by a public perception that profits and dividends were headed even higher. His own private fortune, and his proven ability to run successful companies, made it certain that Sir Mortimer would be able to raise the funds needed to purchase Hiram Walker.

On December 3, 1926, the *Financial Post* ran a story that claimed a source inside one of the two companies interested in buying Walkers had advised the newspaper that the deal between Sir Mortimer's Industrial Alcohol Company and the Walker brothers had been worked out. All that remained were a few formal details. Even the financing, which involved some New York interests, had already been arranged. No mention was made as to the identity of the other company. For reasons never publicly explained, Sir Mortimer decided not to proceed with the deal and the way was open for Harry Hatch, the other interested party, to make his move.[9] Hatch did not waste time and, on December 22, took the train from Toronto for Windsor, arriving at 4 p.m. By 11 p.m, Harry Hatch, Harrington Walker, and Hiram Walker had affixed their signatures to the biggest commercial deal made in Canada during 1926. Although Hatch, as usual, kept a low profile, refusing photographs or long interviews, he displayed a fine sense of the dramatic by signing the papers on the third anniversary of his purchase of Gooderham and Worts. Both deals were signed late in the evening of December 22.[10]

The purchase price of $14 million was arranged by a bank

loan of $4 million and the issuing of 400,000 shares with a par value of $25 each. Of these shares, only 160,000 were made available to the general public. This raised an additional $4 million. The remaining 240,000 shares were issued to Harry Hatch, the Walker brothers, and associates of Harry Hatch from Gooderham and Worts. The sale of these shares raised the balance of $6 million.

It was a period of heady optimism when even grocery clerks were making killings on the stock market. Shares of Hiram Walker came on the market on January 24, 1927, and immediately traded at a premium of $10 above the issue price of $25. By April, those investors who had been well enough connected to buy the shares at $25 saw their profits more than double, with the stock trading above $60 a share. In bidding the price so high, so quickly, investors displayed a well-deserved confidence in Harry Hatch. He had made Gooderham and Worts extremely profitable, and he had bought Walkers at close to a fire-sale price.

The assets of Hiram Walker included a plant and equipment valued at $4 million, reputedly one of the finest and most modern on the continent. Its nineteen acres included 1,400 feet fronting on the Detroit River, where the company had its own export dock. Strategically, this location, directly across from Detroit, could not have been better. Sixty-five per cent of Canada's whisky exports to the U.S.A. made their entry via the Detroit River route. The rum-runners crossed the mile-wide river too quickly for the border patrol boat crews to catch more than a small number of them.

In addition to a strategically placed distillery, Hatch also acquired 4 million gallons of matured stock. No other distillery in Canada had such a large supply of aged whisky. (When Bronfman purchased Seagrams in 1928 they had only a tenth of this amount in stock.) At an average value of $5 a gallon, the minimum value of this stock was $20 million. Included in this bonanza were some of the most widely recognized brand names in the world, one of which, Canadian Club, was the best-selling whisky in Canada, with a reputation that was – and is – world wide.[11]

It is standard practice when purchasing a business to pay for something that is loosely described by accountants as "goodwill." This includes all those intangibles that go into making a company successful but that are difficult in themselves to evaluate. They include copyrights, trade marks, public recognition of the product, in-place organization, quality and experience of existing personnel, and all those variables that make a business profitable. In assessing the value of a corporation's goodwill there are a variety of complicated formulas, but a very general rule is simply to take two or three years' annual before-tax profit. As the profit at Walkers had been averaging $1.5 million a year, goodwill should have been worth at least $3 million. A fair price for the company would have been: land, buildings, and equipment, $4 million; accounts receivable, $1 million; the stock of aged whisky, $20 million; goodwill, $3 million – for a total of $28 million.

When Sir Mortimer Davis turned down the opportunity to buy Hiram Walker for less than $15 million, he revealed a lack of confidence in the future of the Canadian distilling industry. The condemnations and sweeping reforms recommended by the House of Commons Smuggling Committee had shaken everyone in the industry, and the sessions of the upcoming Royal Commission promised to be even more ominous. Even the aggressive Bronfmans had looked at Hiram Walker and had then backed off, perhaps fearing that the absorption of so large a company would over-extend their financial resources.[12] There was a general apprehension that the Royal Commission would uncover practices that might force King's government to cooperate actively with the Americans to stop rum-running. There was also a concern that the government might decide the industry owed it hundreds of thousands of dollars in unpaid excise and sales taxes.

The Canadian Industrial Alcohol Company was more vulnerable to this charge than was Gooderham and Worts. The Hatches exported their production via lakes Erie and Ontario, openly declaring the United States as the destination and paying the $9 a gallon excise tax. Corby's and Wiser's, unwisely as it transpired, shipped a large proportion of their exports to Vancouver or Halifax, where they were transferred to ocean-going vessels for delivery to Mexico, Central America, Cuba, and other countries where importing of liquor was legal. By selling to such countries, the Canadian Industrial Alcohol Company was able to avoid paying the excise tax. Sir Mortimer knew the real destinations of those boats were ports in the United States and Canada and that the landing certificates submitted by his employees to government officials were false. Even worse, he knew the Royal Commissioners had hard evidence proving this and expected his company might have to pay hundreds of thousands of dollars to the government in back excise taxes.* This by itself does not explain why Sir Mortimer backed off Hiram Walker while Harry Hatch took the plunge. Sir Mortimer had much greater financial resources than did Hatch and, even after paying excise tax penalties, could have raised the necessary $14 million without diffi-

---

*The Commissioners presented their final report to the House of Commons on January 27, 1928. They recommended the Government take action in respect of sales and excise taxes, to recover $86,078.04 from Wisers, and $973,667.23 from Corbys. The levy on Corbys was larger than on any other distillery. As Gooderham and Worts had always paid the excise tax, the Commissioners could only recommend they be pursued for the recovery of the sales tax which amounted to $192,189.64. In making these recommendations, the Commissioners assumed – quite incorrectly – that all exports were being short-circuited back into Canada and were therefore subject to sales tax.

culty. The explanation may lie in the climate of apprehension that permeated the industry and the fact that, in contrast to the youthful and confident Hatch, Sir Mortimer Davis was older, his drive and energy on the decline. Perhaps in recognition of the threat Hatch now posed, he promoted Billy Hume, Corby's general manager, to the position of vice-president. But Hatch and Hume had been friends since the days when Hatch had been sales manager at Corbys. A week after his promotion by Sir Mortimer, Bill Hume resigned to manage Harry Hatch's Hiram Walker facility.[13]

With the competent Corbyville native running Hiram Walker, Hatch now moved aggressively to expand Gooderham and Worts. It was in the middle of the Royal Commission's hearings and almost everyone in the industry was running for cover. Rocco Perri decided to disappear rather than testify, W.M. Egan, a wealthy Windsor lawyer with connections high in the Liberal Party, left the country permanently, and one brewery president, Herb Kuntz, when put on the stand, openly admitted to regularly breaking the OTA in order to sell his product.[14] Others suddenly got sick or left the country on vacation. It was a time to lie low, but instead Hatch began an ambitious building program, spending more than $3 million to expand storage and bottling facilities at Gooderham and Worts. One of his new buildings, which could hold 1,250,000 gallons, was the largest of its kind in Canada. When he had finished, Gooderham and Worts had storage capacity for 3,250,000 gallons, and a production capacity even greater than Hiram Walker's.[15] Shortly thereafter, Hatch combined the two companies into a new corporation, Hiram Walker-Gooderham and Worts. The *Toronto Star* immediately dubbed him, "King of Canadian Distillers." This was not more hyperbole; the production and storage capacity of the new corporation was far larger than Distillers Corporation-Seagrams, and somewhat larger than Sir Mortimer Davis's Canadian Industrial Alcohol. By mid-1927, Harry Hatch, at the age of forty-four, had made it to the top of the mountain. He was president and chief executive officer of the largest distilling corporation in the British Empire, perhaps in the world, and one of his companies, Gooderham and Worts, boasted the Royal Family's Coat of Arms, and the inscription, "By Appointment to His Majesty King George V."

His was an astonishing vault into the corporate elite, one that is not sufficiently explained by his competitor's concern that the Royal Commission, by uncovering so much corruption, would force the Liberal government into taking some remedial action. It was unlikely such action would be so severe as to seriously damage the liquor interests. For one thing, they were very large contributors to Liberal coffers – a fact established by the Royal Commission – and, for another, they brought more than $20 million U.S. into Canada every year. They also provided employment for plant workers, fishermen, smugglers, dock workers, and countless others. Clearly, if the government did anything it would more likely be for appearance than in order to eliminate the thriving rum-running industry. Sir Mortimer Davis and the Bronfmans were well connected within the Liberal Party, as was Harry Hatch. It is unlikely any of them were greatly concerned about the government destroying their business.

There is another explanation, which fits the facts available. Neither the Bronfmans nor Sir Mortimer would have bought Hiram Walker unless they were reasonably certain they could deliver its large production to American buyers. Both firms got their product to market primarily through ocean-going vessels, which, after the dispersal of Rum Row by the coast guard in 1925, were less able to deliver large quantities. It was for this reason that the Detroit River had become the focus of smuggling activity, with an estimated 65 per cent of Canada's whisky exports entering the United States via this route. This in turn led to an increase in coast guard and border patrol forces on the river, which would explain the large stocks of aged whisky on hand at Hiram Walker. At the time Hatch bought the company, all but half a million of its 4.5 million-gallon storage capacity had been filled. This huge stock of liquor was an enormous asset, but only provided it could be sold and delivered to American buyers. There was no lack of demand in the United States. The problem was the increasing strength of the coast guard and border patrol, which was making it more difficult to maintain the volume of liquor being moved across the Detroit River. This constriction of the booze funnel into America may have caused the whisky produced by Hiram Walker to back up, filling their storage racks. If this was the case, it helps explain why Hiram and Harrington Walker were willing to sell the family firm for half its real value.

Delivery of large quantities of whisky across the Great Lakes was the one route open to Harry and Herb Hatch, but not to Sir Mortimer Davis or to the Bronfmans. The Bronfmans were based in Montreal, and so it was natural they would rely on ocean routes and ships. It was not until their acquisition of the Seagram plant in Waterloo that the Bronfmans were in a position to make use of rum-runners on the lakes. At the time of the negotiations to purchase Walkers, only Herb Hatch and Larry McGuinness had a large network of rum-runners already in place on the Great Lakes.

When Sir Mortimer Davis had hired Harry Hatch as sales manager in 1921, the Corby plant had been in the doldrums, operating at a fraction of its capacity. The Deseronto native had been able to increase sales from 500 to 50,000 gallons a month, an increase of 1,000 per cent. This amazing performance resulted from Hatch's contacts in the United States and from his abilities as a salesman. It was during this period that Herb Hatch and Billy Hume, manager of the Corby plant, developed their contacts with the men who would recruit the Great Lakes' rum-runners, and, in particular, those on Lake Ontario. As Corby's was the only operating distillery on the lake, they had little competition for the services of these men, who included Earl McQueen, Grant Quick,

Claude "King" Cole, Ben Kerr, Mac Howell, and Rocco Perri. These men dealt with Herb Hatch and Larry McGuiness, not Sir Mortimer Davis. Consequently, when Harry Hatch left Corby's at the end of 1923 to restart Gooderham and Worts with his brother, Herb, the new company had no difficulty in finding rum-runners to get its product to the American market. Not all switched allegiance, but enough did to cause Corby's to reduce shipments from the Belleville harbour to twenty-five or thirty a year. The chief customs officer at Belleville, Major Albert Geen, testified at the Royal Commission that "there was not much traffic out of Belleville by water after 1923," and that, thereafter, "Corby's shipped by rail, mostly to Halifax and Vancouver."[16]

Sir Mortimer Davis had not been happy to lose his dynamic sales manager, particularly when he was leaving to go into competition with Corby's and Wiser's. The two men had never been friends and the parting was not amicable.[17] Sir Mortimer realized that Harry Hatch would use his American contacts to develop sales for Gooderham and Worts, and also that Herb Hatch would use his personal contacts with the liquor exporters to try and recruit them into the service of Hatch and McGuiness.

That so many defected to the Hatch brothers is not surprising. Herb and Harry had much in common with the liquor exporters. Of humble, rural Ontario origins, they knew boats and seamanship and could converse with the rum-runners in their own earthy language. Unlike the rough-hewn Hatch brothers, Sir Mortimer Davis was an urban, Jewish sophisticate. The socialite industrialist had nothing in common with the rural and small-town people who handled the liquor exports. On the other hand, Harry Hatch, who eventually made even more money than Sir Mortimer, remained a life-long friend of Claude Cole and J. Earl McQueen, both rugged outdoorsmen.

In the years between his acquisition of Gooderham and Worts and the purchase of the Hiram Walker company,

Herb Hatch suborned the Whitby-area fishermen into "Hatch's Navy," thereby enabling Gooderham and Worts to move enormous quantities of booze across the lake. As this operation remained covert, neither the Bronfmans nor Sir Mortimer had any idea how Gooderham and Worts's product was being exported.[18] Tactically, this gave Hatch a major advantage in his negotiations with the Walker family – he was the only potential buyer who believed he could get their booze into the American market.

It is reasonable to conclude from the evidence that Sir Mortimer backed away from buying Hiram Walker because he lacked an organization capable of getting its production into the American market. His former employee, Harry Hatch, had access through his brother, Herb, and his partner Larry McGuiness to an organization that could do the job. In fact, the firm of Hatch and McGuinness dominated rum-running on the Great Lakes.[19] This enabled Harry to buy Hiram Walker in the deal of the year, raising him to the top of the Canadian distilling industry. The old king, Sir Mortimer Davis, retired to his private estate at Golfe-Juan on the French Riviera, where he could escape the Quebec winter and also avoid the embarassing questions of the Royal Commissioners. He died there a year later. It was appropriate that the new king would stay on in Canada to face some of the best legal minds in the country. The commissioners spared no one in their probe into the venality permeating the liquor industry.

16

TURNING POINT

No one seriously believes that small-fry scallywags could systematically pilfer public funds and violate a national trust WITHOUT THE INDULGENCE OF THOSE AT THE SOURCE OF AUTHORITY. IF THERE IS NO OTHER WAY TO BRING THEM TO ACCOUNT, MINISTERS OR EX-MINISTERS, SENATORS OR MEMBERS OF PARLIA-MENT WHO TRY TO HIDE BEHIND PARLIAMENTARY PRIVILEGE MUST BE IMPEACHED.

> Grattan O'Leary
> *Maclean's*, June 15, 1926

Bribery, official corruption, huge profits in the liquor indus-try, evasion of taxes, these were the stories dominating the pages of Canada's newspapers during the winter and spring of 1927. The Royal Commission on Customs and Excise kept the presses of the nation humming as it marched across the land from Victoria to Charlottetown. It moved like some majestic battleship, ploughing through a barge canal, its bow wave churning up the scurf.

At the commission's hearings, citizens from the highest to the lowest were called upon to step into the witness box and, under oath, answer the probing questions of some of the sharpest legal minds in the country. Joe Burke of Port Credit, Ben Kerr, Rocco Perri, Bessie Starkman, Nick Vandeveer, even Herb and Harry Hatch, all put their hands on the Holy Bible and swore to tell the truth, the whole truth, and nothing but the truth. Some, like Rocco and Bessie, were quickly exposed as liars and perjurers. Meanwhile, the liquor exporting business continued unabated. The corporations paid more attention to the technicalities of the law but otherwise little seemed to change.

On Lake Ontario, the annual battle between the coast guard and the smugglers was slow in getting underway, chiefly because spring break-up had come late. Fittingly, it was chief bo'sun's mate Merle McCune who made the first capture of the season. It occurred shortly after midnight on May 1, 1927. McCune was cruising east of Oswego in picket boat *CG-2207*. With him were machinist mate M.F. Moss and surfman C.A. Sprague. At 12:15 a.m., they spotted two boats running without lights about four miles out from shore. As was the practice when searching for rum-runners, McCune had earlier doused the running lights of *CG-2207*. The three boats converged in the darkness. McCune waited, expecting any second that the rum ships' crews would spot him and make a run for it. Finally, when he was almost on top of the two black ships, McCune switched on his lights. At the same moment surfman Sprague trained the picket boat's spotlight on the quarry. Merle McCune identified himself and, using the hailer, called on the rummies to "round 'er up there." When they failed to respond, he fired two revolver shots into the air. The two boats immediately stopped and *CG-2207* drew up alongside the smaller of the two black ships, ordering her crew to come aboard. The two Canadian rum-runners offered no resistance, but while the crew of one was being handcuffed and their craft boarded, the other boat slipped quickly away. McCune was short handed; one of his crew was aboard the captured rum ship, the other guarded the two prisoners. In spite of these handicaps, the chief bo'sun spent considerable time searching the area, but in the darkness could not locate the miscreant.

It had been a good night's work. The captured rum-runner was a beauty. Twenty-eight feet long, equipped with a self-starter, optional under-water exhaust, and a forty-horse-power Scripps engine, it appeared to be brand new. The cargo, consisting of 100 bags (2,400 bottles) of Canadian ale, was protected by a waterproof canvas cover. The men arrested on board this fine boat had helped to build it. They were Napoleon "Nap" Goyer, age thirty-seven, and his brother, Lawerence "Gilly" Goyer, twenty-two.[1] Both men were bachelor fishermen from Belleville, members of a large family of three sisters and eight brothers, most of whom were prominent local athletes. Nap Goyer had served overseas in the war and was unconcerned by the prospect of jail. But Gilly Goyer feared his arrest might end his chances of a career in professional hockey. He had been the leading goal scorer in Belleville's OHA team the previous winter.

Both Nap and Gilly were working for their older brother Archie, who had been in charge of the boat that escaped. Over the winter they had assisted him in building the new boat. Archie, age forty, was the family entrepreneur. A barber by trade, he also fished, and for the past few years had operated a liquor export business. It provided him with the money to buy his wife, Ethel, a diamond ring, which was the envy of the Foster Ward neighbourhood of Belleville. She and her daughter also sported beautiful full-length Persian lamb coats. These baubles, while impressive to his neighbours, were small change to the handsome barber. He reserved his big money for his real passion – gambling.

Like most small cities of that era, Belleville's merchants closed up shop every Wednesday at noon. After persuading their wives of their need to stay at the store to deal with some pressing problem, those merchants of a sporting bent would then congregate in the upstairs room of Eddie Thomas's cigar store for an afternoon of high-stakes poker. Archie Goyer would be there, the bon vivant of Foster Ward, matching wits and bets with some of the city's wealthiest citizens.[2]

The Goyers were a close-knit clan, and Archie wasted no time in raising the $2,400 bail money necessary to gain Nap and Gilly's release.[3] Two days later, Archie Goyer was himself in jail. He and his helper, Big Bill Moy, were captured by George Jackson, commander of the Oswego coast guard station, who was in charge of *CG-2207*, the same picket boat used to catch Nap and Gilly Goyer only six days earlier. Machinist's mate Merville Moss had the distinction of participating in both captures.

George Jackson's report to the commander of the Ninth District revealed some of the tactics used by rum-runners and some of the problems he and his men faced. He had been trying to capture Goyer's boat for three years, but it had always stayed within the law. In other words, the rum-runners had always had time to jettison their cargo. The system whereby Canadian customs reported all outbound boats laden with contraband was also deficient. Under the system, notice of the clearance was phoned to the collector of customs at Rochester who in turn informed the border patrol at Oswego. No one notified the coast guard.

The forty-foot cabin cruiser, when captured, bore the name *Imp*, but inside Jackson found two sets of name boards, bearing the names *Sonora* and *Guy* respectively. This enabled the boat to clear Canadian customs under one name and, before reaching American waters, change its name to something else.[4]

The seizure was a major blow to Archie Goyer. He had lost 100 bags of ale on the first seizure, and a further 225 bags on the second, for a total loss of 7,800 bottles. In addition, he had had to post bail money for his brothers, and had lost two excellent boats. Nevertheless, he was able to raise his own bail money. Big Bill Moy was left to languish in jail. Archie may not have trusted him to appear for trial or he may have run out of money. Whatever the reason, Moy remained in jail from his arrest on May 7 until his trial in late October.[5]

Sometime before their trial, Gilly Goyer had signed a contract to play hockey for the New Haven team of the American Hockey League. The team hired a Boston lawyer to defend the popular athlete and, on October 21, he was fined $450 by Judge Frederick H. Bryant. Two days later, Judge Bryant fined Nap Goyer $400. This was the end of rum-running for the two Goyer brothers; Nap returned to commercial fishing, while Gilly pursued his hockey ambition.[6] For a while, Archie stuck with the liquor-export business but, wisely, no longer went himself. At the auction in Rochester basin, he was able to buy back the *Imp* for just $600.[7] Another boat was purchased from Ralph Boulter, a neighbour on South Front Street, who was also a boat builder and liquor exporter.[8] Goyer then hired two seamen from Nova Scotia, Clarence Robinson and John Burque, who were each to receive $75 per trip.

On June 15, 1927, the two Nova Scotians landed 200 bags of beer at Lashers Landing, twenty-five miles west of Oswego. Waiting for the load were three men with a hay rack, a team of horses, and two touring cars. The leader of the group was Edward "Peg Leg" Jones, a one-legged man from Lacona, New York. Unknown to these men, Chief Collector Andrew Wiedenmann and his officers had been watching the spot for three weeks. George Jackson was offshore in picket boat *CG-2207*. This joint operation was a complete success and all five men were arrested. Unable to post the $10,000 bail, Burque and Robinson languished in jail for two months before coming to trial. Both men were first offenders. Burque, who had a wife and seven children, claimed he took the job as driver or "puller" of the beer boat because there was no work to be found in Nova Scotia. The judge fined each man $150 and set them free.[9]

The two Nova Scotians promptly went back to driving for Archie Goyer. Within three weeks they were caught again, this time by Bo'sun Bill Paeny on the *CG-2207*, a boat that had been involved in more captures than any other coast guard vessel on Lake Ontario.[10]

Burque and Robinson went to jail and later received stiff sentences. Archie Goyer lost the *Imp* for a second time, as well as its load of 150 bags of Canadian ale. It was the final blow for the gambling barber. He had lost four boats over the course of a single summer, as well as four loads of ale totalling 13,800 quarts. He had had to post bail for himself and his two brothers and pay the fines of his pullers, Burke and Robinson. Through a combination of luck and persistence, the coast guard, cooperating with the customs border patrol, had made beer-running too expensive for Archie Goyer. He quit the business.

The Foster Ward smuggling fraternity had lost one of its more colourful members. Gone, too, were Charlie Mills, serving his sentence at the federal prison in Atlanta, Georgia, and Wild Bill Sheldon, who was completing his sentence at Munroe County Penitentiary in Rochester. Although reduced in numbers, the fraternity was still fairly active. Doc Welbanks, Ralph Boulter, and Earl McQueen were all operating liquor export businesses, employing local wharf rats as pullers. In May 1927, McQueen purchased a new forty-one-foot cruiser, the *F.B. Wright*, while Doc Welbanks owned three boats, all more or less steadily engaged in the trade.[11]

The coast guard and border patrol were able, with luck, to put medium-sized operators like Goyer out of business, but they could not reach the big operators. Men like Rocco Perri were too rich to be seriously damaged by the occasional loss of a boat and load. In any case, the coast guard had no success against Perri's fleet of fifty fishing boats. By adopting Herb Hatch's method of carrying the booze inside a fish net slung under the boat, Perri's fleet successfully avoided capture. Ontario police had more success on the highways and, over the years, captured several of Perri's trucks.

The ending of Prohibition in Ontario was the first major setback for Rocco Perri and Bessie Starkman. This was followed by the Royal Commission, which called on them to testify at its sittings in Toronto. Bessie went through a gruelling cross-examination, but Rocco could not be found. Bessie claimed not to know anything about Rocco's business, or even of his whereabouts. When asked about all the long distance phone calls to Gooderham and Worts in Toronto, she claimed that friends of her husband, whom she could not identify, frequently came in and used the family telephone to make calls about which she knew nothing.

The distinguished lawyer and King's Counsel R.L. Calder came up against the impeccably groomed Bessie Starkman and, for a while, came off second best. She answered all his questions with either "No" or "I don't know." In frustration, Calder rebuked her: "You had better wait until I finish my questions; otherwise I shall have the impression that you are prepared to say No to everything I ask you." Bessie blurted, "Oh no!"[12]

Eventually, Calder was able to trip her up when she maintained that all she had in bank accounts was $98. The commission had evidence of several bank accounts. Using different combinations of the names Perri and Starkman, the crafty Bootleg Queen had accumulated $841,000 in various Hamilton banks. Like everyone appearing before the commission, Bessie had made her statements under oath; she was therefore guilty of perjury. Her husband was subsequently located and subpoenaed by the RCMP. Forced to testify before the commission, Rocco suffered an almost total memory loss. Where was he last week? He wasn't sure. Was he not in Welland? He might have been, he couldn't remember. And so it went. At one point, Counsel inquired rather sardonically if Rocco remembered where he was last night. The cool, little Italian (he stood barely five feet four inches) almost blurted he didn't remember, then smiled, and replied he had been at home. The commission lawyers kept coming back to the interview he had given the *Toronto Star* in which he claimed to be "King of the Bootleggers." Rocco ducked, dodged, hedged, and finally denied he had understood the statement the *Star* had made him sign before printing the interview. As a result of this testimony, the commission decided to lay charges of perjury.[13]

Shortly thereafter, in May 1927, Rocco and Bessie disappeared to avoid standing trial. The commission prepared to seize their property. Unable to operate their export business while in hiding, the couple reappeared and on November 18, 1927, were indicted in a Toronto court. They were each charged with eight counts of perjury and were released on bail of $10,000.[14]

Early the following year, the pair came to trial. The clever Bessie was able to win an acquittal, but Rocco went to jail for six months. It was the first time the millionaire bootlegger had spent more than a few nights in jail.[15]

The Royal Commission on Customs and Excise had a major impact on the beer and liquor industries. As a result of its recommendations, a number of breweries failed to get their licences renewed until they had brought their sales practices into line with the Ontario Temperance Act. The customs service was reorganized and several corrupt or incompetent officers, including the chiefs at Windsor and Toronto, were removed from their posts.

Acting on the commission's report, Parliament passed four laws dealing with the customs department, among them an act to give the minister power to cancel brewers' and distillers' licences. The management of the O'Keefe brewery had burned its books rather than turn them over to the commissioners; the minister used his new powers to suspend their licence. In so doing, he served notice that the government fully intended to use its new powers; if the brewers and distillers wanted to stay in business, they would have to clean up their act. Their free-wheeling days were over. The government also began legal action in the courts to recover millions of dollars from the distillers and brewers for back payment of sales and excise taxes.

The hearing held by the Royal Commission brought into the open many of the practices used by distillery executives to circumvent Canadian law. Herb Hatch admitted that he and Larry McGuiness operated an office at Niagara Falls, New York, from which they forwarded orders to Gooderham and Worts in Toronto. Technically, they were operating within Canadian law because their orders were for delivery outside of Canada. The commissioners were able to show that some of these export orders were fraudulent. Hatch had simply phoned a telegraph office at Niagara Falls, New York, and paid them to send telegraph orders to Gooderham and Worts for delivery to a J. Penna at Wilson, New York. J. Penna was a pseudonym for the Hamilton bootlegger, Rocco Perri. This information was the basis for the government's case against Gooderham and Worts for the recovery of $439,744.05, representing unpaid sales tax for a twenty-eight month period. The Supreme Court tried the case in Toronto where Judge J.A. Grant awarded the government $439,744.05, plus interest at five percent.[16]

Unhappily for Herb and Harry Hatch, this setback was followed by yet another, this one emanating from the United States. By testifying under oath before the commission that they had been soliciting orders for delivery to the U.S.A., Herb Hatch and Larry McGuiness were admitting they had been violating American prohibition laws. In filling these orders, the executives at Gooderham and Worts were admitting that they, too, were violating these laws. There was nothing unusual in this. All of the brewery and distillery executives brought before the Royal Commission had been anxious to prove they had not been selling to bootleggers in Canada but to an export market. Most acknowledged that these exports were for the United States, but not all. Sir Mortimer Davis had tried to avoid both the excise tax and the sales tax by claiming that the Corby and Wiser distilleries were not selling to the U.S.A but to Mexico, Cuba, and various other southern countries where the importation of liquor was not illegal. The commission exposed this as a fraud.

As this testimony had been made under oath, it provided American Treasury officials with legal proof that these companies and their officers were knowingly breaking American liquor laws. Sir Mortimer Davis had retired to his villa in the south of France, but Harry Hatch was conveniently close at hand in Toronto. Moreover, the evidence against Hatch's companies was more clear-cut. The Treasury Department decided to ignore the Canadian Industrial Alcohol Company and Sir Mortimer Davis, and concentrate its efforts on Harry Hatch, the new King of the Canadian liquor industry. On December 4, 1928, the Federal Grand Jury, meeting in Buffalo, issued indictments against thirty Canadian firms and individuals for conspiring to violate American prohibition laws. A number of Americans were also indicted, including employees of telegraph, railroads, and banking firms.

The most prominent Canadians indicted were Harry Hatch, Herb Hatch, and Larry McGuiness. If any of these men entered the United States and were recognized, they would almost certainly be arrested and brought to trial. This put a crimp in the sales activities of Hatch and McGuiness. For Harry Hatch, it was far more than an inconvenience. He had recently entered the field of thoroughbred horse-racing and was planning on entering his horses on American tracks. If he did so, he risked having his expensive racehorses seized by American authorities.

Equally galling to Harry Hatch was the social stigma. He was a major power in the distilling industry who travelled extensively and had business contacts in the U.S.A, the British Isles, and South America. When a reporter from the *Toronto Star* called to discuss the American indictments, he found his questions routed through a secretary who relayed the questions to Hatch. He in turn invariably replied that he "did not wish to comment on the matter." The reporter's questions became more direct, "Will you stand trial?" The president of Hiram Walker-Gooderham and Worts hung up.[17] All further attempts by the press to obtain an interview were denied.

It is unlikely the American officials ever expected to bring the Hatch brothers to trial. Their real purpose was to bring pressure on Canadian politicians and force them to prohibit the export of booze to the United States from Canadian ports. Prime Minister Mackenzie King did not oblige them. His government was no doubt influenced by the generous contributions made to Liberal Party coffers by the liquor interests. The influence of these interests is revealed by a letter sent by Canada's outstanding senior public servant to the government's representative in Washington, the Honourable Vincent Massey:

Ottawa, 2nd April, 1929.

Personal and Confidential

My dear Mr. Massey:

I have your inquiry of March 28th as to the Canadian distillers' indictment at Buffalo. I believe that with this information on hand you would be in a position to approach the Attorney General informally to ascertain whether the indictment could be squashed...I think it would be desirable that it should be squashed, but in view of all the circumstances surrounding this particular transaction and the general liquor smuggling controversy, it does not seem desirable at present at least to put the United States Government in a position where it could be announced that the indictment would be squashed as the result of a request by the Canadian government.

Yours sincerely,
O.D.Skelton[18]

As it turned out, the indictments had little effect on Harry Hatch or his companies. During the fiscal year ending August 31, 1929, Hiram Walker-Gooderham and Worts increased its net profit a full 20 per cent to $4,117,668.[19] Business was running so smoothly and profitably that Hatch decided to turn the president's job over to Bill Hume, thereby enabling Hatch to devote more time to his horse-racing interests. Harry Hatch retained his position as chairman of the board of directors, where he was able to oversee major policy-making.

While the profits for the liquor companies were still booming, the situation for the ordinary rum-runner was changing rapidly for the worse. The scathing denunciation of the Canadian customs service by the Smuggling Committee led, in May 1927, to a complete reorganization of the Preventative Service. This branch of the Customs Department was responsible for preventing smuggling into Canada. The situation on the Great Lakes had been laughable – one man for the entire province of Ontario. An experienced and capable officer, George Fowler was appointed divisional chief for the area from Kingston to the Manitoba boundary. Fifty-five men were recruited for the sole purpose of preventing smuggling within this territory. At the outset, they were provided with a dozen fast automobiles and, at Fort Francis, one fast patrol boat.[20] By 1932, when the Preventative Service was absorbed into the RCMP, it numbered 246 officers and men, and included in its equipment some thirty-two patrol boats. Most of these served along the Atlantic coast, but a few were deployed to the Great Lakes.[21]

These actions by the Canadian government, together with the continued increase in the numbers and equipment of American prohibition enforcement agencies, ushered in the most violent period of rum-running. In 1928, the coast guard was just one boat short of capturing as many rum ships on Lake Ontario as they had managed in the previous three years combined. As a consequence, during 1928 many old-time smugglers decided to call it quits. The business was too risky, the odds on capture too high, the fines too heavy, and the probability of a long prison sentence, if captured, almost certain.

One man exulted in the greater risks. Ben Kerr crossed the lake more frequently, usually three or four times a week, and often alone. In the winter, when one of the *Pollywog*'s two motors gave out, he refused to lay up for repairs but continued the crossings, relying on the one remaining motor to get him through the ice. As the war with the coast guard heated up, he pushed himself even harder, reaching closer than ever before to the outer limits of his luck and ability.

Few rum-runners crossed the lake more than once a week, but at Main Duck, Kerr often encountered Bruce Lowery, a newcomer to rum-running but one who was every bit as persistent as the Hamilton plumber. Like Kerr, Lowery crossed the lake in all seasons, including winter, and frequently did so alone. Of average height, Lowery possessed a sturdy frame developed from a lifetime of hard labour as a commercial fisherman. A decade younger than Kerr, he was at least as capable a mariner, and, as events would prove, the possessor of such daring coolness under fire, and just plain luck, that today his exploits are still recounted in the beverage rooms, on the wharfs, and around the kitchen tables of Prince Edward County.

Lowery's entry into rum-running would have been less noteworthy but for the zeal of coast guard Captain Richard Herline, and the pugnacity of Doc Hedley Welbanks. The cigar-chomping horse doctor was the man who had recruited

Lowery into rum-running in the first place. Much to the friendly fisherman's chagrin, the burly veterinarian's vengefulness and parsimony brought them both a lot of unwelcome publicity when the Doc hijacked the rum boat *Rosella*. The trial and publicity resulting from this episode had a disastrous effect on Lowery's personal life. His engagement to an attractive Free-Methodist girl from Picton was one of the casualties of his connection with the irascible Doc Welbanks.

17

DOC WELBANKS
HIJACKS A BOAT

"This was a high-handed act of piracy for a United States cutter to come into Canadian Waters and seize a Canadian boat."

Magistrate Mikel
October 26, 1927[1]

Over the years Hedley Welbanks had hired many different men to drive his whisky boats. Some of these men he recruited from among the wharf rats in Belleville, the city where Welbanks lived and carried on his veterinary practice. But there were problems with this source; many of the men were unreliable, drinking too much and not showing up when needed. It was also getting harder for him to persuade them to risk jail or a coast guard bullet for $75 a trip. With the supply of good men drying up in Belleville, he decided to recruit from among the sturdy farmers and fishermen of Prince Edward County. It was a smart move. The Doc's parents were prosperous and well-known farmers from Milford, a small village located ten miles south of Picton. Milford was only three miles from Port Milford, then a hamlet of about a hundred souls perched on a low hill overlooking the waters of South Bay and today a ghost town. For generations the people living around South Bay had earned their livelihood as commercial fishermen. These sturdy individuals knew the waters from the Upper Gap to Main Duck as well as any farmer knew the path to his own barn. They could read the lake and anticipate its moods. Most important, they had learned how to survive the sudden storms that gathered in the area and erupted with deadly swiftness. These skills made the fishermen ideal candidates for the increasingly risky job of rum-running.

In the close-knit rural communities of Prince Edward County, word spread quickly that Doc Welbanks was looking for a man to drive one of his rum-running boats. Welbanks was, and still is, a county name. A fisherman from the county, who might hesitate to approach a stranger in Belleville about such a job, would feel less uncomfortable asking the Doc about it. One of the first to approach Welbanks was Ken Peterson of South Bay, known as Coo Peterson to his friends. Peterson's parents were respectable, church-going people. Even better, the father had been a commercial fisherman all his life. But Welbanks hesitated. He knew that Ken's older brother, Herb, was a hopeless alcoholic. And although Ken was only eighteen, he had already been arrested four times for offences ranging from disorderly conduct to breaking the Ontario Temperance Act.[2] The raw-boned youngster was tough and clearly had the nerve for the job, but he would be difficult to control and probably unreliable. Welbanks turned him down.

Several farm-hands and wharf-rats applied, but Welbanks turned them all down. He was looking for an expert fisherman, a man he could rely on, someone who would make good money for them both. That so few applied was largely due to the religious make-up of Prince Edward County. The Methodist Church and its off-shoot, the United Church of Canada, were dominant throughout the area. Both churches were staunch supporters of total prohibition, vehemently opposed to the liquor traffic in all its forms. Their influence was manifested in the province-wide plebiscite held in 1924. Voters in the neighbouring cities of Kingston and Belleville split almost evenly on the question of prohibition, but the county supported the OTA in overwhelming numbers, voting six to one against government sale of alcohol. Any fisherman who got involved in rum-running would face the disapproval of his friends and neighbours. Doc Welbanks knew all this but hoped the decline of the fishing industry, combined with the lure of good money, would be a sufficient attraction.

Word of the Doc's search reached Bruce Lowery in Milford, where he was living with his mother and younger brother, Jimmy. Twelve years earlier, Lowery's father and two of his brothers had perished in a house fire. Lowery had been able to save two-year-old Jimmy, who had been sleeping in an upstairs bedroom. Despite valiant efforts, he could not get back into the downstairs where the fire had started. The frame house burned up, taking three lives and almost all the family's possessions. Only the day before, his father had sold his fishing boat, nets, racks, and other equipment, intending to move the family to Western Canada. The money burned up in the fire. At twenty years of age, Bruce Lowery assumed the responsibility of supporting his mother and younger brother.[3]

Over the next twelve years, Lowery worked first as a fisherman's helper at Main Duck Island then, after a year overseas with the Eastern Ontario Regiment, he returned to Main Duck and used his savings to buy his own fishing rig. While he was overseas, he regularly sent his mother half of his monthly pay cheque.[4] The army fed and clothed him and, as he neither smoked nor drank, he was able to save what little money remained. Buying his own rig had been his ambition since the death of his father and two younger brothers.[5]

While he was at Main Duck, Lowery frequently met various rum-runners, but at no time had he joined them. His older brother, Martin, who sometimes worked for Bruce, did make a number of trips. At $50 a trip, he could make more in one night than he made in two weeks of back-breaking labour as a fisherman's helper.

In 1924, King Cole advised the fishermen on Main Duck that he would be raising their rent in 1925. This rankled some of them. They knew Cole was wealthy and that he was making big money by using Main Duck as a depot for rum-runners. Bruce Lowery and three others decided to strike out on their own. The four fishermen bought a piece of land on the south shore of Amherst Island where they built four cottages, a dock, four net-houses, and an ice-house. For the next two years, they struggled to pay their bank loans as the price of fish fell and catches declined. Some of the men were tempted to give it up and go rum-running with Charlie Mills, a frequent visitor at Amherst Island. A few of the fishermen and their helpers did so, including Babe Cole of Main Duck, and Garfield Thomas of Amherst. By 1926, Martin Lowery was making a few irregular trips running beer and whisky out of Kingston.[6]

Bruce Lowery, Methodist, non-smoker, infrequent drinker, and hard-working fisherman, began to think seriously about getting into rum-running. His tall, dark-haired sister, Naomi, tried to talk him out of it, pointing to the killing of Leo Yott by the coast guard, and the long prison sentence received by Charlie Mills. Both of these events occurred in 1926, the year Lowery made up his mind. The fishing industry was in the doldrums, and he was finding it increasingly difficult to support his mother and younger brother and to keep up the payments on his share of the Amherst Island fishing venture. Adding to his financial problems was his determination to marry Letty Hicks, a young Picton woman he had been dating for sometime. A slender, sensitive woman, who was well educated for the times, Letty was also a Free Methodist and therefore opposed to the liquor trade. Lowery knew her parents were even more opposed and would end the engagement if they learned he was running booze. But he was thirty-two years old, well past the age when most men marry. Perhaps he could make enough from rum-running in one year to solve his financial problems, get married, and go back to fishing.

One the day of decision, Bruce Lowery cranked his old Star sedan into life, and drove north on the Milford road towards Belleville. Earlier, he had telephoned Doc Welbanks who had volunteered to drive to Milford. But Lowery did not want to discuss the job where his sister, mother, or younger brother might overhear. The meeting was to be held at Doc Welbank's house on James Street.

Isabel Welbanks ushered Lowery into the family kitchen. She knew about her husband's rum-running activities but didn't like to think about them. Isabel was pleasantly surprised by the polite, smiling fisherman. He was not what she had expected.

The beefy vet was not surprised. He had already made inquiries of his relatives at South Bay who told him Lowery was highly regarded. His action in saving the life of his younger brother from the house fire was well known. The South Bay residents also spoke of his feat in surviving the great storm of 1924. He had been piloting his open fish boat from Main Duck to Long Point, a distance of twelve miles, when the hurricane had struck. It had levelled trees on False Ducks and Long Point, torn the wooden railing off the Long Point Lighthouse, flattened a barn, and turned that section of the lake into a boiling, churning, maelstrom.

Three men and a boy had been in the boat with Lowery when what should have been an easy hour and a half trip, turned into a marathon of survival. Water poured into the boat, first from the stern, then from the bow, and the men bailed without rest to avoid swamping. This went on and on for eight exhausting hours. At one point, a giant wave crashed over the stern extinguishing the engine and the boat began to broach-to. The young boy, Francis Welbanks, thought they were a "gone goose." Bruce doused the engine with gasoline and set it on fire. The motor coughed into life. Eventually, they made it to the lee of False Duck Island and from there to safety. Francis Welbanks credits their survival to Bruce Lowery's skill with a boat. "He was," he states simply, "the best on the lake."[7]

In the spring of 1927, Bruce Lowery made the first of many trips across the lake in Doc Welbanks's old fish boat, the *Rosella*. It was thirty-eight feet long and powered by a two-cylinder Fairbanks engine, with an exhaust pipe that went straight up into the air. You could hear the boat coming for a long time before you could actually see it. Using this comical old rig, Bruce went across to Oswego in daylight, sailing in right under the noses of the customs and the coast guard, who never suspected such an old crock would actually be used to smuggle beer and whisky. The strategy worked; Lowery made sure he acted like a fisherman and that the *Rosella* looked like a fishing boat. By crossing during the day, he also avoided the coast guard picket boats, which usually patrolled at night.[8]

The system worked well all spring and on into the summer of 1927, but was brought to a sudden end by the unexpected appearance in eastern Lake Ontario of *CG-121*. This was the patrol boat that had been used so successfully on Lake Erie two years before, where it was involved in five major captures in a single summer. The rum-runners never knew where or when they might encounter one of these six-bitters. They were designed to be away from port for a week at a time, and so could roam the lake freely.

The patrol boat and its crew had been transferred to Sackets Harbor, due east of Main Duck Island, to assist the three picket boats already on the lake.[9] Tactically, it made sense for the smaller picket boats to patrol the American shore, leaving Captain Herline in *CG-121* to lurk in and around the waters off Main Duck. In the late afternoon of July 26, 1927, he was cruising in the waters between Galloo and Main Duck islands when he spotted "a long low neutral colored craft" edging between the two islands.[10] At this point, accounts of the incident start to differ. Herline and his crew claimed the rum-runner was in American waters about twenty-six miles from Oswego. Lowery and ten other witnesses claimed he was north of Main Duck, clearly in Canadian waters.

Lowery and his crewman, Ernest Warren, spotted the cutter steaming towards them and made an abrupt 180-degree turn to keep well to the north of the American boundary. The cutter could make fifteen knots, the *Rosella* no more than seven or eight. In a matter of minutes the six-bitter had drawn alongside and Captain Herline was shouting, "Round her up there." Lowery looked up to see a machine gun trained on his boat, "Do you know where you are?" he demanded. "Never mind that, round up," was the response.[11] Grudgingly, Lowery submitted to being handcuffed and taken aboard the cutter. The *Rosella* was towed to Oswego, where the coast guard placed the boat and the cargo of 110 bags of beer and forty bags of liquor under seizure. Lowery, who gave his name as Fred Sprung, was escorted to the Oswego County jail along with Ernest Warren. Bail was set at $1,500 each and the hearing scheduled for August 6, 1927.

The evening before the hearing, Doc Welbanks arrived in Oswego driving a forty-foot launch containing several passengers. They included Wesley Thomas and Jim Hutchinson, lighthouse keepers at Main and False Duck islands respectively, Freeman Cory, a commercial fisherman from South Bay, and Reverend Ernest Lee from Kingston. The minister had been with a group picnicking on Main Duck Island at the time of the seizure. All of these people were put up at the Musico Hotel and provided with a big meal and free drinks, all at Doc Welbanks expense. The following day, each witness was called upon to testify by Commissioner Charles Bulger. The mass of evidence clearly favoured the defendants, the testimony of two church ministers being particularly convincing. Fred Sprung and Ernest Warren were set free. Commissioner Bulger also ordered the coast guard to return the *Rosella* and her cargo to Doc Welbanks. Up to this point Lowery had managed to conceal his real identity from the press and, more importantly, from the parents of his intended bride.

Welbanks soon discovered that he hadn't really won. The hearings had taken place on August 30, a full month after the seizure, during which time the coast guard had turned the *Rosella* over to customs. Commissioner Bulger, it seemed, had no authority with customs, and, instead of returning the boat and cargo to Welbanks, the collector of customs served notice that, in twenty days, the boat would be sold at public auction.

This greatly vexed Doc Welbanks who was known to be close with a dollar. He had spent all that money entertaining the witnesses a Musico's, a notorious dive which stood on the site of the present Ferris Hotel. And for what? It was beginning to look like the liquor was gone for good, and if he wanted his boat back, he would have to bid for it. Understandably annoyed, he travelled to Rochester and bid $350 for his own boat, only to be out-bid by Dwight Palmer, an American fish buyer. Thoroughly disgusted with the American system of justice, Doc Welbanks returned to Belleville and made plans to get justice his own way.

The Palmer Fish Company made some repairs to the *Rosella*, added a new cabin, and renamed her *Verna*. On October 10, 1927, the *Verna* was put into service, hauling fish to Rochester. Her first stop was at Deseronto, where she picked up a load of fish. Three days later the *Verna* put in at Brighton for gasoline and, as the lake was stormy, her two crew-members decided to stay over for the night. Someone phoned Doc Welbanks anonymously, instructing him where he could find his boat. There was a hurried consultation between Welbanks and Major Geen, head of the local customs office. Shortly thereafter, Doc Welbanks, toting his army service revolver, took off for Brighton accompanied by customs officer Fred McLeneghan. Had Major Geen known Welbanks was packing a gun, he would never have allowed McLeneghan to accompany him. Nevertheless, the fact that he did send McLeneghan to assist Welbanks illustrates the alliance that existed between the customs service and the liquor exporters.

The two men arrived at the Brighton pier a little after midnight. The *Verna* was tied up and her crew asleep. Welbanks boarded the boat with gun drawn, roused the crew, and informed them that he had a Canadian customs officer with him and was retaking possession of his boat. Fred McLeneghan realized he had made a mistake in coming as soon as he saw the big revolver and wisely remained in the car throughout the seizure.

Welbanks's high-handed action, especially in brandishing his gun at the two Americans, touched off a minor diplomatic row. The OPP arrested both Welbanks and McLeneghan and charged them with theft. Major Geen wiped the egg off his face and called on his supervisor for advice. Dwight Palmer went to Ottawa, where he was treated with great politeness by the minister of customs. At Rochester and Oswego, the seizure was headline news and sent the politicians scrambling. Major Geen had instructions not to make any statements to the press. He was in a difficult situation. The customs department could not support the use of a gun against innocent American citizens but, at the same time, could not be too sympathetic to the Americans when it seemed clear that they had no right to the boat in the first place.

When the case came before Magistrate Mikel, he attempted to duck it, saying, "My view is, that I do not wish to try this case," and, as if to explain, "It would not be wise for me to determine whether the United States authorities had the proper right to seize this vessel."[12] The trial was adjourned, giving Mikel time to get some legal advice and the lawyers time to ponder the complexities of a highly unusual case.

The trial was held late in October and took two full days. The small court room was packed with curious spectators and a long parade of witnesses. C.A. Payne, defence attorney for Doc Welbanks, maintained that his client could not be guilty of theft because the boat was his own property. It had been seized illegally by the coast guard, and an American judge had recognized Doc Welbank's title to the boat by ordering it returned to him. It was clear that if Welbanks won his case, customs officer McLeneghan would be automatically acquitted.

Crown attorney Bryson Donnan produced a bill of sale from U.S. Customs to the Palmer Fish Company as evidence that it had "right and title" to the boat. If it had title, then Doc Welbanks had committed a theft. The two crew members then testified, describing how Welbanks had boarded the boat with his gun, told them there was a customs officer in his car, and sent them packing. Both men stated that the customs officer had neither left the car nor spoken to them.

Defence attorney then called on several witnesses, many of them from the original trial at Oswego. Bruce Lowery was the second last to testify. This time he had to use his real name. The Belleville newspapers printed it and word got to Letty Hicks's parents. Bruce and Letty's engagement was off.

Doc Welbanks was the last to testify. He insisted on laying the majority of the blame for the repossession of the *Rosella* on the shoulders of Major Geen and customs officer McLeneghan.

By implicating the customs department, the stubborn horse doctor managed to embarrass the Canadian government, which was under pressure from the American government to end the export of Canadian liquor to the U.S.A. It is clear that some sort of a deal had been struck before the trial, because defence attorney C.A. Payne repudiated the testimony of his own client, advising Magistrate Mikel that Welbanks was ready to take the blame for the repossession and to absolve the customs department from any responsibility. Welbanks was then recalled to the stand and questioned by Magistrate Mikel: "You have sworn that McLeneghan accompanied you for the purpose of seizing the Rosella?" Doc Welbanks, who clearly didn't trust lawyers or the judicial system, replied that he didn't know if McLeneghan was there just to supervise or to seize, and then with a parting shot at his own lawyer stated, "I guess McLeneghan wasn't along for a night ride."[13]

Magistrate Mikel rendered his verdict the next day. He dismissed all charges against the accused, noting that for theft to have occurred, Welbanks had to take the property "without colour of right." As the coast guard had seized the *Rosella* in Canadian waters, they had taken it illegally. No United States agency or department could give the Palmer Fish Company title to the boat as title still resided with the legal owner, Doctor Hedley Welbanks. The Magistrate went on to censure the coast guard, calling their action "a high-handed act of piracy."[14]

There was further skirmishing. Dwight Palmer obtained a temporary injunction preventing Welbanks from taking possession of the boat. An armed guard was placed on the *Rosella* to deter the combative veterinarian from staging another hijacking. But this time Welbanks used the court to enforce his claim and, on November 5, 1927, the *Rosella* was turned over to Doctor Welbanks. In commenting on this development, the *Daily Intelligencer* wryly observed that, "the Rosella will now resume its former duties as a fishing craft."[15]

Other than the newspaper reporters, who got some good stories, there were no winners in the *Rosella* affair: the customs department was embarrassed; Doc Welbanks spent a night in jail, paid out money to lawyers, and failed to recover a boatload of booze; the coast guard was told to stay out of Canadian waters; Dwight Palmer was out the money he had paid for the *Rosella*; and Bruce Lowery wasted a month in jail and lost a fiancée. In addition, Doc Welbanks and Bruce

Lowery had come to the parting of the ways. First, because after Lowery had been arrested and was awaiting trial, Welbanks had refused to post his $1,500 bail, and second because, at the trail, Lowery had seen Welbanks betray the very customs officers who had tried to help him. Now the Doc had a boat but no one to drive it. Fortunately for Welbanks, an old rum-runner was back in town. Charlie Mills had returned in October after serving his year in the Atlanta prison. About the middle of November, Mills bought the *Rosella* from Welbanks, re-christened her the *Lindy*, and sent her off to Oswego with a cargo of ale.[16] Bruce Lowery was in the pilot house.

It was a good arrangement for Mills, who feared crossing the lake after October and also knew that a second arrest would likely result in an even longer sentence than the one he had just served. Jennie Batley, the vivacious widow who frequently crossed the lake with Mills, provided a special incentive for him to stay out of prison. During his stay in the Atlanta penitentiary, Jennie had been pursued by an amorous Belleville detective. On his release from prison, Gentleman Charlie had threatened to "blow a hole" in the policeman if he continued his attentions.

For Bruce Lowery, the good pay offered by Mills gave him the opportunity to get enough cash together to buy his own boat. Although Lowery was crossing the lake in the stormy season, the *Lindy* now protected him from the elements. During the brief time they had owned it, the Palmer Fish company had obligingly installed a pilot house and overhauled the engine. Even with these improvements, the thirty-eight-foot former fishing boat was still underpowered and slow, capable of no more than seven or eight knots. Consequently, Lowery planned his routes so that he could lay over at Main Duck if a winter storm blew up.

During the winter the island was nearly deserted. The fishermen left at the end of October, leaving only the two caretakers of King Cole's livestock and buildings and the lighthouse staff. Wes Thomas and Charlie Stewart, his assistant lighthouse keeper, stayed only until mid-December when shipping ceased. They then shut down the light and returned to the mainland to spend the winter with their families. Wes Thomas remembers Bruce Lowery stopping in to visit one particular stormy day in early December.

Lowery was known to brave the lake in weather that would send most men scuttling for a safe harbour. He would have known the day before his departure that a storm was brewing, simply by using the old sailor's trick of standing with his back to the lower winds and noting the direction of the upper winds. If they were from his right side, the weather was clearing, if from his left, he could expect deteriorating conditions and, possibly, a storm. In the morning, before leaving the government dock in Belleville, he would note the direction of the wind and, during the next several hours, would watch for any shift in direction. A backing wind, shifting from southwest to southeast, signalled a low pressure front, and the imminent arrival of sleet or snow flurries.

In the seven hours it took for Lowery to sail from Belleville to Main Duck that December day, the wind had freshened, icing the blue-green lake with sparkling white caps. A leaden sky pressed down ominously, forcing the surface wind to back and veer abruptly. The lake was beginning to churn and spit. There was no point in continuing in such weather. In a few hours, the worst of the storm would be over and Lowery could finish his journey to the American shore after dark. He actually preferred to cross the lake at this time of year because the coast guard were less likely to venture out in their small picket boats.

When Lowery turned into Schoolhouse Bay at the north end of Main Duck, he noticed a sleek cabin cruiser, bobbing gracefully in the lee of the wind. He recognized the *Pollywog* from its low silhouette and curtained black cabin: Ben Kerr was already ashore visiting with Wes Thomas. Bruce Lowery joined them to wait out the storm and spin away the hours trading stories with the legendary rum-runner.

Late in the afternoon, the men heard a pistol shot and went outside to investigate. A medium-sized open motorboat was disabled and drifting helplessly about a mile off the island's rocky north shore. One of the men in the boat had fired his revolver in an effort to attract rescuers. A full-scale winter storm was developing: increasingly violent waves slapped and slashed at the steep north shore and intermittent squalls of snow blotted out any view of the boat and its hapless occupants. Each time the snow cleared, the men on shore could see that the boat was being blown closer and closer to the north shore, which, for a distance of several hundred yards, rises vertically to a height of fifteen feet above the water's edge. When it reached this cliff, the drifting boat would be quickly dashed to pieces on the rocks. Its occupants, already numbed by the winter air, would not last more than a few minutes in the icy water.

None of the men ashore recognized the boat, and Ben Kerr flatly refused to chance such a sea for strangers. But Bruce Lowery, the ex-fisherman, lived by a different creed, a belief that you always help a fellow mariner in distress. Setting out in *Lindy*, he headed directly into the stiff winds, which by now had backed into the north. At the northwest end of the island, he swung southwest, taking the waves on his aft quarter. Because *Lindy* was underpowered, there was a danger she would yaw to starboard and be broached by the heavy seas. Drawing on all his skill as a sailor, Lowery manoeuvred the *Lindy* close enough to the disabled boat to throw a line to its crew. The attempt failed and he prepared to manoeuvre for a second pass. This time, the seas intervened, and Lowery barely managed to avoid capsizing. He was preparing for a third attempt, when a giant wave washed over *Lindy*'s stern, extinguishing the two-cylinder Fairbanks motor. As he had done during the storm of 1924, Lowery poured gasoline on the engine and set it on fire. It was a risky procedure, but it dried the motor sufficiently for Lowery to coax one cylinder back to life. By this time, the men in the boat were too numbed to catch the line. Lowery concentrated on navigating the half-crippled *Lindy* northward into the wind, in an effort to round the tip of Main Duck and reach the safety of the island's main harbour. Even on two cylinders the *Lindy* was underpowered for the task but, by quartering into the waves, the skilful mariner gradually worked his way around the point and, sometime after nightfall, arrived back in harbour where he anchored to ride out the storm.

In the meantime, Wes Thomas had been lowered by a rope down to a ledge at the edge of the water. During a lull in the storm Wes was able to tie a rope around each man in turn and Charlie Stewart hauled them to safety. The fifth and last man had just been tied and hauled up when the storm again lashed into full fury. As Wes Thomas scrambled to the top of the cliff, the boat at its base was dashed to pieces.

Years later, while recounting the story for a reporter from the Picton *Gazette*, the venerable lighthouse keeper remarked of Bruce Lowery that, "his courage and audacity were second to none who crossed the lake."[17] Wesley Thomas proved his own courage that stormy night and was directly responsible for saving five lives. The rescued men were rum-runners from the United States.

A few days after the incident, Wes Thomas returned to South Bay to spend the winter on the mainland with his family. Both Ben Kerr and Bruce Lowery continued to cross the lake. In winter, because the Bay of Quinte freezes over, the rum-runners shifted from Belleville to other ports. Ben Kerr shifted his operation to Presqu'ile Point where he rented a cabin from Grant Quick. A busy summer resort area, Presqu'ile Point was largely deserted in winter, enabling Kerr to carry on his activities undisturbed. The isolation of the point appealed to Kerr, who often used the cabin in the fall. Summer, when the place was busy with tourists, was the only time he avoided the place.

The more gregarious Lowery shifted his operations to Kingston. During the short period its harbour froze over, he worked out of Bath, some fifteen miles to the west. By this time he had severed his connections with Charlie Mills and was on his own. He carried beer for a variety of companies but carried whisky only for Gooderham and Worts.

At Kingston, the amiable ex-fisherman made the acquaintance of a small group of rum-runners, including Wild Bill Sheldon, Tony Kane, Cecil Phillips, Bill Dowie, Bill Circle, and Vic Sudds. Sudds was also an ex-fisherman and became a close friend, occasionally travelling with Lowery across the lake. During the years when the coast guard mounted its all-out war on booze-smugglers, Lowery and Sudds were considered an unbeatable combination; if no one else could get through, they could.

Except for the winter of 1925, the coast guard always stopped their patrols in late December. This removed one of the risks for those venturesome enough to cross the lake in winter. Lowery and Kerr still had to guard against being captured while unloading on shore, but their main concerns were the lake and the weather. Kerr's boat, the *Pollywog*, had twin engines and an enclosed cabin that afforded some protection from the wind and cold. Lowery had purchased a new boat which he named *Scout*. It was small for a rum-runner, no more than twenty-five feet long, but powered by a Scripps engine and very fast. By careful packing, Lowery was able to load ninety bags of whisky aboard this small craft. He used the *Scout* to cross the lake all winter; his only protection from the elements being its windshield, his oils-licker, and an unusual ability to endure cold.

Today, almost sixty years after Bruce Lowery left Prince Edward County, it is easy to find people to talk about him. One tale concerns his return to Kingston so encased in ice, he had to be chopped free of his boat.[18] Another deals with his stopping in at Main Duck one January and going to King Cole's house, where the two caretakers beat the ice off him with sticks while he stood by the wood stove sipping hot coffee.[19]

The surviving fishermen and rum-runners from the county have clear recollections of both Bruce Lowery and Ben Kerr. They view them as the most persistent of all the rum-runners who hung out at Main Duck. They knew Lowery better than they knew Kerr, partly because Lowery had been one of them, but also because Kerr was naturally reticent. Nevertheless, they observed that Kerr had an exceptional ability to forecast the weather, whereas Lowery had superior boat-handling skills and an uncanny knack of navigating with pinpoint accuracy under the most adverse conditions. Although outwardly congenial, Lowery possessed a streak of ruthlessness that was probably equal to Kerr's. Both men were close-mouthed when it came to their rum-running activities, keeping their crew members in the dark about departure times and destinations until the last possible moment.

In addition to their abilities as mariners, both men were natural athletes. Lowery was known for his outstanding swimming ability. It is said around South Bay that he could swim as fast and as far under the water as he could on the surface, a talent he used on at least one occasion to escape from the coast guard. Not much is known of Kerr's youth, but in his forties he moved with the easy grace of an athlete, and was known as a first-class snooker player.

Although the Hamilton plumber was extremely well organized, to the point of fussiness, in one respect he was more lax. Lowery never drank when rum-running and did not allow his crew to drink. He demanded total sobriety before starting a trip. Kerr, on the other hand, permitted drinking on the *Pollywog* and, although he never overimbibed, would drink a certain amount of whisky while on the lake.

The war on the lakes, which peaked during 1928 and continued for another eighteen months, caused a number of rum-runners to give it up as too risky. A very few, Kerr and Lowery were among them, not only did not quit, but responded to the greater demand for their services by increasing the frequency of their trips. From 1928 onwards, rum-running became a highly dangerous activity. Coast guard captures rose dramatically, as did the incidence of drownings and hijackings. Given the willingness of Kerr and Lowery to take these risks, it was inevitable that one of them would not survive the war on the lakes.

18

WAR ON THE LAKES

In other cases, particularly Olcott, New York., no ordnance [guns] were removed for the reason that smugglers in the area had been firing on coast guard patrol boats. During the month of July, approximately 5,000 rounds of machine gun and rifle ammunition were fired at rum-runners operating in the western end of Lake Erie and the Lower Detroit River.

Commander N.W. Rassmussen,
Ninth District U.S. Coast Guard, 22 August, 1929.

Three months prior to writing the above memo to the commandant of the coast guard, Norman Rassmussen suffered a breakdown from overwork.[1] He had received his posting to the Ninth District early in 1928, just as the Great Lakes became the chief battleground in the war between the smugglers and the coast guard. In this battle, Rassmussen was in command of the largest naval force the United States has ever placed on the Great Lakes.

During the War of 1812, a total of forty-one American warships were in service on the Great Lakes. At no time during the conflict were all of these ships in operation as they were constantly being sunk or seized by the British. It is unlikely that at any one time the American navy ever exceeded thirty warships.

In the early days of Prohibition, the coast guard had no armed vessels on the Great Lakes and so was virtually powerless to stop the rum-runners. The force, which numbered 4,295 officers and men in 1920, was quickly expanded until, by the summer of 1927, it numbered 11,425 men in all ranks. On the lakes, the service remained without significant armed vessels until the fall of 1924, when the first of the seventy-five-foot patrol boats and smaller picket boats began to appear. Their numbers were increased slowly over the next three years, and in 1928, the coast guard's success on the Atlantic enabled it to transfer large numbers of cutters to the Great Lakes. In the fall of 1929, an inventory of men and vessels was compiled at the request of the National Commission on Law Enforcement. It disclosed that the service had deployed 223 vessels to the Great Lakes, made up as follows:

> *Seminole*, first-class cutter, 188 feet long, 4 guns.
> *Crawford*, 125-foot patrol vessel, one 6-pound gun.
> *Chippewa*, 88-foot tug, small arms.
> Twenty, 75-foot patrol vessels, each with a one-pound cannon, a Lewis machine gun, and small arms.
> *AB-18*, 52-foot patrol vessel, small arms.
> *AB-1*, 80-foot patrol vessel, small arms.
> *AB-13*, 45-foot patrol vessel, small arms.
> *AB-17*, 45-foot patrol vessel, small arms.
> *AB-12*, 40-foot patrol vessel, small arms.
> Twenty-nine, 35-and 36-foot picket boats, each with a 30-calibre machine gun and small arms.
> Fifty-four motor surfboats, small arms.
> Forty-three motor lifeboats, small arms.
> Sixty-nine rowing surfboats, small arms.

The larger ships operated on Lakes Superior and Michigan, and most of the six-bitters and picket boats were assigned to Lakes Erie and Ontario. A force of 900 to 1,000 men was required to man the Great Lakes fleet.[2]

The customs border patrol provided another sixty fast speedboats, armed with machine-guns, to patrol the Detroit River.[3] E.R.Norwood, who was assigned to co-ordinate the various forces – customs border patrol, coast guard, and federal agents – operating at Detroit, commanded between 700 and 800 men alone.[4] These forces were augmented by federal agents and customs officers stationed at various centres along the lakes. These were mostly land-based forces, but at Youngstown, New York, the eighteen-man border patrol station boasted the "Grey Goose," a coastal-sized boat, mounting a machine-gun on its foredeck. Manned by a crew of six, it patrolled parts of both Lake Ontario and the Niagara River. All told, the rum-runners faced a formidable force. Commenting on the situation in an editorial dated April 9, 1928, the *Globe* observed that:

> The Niagara Frontier promises to be livelier than it has been any time since the War of 1812. A patrol fleet of 250 boats is to be put into commission stationed at two-mile intervals and their efforts are to be reinforced by aeroplanes and radio equipment. Messages will be flashed along the route when liquor-laden boats start out from the Canadian side and the chase will be on.

The reporter didn't get all his facts straight. He exaggerated the number of boats, and aeroplanes would not be in regular use for another three years, but otherwise the story was correct.

Faced with this well co-ordinated and massive force, the rum-runners had to develop new tactics and strategies and, like their adversaries, they had to cooperate with one another. When the rum fighters concentrated at Detroit, as they did in June of 1929, the big liquor exporters shifted their smuggling activity to Bridgeburg on the Niagara River. When the coast guard shifted forces from Detroit back to Buffalo, the rum-runners abandoned Port Colborne on Lake Erie for Lake Ontario.[5] By deploying the rum fleet in this way, the exporters were able to keep the booze flowing, but at a cost. Arrests of rum-runners went up dramatically, as did seizures of boats and cargoes. All of this added to the cost of "exporting," driving up the price of liquor on the American side.[6]

The massive shift of American prohibition forces to the Great Lakes coincided with a stepped-up campaign by the Ontario government. Beginning in the fall of 1927, the OPP launched a harassment campaign to close down the river-front dives in Windsor. So successful was this campaign, it caused one reporter to observe that the formerly wide-open Border City was now as dull as Toronto.[7]

The following year, the government attacked on a different front, this time hitting directly at the big liquor exporters. Operating on the premise that the accumulation of large stocks of liquor at the export docks was contrary to the Canada Temperance Act, the chairman of the Ontario Liquor Control Board, Sir Henry Drayton, ordered the OPP to seize $500,000 worth of liquor stored at two docks in Windsor. A month later, on August 11, 1928, the raids were repeated, this time against all thirty export docks in the Border Cities area. The value of the liquor confiscated was placed at several millions of dollars. These raids continued throughout the year.[8] The liquor exporters were in a conundrum. They ordered booze by the carload from the distillery in anticipation of shipping it directly across the river to Detroit. But frequently when the liquor arrived, they discovered the border patrol and customs service were out in such force it was impossible to move the booze across. If the liquor was not exported almost immediately, the OPP would sieze it.

The federal government had not interfered with the liquor export business up to this point. But now, under pressure from the Ontario government, and with public opinion finally aroused by the findings of the Royal Commission on Customs and Excise, it agreed to act. An accord was reached with the Ontario government whereby the number of Border City export docks would be reduced from thirty to ten. No other export docks were to be opened in Ontario without the consent of the provincial government. These two decisions made it more difficult for the rum-runners at Windsor to cross the Detroit River undetected. The coast guard and the border patrol now had twenty fewer locations to keep under surveillance. Some rum-runners reacted by arming themselves in an attempt to drive off their pursuers. The OPP responded with a public announcement that the carrying of guns on Canadian waters was a violation of the Criminal Code.[9] This was followed by rigid enforcement of the regulations prohibiting the return to Canada of booze once it had cleared customs. On a single day, rum-runners, unable to penetrate the coast guard blockade off Amherstburg, had to dump 3,000 cases of liquor into the lake to avoid having the cargo seized by Canadian customs when the boats returned to port.[10]

The efforts of American enforcement agencies, combined with those of the OPP, reduced smuggling out of the Border Cities area dramatically. The 150,000 cases that had crossed the Detroit River each month during the summer and fall of 1928, declined to just under 50,000 cases by September 1929.[11]

Some liquor exporters saw the handwriting on the wall and began to diversify into other activities. Three millionaire liquor exporters, Jim Burns, Marco Leon, and Harry Low, turned their talents and considerable fortunes to large-scale real estate development, including the financing of the Dominion Square building in downtown Montreal. Begun in 1928, this massive project eventually covered an entire city block.

Individual smugglers lacked the capital and business expertise for such grandiose projects. At Port Colborne, the largest rum-runner was Aaron Vandeveer, father of Amos "Nick" Vandeveer. Aaron and Nick employed several boats over the years, losing the occasional load but generally keeping ahead of the Coast Guard. However, the tactics that had worked when they had to contend with one six-bitter and two picket boats would no longer suffice; the coast guard posted forty patrol boats to Buffalo in 1928. In response to this massive build-up, Aaron acquired the *Over the Top*, reputed to be the fastest boat on Lake Erie. With it he would lure the coast guard into chasing him, while the slower boats in the rum fleet delivered their cargo elsewhere. It was a risky business and eventually cost Aaron his life. Aaron was probably shot in the dark while trying to escape the coast guard.[12] He had been missing for sometime when his bullet-ridden body washed up on shore. His son Nick carried on the business but wisely hired others to do the driving.

In 1926, Nick lost a thirty-three-foot speedboat to the coast guard who diverted it to their Erie station fleet as *CG-2248*. It was powered by a twelve-cylinder Liberty airplane engine which gave it a top speed of thirty-five miles an hour, making it the fastest picket boat in service on Lake Erie. On the night of March 30, 1928, while the *CG-2248* was in drydock waiting to undergo repairs, it mysteriously caught fire and was destroyed. An investigation pointed to arson.[13] The war on the lakes was heating up.

The build-up of coast guard forces at Buffalo had the intended effect, and Port Colborne declined as a liquor exporting centre. The fleet of nineteen launches that operated from the port in 1926 was down to less than half a dozen three years later.[14] Nick Vandeveer lost a number of boats during this period, including the thirty-foot *Alma* and the fifty-foot *Wyandotte*.[15] The crew of another of his boats, the *Lady*, had to dump her load of whisky overboard to avoid capture. Later that summer, the *Lady* was seized along with

236 cases of Canadian ale, a 1925 Cadillac, and a 1929 Chrysler.[16]

The reverses suffered by the Vandeveers were typical of the rum-running fraternity during the latter years of Prohibition. The reorganization of the OPP and the strengthening of the Canada Customs Preventative Service were responsible for this in part, but the greater numbers of U.S. coast guard patrol boats was the major factor. Their anti-smuggling efforts were made even more effective when Washington sent William J. Kelly, the service's best undercover agent, to work Lakes Erie and Ontario.

Ideally suited to working undercover, the gregarious Kelly was quite probably the best intelligence agent in the service of the coast guard. A true Irishman, he could party all night with his unsuspecting hosts, smoking Murads and enjoying their fine red wines. The next day, the observant Kelly would write detailed and cogent reports, which often led to the destruction of entire smuggling rings. For several years, he posed as Walter Prendergast, businessman and *bon vivant*, operating out of Havana, Cuba. In Washington, he was almost as famous for his astronomical expense accounts as for his ability to unravel the complicated dissemblements of the smugglers. When writing to Charles Root, his superior in Washington, he invariably signed off with some reference to the famous movie actress, Mary Pickford. A typical close would read, "Mary Pickford joins me in wishing you and Mrs. Root a very happy Christmas" or on another occasion, "With best regards to you and Mary Pickford and to all whom I may know." The fun-loving Kelly, who clearly relished the Cuban life-style, could hardly have missed the irony in his being plucked from that languidly corrupt island for a mid-winter posting to Canada, Mary Pickford's original home.[17]

The northerners were no more a match for him than the Cubans. Within weeks, he had broken one of the largest bootlegging rings in northern Pennsylvania. Working from leads supplied by Lewis Hannah, the one man arrested during the unloading of Vandeveer's boat, Kelly was able to obtain indictments against ten others, including Spike Munroe and Phil Latona. For eight years these two bootleggers had been able to avoid arrest. Kelly brought them to trial.[18]

His work in Erie, Pennsylvania, and Port Colborne finished, the peripatetic Kelly next reported to Niagara Falls. Here, he noted that clearances from Bridgeburg, Ontario, for the month of August were 7,000 cases of whisky, 12,000 cases of ale, and 500 cases of wine. In liquor exports, Bridgeburg was second only to Windsor. The smugglers had developed a system that made the job of the coast guard nearly impossible. The black boats would load up at Bridgeburg and then anchor near the middle of the Niagara River, but well within Canadian waters. Young lads, fifteen and sixteen years old, were hired to row out to these boats, take on fifty case loads, and row them back to the American side. Kelly reported that, "one can stand on the Peace Bridge and see all of this without trouble."[19] If a coast guard boat suddenly appeared, the load was so positioned in the rowboat that the rower could quickly flip the boat over, sending the load to the bottom.[20] In this way, the smugglers avoided arrest. The problem for the coast guard was compounded by the large number of small fishing boats and pleasure craft on the river, making it difficult to spot those that might be carrying contraband. What seizures were made usually occurred on shore where the border patrol kept watch for suspicious-looking automobiles.[21]

These rowboats were employed only during periods when extra patrol boats were assigned to the Niagara Station. During normal times, the rum fleet cruised along the Canadian side of the Niagara River and, when the signals from shore indicated all clear, would dash to the American side, unload quickly and dash back. When pursued by the coast guard, they often unloaded at Navy Island, intending to pick up the booze at a later date when the coast guard was less in evidence. Unfortunately for the smugglers, the OPP got wind of this tactic and began raiding the island and seizing the contraband.[22] This forced those rum-runners who could not penetrate the coast guard's blockade to drop their load into the water. Later they would return to retrieve it. There was always the risk that some bootlegger or thirsty farmer had beaten them to it.

Dumping the load overboard became more and more prevalent during the "war" years. In all cases, the smugglers would try to unload in shallow water; six to twenty feet was considered ideal, as the deeper the water the more difficult the load was to find. If the water was too shallow, there was a danger the load would be discovered by bathers or fishermen. Near Munroe, Michigan, a group of smugglers unloaded their liquor in shallow water, a few hundred yards off the Lake Erie shore. A strong wind came up, gradually driving the waters several hundred yards offshore. The following morning, lakeshore residents could hardly believe their eyes or their good fortune. Bags of beer, whisky, and wine were scattered along the beach. One old-time fisherman opined he had "his best catch in forty years."[23]

If forced by bad weather or by the coast guard to turn back, rum-runners would also heave their loads over board off the Canadian shore. To return the contraband to a Canadian port was to risk arrest for short-circuiting by the OPP, the local police, or the newly re-organized and strengthened customs preventative service. It was much safer to cache the booze in familiar waters for retrieval and delivery to the States later.

On other occasions, the smugglers might get close to the American shore and receive a signal that it was not safe to land. The lake might be too rough to unload or the boo-tleggers might suspect they were under police surveillance. The cargo would then be unloaded into the water about a mile offshore. If the whisky was still in wooden cases, these would be broken open and the bottles repacked into potato sacks, two cases or twenty-four bottles to a sack. A line would be attached to each sack, using a half-hitch knot, and a bag would be lowered every twenty-five to fifty feet. The "rum line" would be attached to all the bags so that in finding one bag, the smugglers found them all.

Later, when conditions were favourable, the smugglers would return and drag for the rum line, much as fishermen drag for fish nets that have broken free from their buoys and sunk. The procedure is simple but effective. Fishermen learned early on that grappling hooks will snag on rocks and ledges and so are useless in dragging for nets. Instead, they use old propellor shafts (or a similarly shaped object), attaching a line about a quarter of the way from one end. This is then dragged at right angles to the set of the rum line. If the propellor shaft fouls a ledge or a rock, it simply up-ends and carries on. When the shaft tangles the rum line, it draws to the surface and the line and flour sacks are hauled aboard. This method was popular with the fishermen-smugglers who crossed Lake Ontario at its western end and landed their loads along the shores of farms in the vicinity of Wilson, New York.[24]

The strengthening of the various prohibition agencies forced the liquor exporters to spend more money on bribes. The large number of enforcement officers made this an expensive procedure, but the alternative – arrest and seizure – was even more expensive. Bribery was most prevalent at the busy export centres of Windsor and the Niagara River. Windsor was the worst. An eight-month undercover investigation by Treasury agents revealed that $2 million a year was being paid out by the distillers and rum-runners to assure safe passage across the Detroit river. One border patrol officer testified there were only three honest men on the force. He explained that a patrol boat crew covering a certain section of the river would provide the rum-runners with a "free night" for about

$500. This allowed the exporters to ship across the river at a certain point with no fear of arrest or seizure that night. Pay scales for a customs border patrol officer ranged from $1,800 to $2,400 a year. One undercover Treasury agent testified he was offered bribes averaging $1,700 a month to cooperate with the rum-runners. One lieutenant, who refused all bribes and vigorously pursued the rum-runners, was offered $50,000 if he would quit the force. He testified that the border patrol was no place for an honest man. Those facts emerged in December of 1928, during a United States Grand Jury at which twenty Detroit-based border patrol officers were indicted for accepting bribes. In announcing the indictments, U.S. District Attorney Watkins made the hopeful observation that, "this is the end of graft on the river," but added the qualification, "on a wholesale basis at least."[25] It was an accurate assessment. There were no more revelations of large-scale bribery, but rum-running continued. Four months later, a Detroit police captain, Joseph F. Burkheiser, was arrested for aiding rum-runners. Burkheiser, who was also harbour master at Belle Isle, had blatantly ordered his subordinates to use police boats to provide safe passage for rum-runners and to protect them from federal and state officers. On three different occasions, the captain had driven a police car loaded with liquor across the Belle Isle bridge. Burkheiser and six of his officers were suspended from the force and charged under the Volstead Act.[26]

At Niagara, undercover agent Bill Kelly reported on a large-scale operator from Bridgeburg, known as Sullivan but whose real name was Sullirano, an associate of Rocco Perri. Sullivan owned a large boat, the *Maroma*, which cleared almost daily from Bridgeburg, carrying 1,200 cases of whisky and ale. The *Maroma* would anchor in Canadian waters near the Peace Bridge where she would transfer her load to speedboats, hauling anywhere from 100 to 300 cases each. The speedboats would shoot across the river to a boathouse near Bird Island. Customs and immigration officers, who were in a position to stop all this, had apparently been paid off. Kelly pointed out to Charles Root, his superior in Washington, that the coast guard was taking the blame for all the Canadian ale and whisky flooding the Buffalo market when, in fact, the liquor was coming in through a portion of the Niagara River not patrolled by the coast guard, but by the border patrol.[27]

The widespread bribery and curruption rankled those police officers who had the integrity to remain honest. These beacons in a venal sea of booze were tarred by the general public with the same brush as their dishonest and prosperous colleagues. Often, when the coast guard made an arrest they were booed by shoreline spectators, who would welcome the captured rum-runners with the cheers normally accorded folk heroes.

Relations between coast guard and rum-runners became more and more bitter in the final years of Prohibition. The rum-runners were earning fabulous wages by breaking the law. Many judges, on the merest technicality, refused to convict or levied ridiculously low fines and short sentences. The coastguardsmen carried out a difficult and often dangerous job for low wages, (in 1929, pay, quarters, and rations for each man averaged $1,263 a year) and got little public support for their efforts.[28] When the rum-runners began shooting at them, as they did in 1928, it was the last straw. In earlier years, a pursuing cutter had always fired three warning rounds across the bows of a suspected black ship. By 1928, some individual patrol boat commanders had abandoned that policy. When they came across a rum ship that did not stop when hailed, they immediately fired at the boat to prevent its escape. The war was on.[29]

On the Niagara River, Maurice McCune was cutting a wide swathe through the ranks of the rum-runners. Like his brother Merle, he resisted all efforts at bribery and, as consequence, had to endure threats on his life, and threats against his wife and daughter. But he did not lose his sense of humour, and he was not deterred. In less than a year, Maurice McCune was directly involved in eighteen captures, most of these on the Niagara River or on its banks. Many of the arrests involved repeaters. The smuggler would be brought before the commissioner, post bail, and return almost immediately to the trade. With so many Volstead infractions crowding the courts, the smuggler's case would not come before the judge for perhaps a year. In the interim, McCune would catch him again, only to have the whole procedure repeated.

One of the repeaters was Carl Anderson, a resident of Lewiston, New York, who had been in the business for several years. McCune caught Anderson on August 31, 1928, and again on September 12 of the same year. Two days later, Anderson came before Commissioner Hall at Niagara Falls for arraignment. He posted bail and was again released.[30]

In the early morning hours of November 29, 1928, Maurice McCune was patrolling the Lake Ontario shore in cabin picket boat *CG-2364*. When he was five miles east of Fort Niagara, McCune spotted the *Bug*, a cabin cruiser which the coast guard had been ordered to seize on sight. McCune fired two warning shots at the *Bug*, which was running without lights, and ordered the rum-runners to "heave-to." There are two versions of what happened after that. According to the crew of *CG-2364*, the *Bug* immediately tried to ram them and, in response, they fired their machine-gun at the cabin cruiser as it flashed by. It then ran up onto the beach. Ed Sahr jumped out of the *Bug* and ran away. Inside the cruiser, Carl Anderson was dead, the top of his head shot off. There was no contraband on board. Inside the dead man's pockets, McCune found papers revealing that the *Bug* had cleared from Niagara-on-the-Lake the day before, carrying 200 cases of Canadian ale.

Sahr, who had been wounded in the shoulder, told a completely different story. In his version, the two warning shots were followed immediately by a burst of machine-gun fire. Anderson had been hit early in the firing as was Sahr, who ducked low trying to avoid being hit again. There was a lull in the firing and Sahr looked up to see that the *Bug* was only a short distance from shore. He ran it up on shore and awaited the coastguardsmen. They arrested him and left surfman Rush on guard while McCune and a crew member went in search of a doctor. An hour later, the two had not returned and, fearing he might bleed to death, Sahr made his way to a farmhouse. The farmer took him to the hospital.[31]

Anderson's violent death occurred at a time when American public opinion in the Niagara area was already aroused and hostile to the coast guard. One of the coast guard crew, Chris Dew, had been involved in the shooting of Joseph D. Hanson the previous May. Hanson was returning home late at night from a business meeting when three men jumped in front of his car, firing their pistols and ordering him to stop. Fearing robbers, Hanson sped by but caught a bullet in the head which, several days later, caused his death. No contraband was found in Hanson's car, nor was there anything to indicate he had been engaged in any illegal activity.

The shooting had sparked a wave of public protest against coast guard violence. Resolutions condemning it were passed by the New York State Automobile Association, the Elks, the United Association of Journeyman Plumbers and Steam Fitters, and the Ancient Order of Hibernians of America. Letters of protest from several United States congressmen were sent to the commandant of the coast guard, Rear Admiral F.C. Billard. An investigation was ordered and coastguardsmen Beck and Jennings were charged with manslaughter. They were awaiting trial when Anderson was killed.

Beck and Jennings were subsequently acquitted on the charges of manslaughter, and a coroner's inquest exhonorated the crew of *CG-2364* in the death of Carl Anderson.[32] This was not sufficient for U.S. Senator Royal S. Copeland, who conducted an unofficial investigation of his own. Stanley Copeland, his son, who was acting for the senator, spoke with the district attorney and with Edmund Sahr. After examining the written transcript of the evidence, he wrote the senator, sending a copy to Rear Admiral F.C. Billard. He concluded that Anderson and Sahr had been hit early in the shooting and went on to disprove various aspects of the coast guard crews' version of events. He ended his criticisms by noting that, "the treatment accorded to Sahr after he was shot, caps the climax of this exhibition of cruel stupidity."[33]

Violence, which before had been largely confined to the Detroit River, now spread to Lakes Erie and Ontario. Bruce Lowery began carrying a .303-calibre rifle, using it to shoot out patrol boat searchlights when effecting his many escapes. As the violence intensified, he began firing at the machine gun operators themselves.[34] For additional protection, Lowery carried sticks of dynamite, ready to be ignited and tossed into any patrol boat that got too close. Wild Bill Sheldon, who never carried a gun, began carrying dynamite, while Gentleman Charlie Mills reluctantly armed himself with a rifle.

It was the Staud brothers who really escalated the violence on Lake Ontario. All the Staud brothers were big and tough as rawhide. Two of the brothers had come to Rochester by way of Nevada, where Ed Staud had dabbled in cattle rustling. This had led to Ed being shot in the neck and left for dead. But he recovered, tracked down his assailant, and dispatched him with a bullet. Ed and his brother, George, then fled Nevada, taking their frontier mentality to Rochester, where they joined their brothers in the liquor business.[35]

Midge Staud was the boss of the outfit. Although the youngest of four brothers, Midge was the entrepreneur and sailor of the family. It was Midge who decided to purchase the *Dorothy*, a beamy, fifty-foot motor cruiser powered by a Stirling motor and two twelve-cylinder converted Liberty airplane engines. This unique powerplant enabled the *Do-*

rothy to outrun most patrol boats even when fully loaded with 1,000 cases of whisky. As a further hedge against capture, Midge armour-plated the vessel's stern and wheelhouse.

Dorothy's first encounter with the coast guard took place in September when the crew drove off picket boat *CG-2330* near Pultneyville, New York. This touched off a spate of activity on the part of the coast guard. Special agent Bill Kelly was sent to Canada to investigate and, in his usual efficient way, Kelly reported on the owners, the location of their operations base (Port Hope), and how they got away with carrying a machine-gun. They stashed the gun aboard a tug some distance from Port Hope and, once loaded, picked up the .50-calibre weapon before crossing the lake. A one-eyed man named Holmes operated the machine gun. The other crew members had long criminal records in Rochester.

Later that September, the *Dorothy* got into another shooting, the patrol boat firing 600 rounds, the rum-runners sixty. Once again, *Dorothy*'s superior speed enabled the smugglers to escape back to Canada. Both these engagements took place near Pultneyville, about twenty miles east of Rochester, a dropping-off place for the Stauds, who supplied the Rochester market.[36]

Other shoot-outs took place at Olcott, New York, some distance to the west, suggesting there was another armed rum-runner on Lake Ontario at this time. The first of these involved *CG-211*, a seventy-five footer armed with a one-pound cannon. In his report of July 24, 1929, chief bo'sun's mate G.B. Lok described the incident:

> No lights were showing on the boat I seen and as soon as I seen no signal from that boat, I ordered to fire a blank from the one-pounder. As soon as we had fired the second blank he started firing at us and headed away due north and firing at us from his stern. I then fired eight service shells at the boat. It was a hard job to fire the one-pounder

because of a sea running at the time and having it all abeam. I gave orders to fire the machine gun, the boat firing at us all the time and as soon as we put on another pan on the machine gun he started firing at us again. I had four men with rifles firing from the deck right at the boat. I knew that at least three or four pans [there are forty-eight rounds to a pan] got him right in the stern as you could see the bullets fly straight up in the air as they hit the boat. They got pretty well ahead of us. I was going full speed from the time I seen him and that was 9:45 daylight saving time until about 10:15 p.m. I kept on firing for a short time sweeping the horizon hoping that we may make a hit.[37]

Lok concluded by noting he had fired two blanks, eight cannon shells, and about 450 tracer bullets during the chase. If this were the *Dorothy*, why was it so far west (at least seventy miles) of the other shoot-outs? The coast guard did not know. A later engagement suggests the armoured boat may have been Hatch's *Spray*. In this later encounter, two rum-runners were seen by Lok coming out of Port Whitby, where Slim Humphreys kept the *Spray*. Lok let the two boats cross into American waters and then took after them in *CG-211*. The boats were headed for Point Breeze, about half-way between Olcott and Rochester. Olcott was a frequent drop-off point for smugglers, so it is possible the two boats were deliberately drawing the coast guard away in order to let slower boats slip through to Olcott.

The crews of the two rum boats seemed not to notice *CG-211* while it steadily closed on their sterns. At the last possible moment, they finally noticed the six-bitter and took evasive action by heading towards a large steamer passing conveniently nearby. Lok was forced to hold his fire for fear of hitting the steamer. The two rum boats then easily outran the cutter and returned to Port Whitby. Commenting on the action, Lok noted, "they must have been very fast boats to cross my bow and still keep a safe distance away."

The origin of the boats, the ease with which they kept a safe distance from *CG-211*, and the fortuitous passing of the steamship, all suggest the two rum boats were playing a diversionary role while the real cargo-carrying vessels were somewhere else. Commander M.W. Rasmussen sent Lok's report to Rear Admiral F.C.Billard with the comment, "this report is typical of many similar cases which have occurred this season."[38] In other words, the patrol boats were being lured on wild goose chases by Slim Humphreys and others on a fairly regular basis.

The Staud brothers' success in hauling Corby's whisky across the lake, despite the coast guard build-up, was not typical. Many of the smaller operators were forced out of business. Charlie Mills, who returned to the trade after his release from prison in the fall of 1927, had lost both his boats by August 1928. In his last escapade, he was forced to beach his boat by a pursuing cutter, which then sprayed the shore area with machine-gun fire as Mills dashed into the woods. He was not hit, but it was one too many close calls for Mills. Gentleman Charlie was fifty years old and he was broke. The one-time stunt pilot took his girl friend and her two sons and moved back to the Niagara Falls area, where he spent the rest of his life farming.[39]

Sometimes the violence was done to the coastguardsmen. Walter Buettner was in command of picket boat *CG-2372* on Lake Erie when he and surfman Thesan captured three rum-runners transferring whisky from a motorboat to a rowboat. Buettner recognized one of the men as Joe Kirkendall, a former member of the coast guard who had gone over to the other side. Kirkendall tried to bribe Buettner, eventually offering him $3,000 to turn the three men loose. When this failed, Kirkendall assaulted Buettner with a beer bottle. Buettner feigned unconsciousness and was able to avoid being thrown overboard. The three rum-runners finally departed after first removing all the ammunition from the picket boat's guns. Kirkendall was later captured and sentenced to four years in Atlanta prison.[40]

Inevitably, the shooting and violence came to involve innocent civilians. John Marsellus, his wife, and three children spent a warm July day fishing off Galloo Island. About 6 p.m. they decided to head home. Marsellus heard a shot but ignored it, not suspecting it had anything to do with his party. A second shot was followed by a third and a fourth. By this time, the alarmed businessman had spotted a coast guard picket boat. In conversation with its captain, he was advised that they had hailed him to stop and, as he had not done so, had fired warning-rounds in his direction. Marsellus claimed that, at that distance, he could not possibly hear them hailing him over the roar of his own engine. Quite properly incensed, he wrote a strong letter of protest to Ogden Mills of the Treasury Department in Washington.[41]

During the same month, the coast guard took shots at innocent civilians more influential than John Marsellus. A yacht flying the burgee of the Buffalo Yacht Club was fired on in Lake Erie during a Sunday afternoon outing. Aboard the yacht were Frank Raishie, law partner to Colonel W.J. Donovan, assistant attorney general of the United States, and a number of leading business executives. A coastguardsman insisted they had signalled the yacht to heave-to. The pleasure boaters protested they had not even seen the cutter until its shells fell close enough to splash water on their deck.[42]

It was inevitable that, sooner or later, one of these innocent civilians would be killed. Congressman Fiorello La Guardia presented statistics in the House of Representatives in the spring of 1929 which revealed that 263 people had been killed by prohibition enforcement officers in the United States. Commenting on these figures, the Kingston *Whig-Standard* editorialized that, "while everyone will sympathize with the desire of the American Government to enforce the

Prohibition law, there should be little sympathy with the action of overzealous agents in deliberately firing upon and killing innocent people who are merely suspected, and often wrongly, of being rum-runners. Such action is inexcusable."[43] Citizens on both sides of the border complained and protested about the indiscriminate use of weapons.

Isolated by a public opinion generally hostile to Prohibition, the coast guard literally stuck to its guns. Machine-guns chattered constantly along the Detroit River, and riverside residents complained so loudly about the racket that Assistant District Commander Johnson ordered coast guard boats on the Detroit River to unload their rifles and machine-guns. This left the officers with just their .45-calibre service revolvers against the rum fleet. When word of this order reached coast guard headquarters in Washington, Johnson's order was quickly countermanded. Chas Root, commander of the U.S. coast guard telephoned Johnson and then, to make sure there was no misunderstanding, sent a written memorandum that advised the chastened officer that both the commandant and the assistant secretary strongly disapproved, and that he was to rescind his order immediately by telegraph. Further, he was to direct that "all vessels of the coast guard be fully armed, together with their crews. While the Department does not wish to have any reckless shooting, its vessels must at all times be fully armed and prepared to repel attacks."[44] Eventually, the president himself would be forced to intervene. In the meantime, it was full speed ahead and damn public opinion.

At Youngston, the border patrol added to the casualties when a Canadian rum boat, on a return trip from a delivery to Olcott, New York, ran into the *Grey Goose*. Although his boat was empty, the Canadian – according to the border patrol – tried to make a run for it. A machine-gun burst from the *Grey Goose* virtually decapitated him.[45]

On Lake Erie, the coast guard engaged in running gun battles with the armed rum boat, the *Uncas*, finally seizing it after wounding two of the crew.[46] In another incident, a Port Colborne barber, Bill Shepherd, was so severely wounded, he spent the rest of his life in a wheelchair.[47] At Windsor the shooting continued nightly, with stray bullets occasionally penetrating riverside homes.

A growing Canadian resentment of the actions of the coast guard was further fuelled by occasional incursions into Canadian waters by armed cutters and patrol boats. Port Credit and Bronte fishermen were astonished when a six-bitter, mounting guns fore and aft, cruised amongst them while the angry fisherman hauled in their nets.[48] A similar incident took place at Main Duck Island where a six-bitter, guns at the bristle, cruised right into the harbour.[49]

In the Canadian House of Commons, opposition MPs called on McKenzie King's government to protest America's violation of the Rush-Bagot Treaty, which limited the number of armed vessels allowed on the Great Lakes.[50] This development was most unwelcome to President Hoover who was hopeful that MacKenzie King, after years of vacillation, would finally ban liquor exports to the U.S.A. Such action would put a stop to as much as 90 per cent of Canada's direct liquor exports to the States. But increasing border violence, combined with coast guard breaches of Canadian territorial sovereignty, threatened to so arouse Canadian public opinion as to dash all chances of King imposing the ban. The Prime Minister would not ban the exports unless he believed the action would be politically popular in Canada. It was, therefore, in Hoover's interests to temporize and to restrain the zeal of the coast guard. He was also under pressure from his own Congress, many of whose members complained of the excessive use of force by prohibition officials. But Hoover was aware that if he moved to restrict the armaments of his prohibition forces, he might damage their already bruised morale. Unlike his defeated Democratic opponent, Al Smith, Herbert Hoover believed in prohibition and was determined to make it work. Consequently, he was more inclined to support and strengthen the efforts of the coast guard, the prohibition agency, and the border patrol, than capitulate to public outcry. As a palliative, he ordered that the seventy-five-foot cutters and other large vessels were to have their cannons removed; the small arms and machine guns would remain.[51] It was largely a symbolic gesture as the big guns could not be used effectively in the close quarters of the Niagara and Detroit Rivers. Even on the Great Lakes, machine-guns had proven more useful than the cannons and were more frequently used in effecting captures.

All the fatalities on Lakes Erie and Ontario had resulted from machine-gun fire, as had all the major captures, including those of Ben Kerr, Charlie Mills, and Nick Vandeveer. A coast guard machine-gun tracer bullet had nicked Ben Kerr under the chin, leaving that middle-aged adventurer deeply scarred.[52] It was a warning to Kerr that, one day, his luck might just run out.

19

TRAVELLING
WITH BEN KERR

Kerr owns the boat that runs from Corbyville distillery to Hamilton, and is known as King of the
Rum Runners.

The Mail and Empire
July 31, 1926

Always hungry for a headline, it was newspaper reporters
who first tagged Ben Kerr with the epithet "King." The title
was appropriate and it stuck.

In any group, this self assured, but reticent, individual
stood apart. His friends were among the elite of Hamilton's
business and sporting community. They admired him for his
business acumen and his willingness to take risks, which his
financial success made unnecessary. Very few liquor exporters continued to smuggle liquor themselves once they could
afford to hire others to do so.

Kerr's coolness under fire extended beyond physical
danger. Called before the Royal Commission on Customs
and Excise, he was put on the stand for two days and subjected to intense grilling by R. L. Calder, K.C., one of Canada's top lawyers. Unlike many others who were called to

testify, he was not intimidated, nor did he take refuge in the evasiveness practised by Rocco and Bessie Perri. Kerr answered directly, admitting that he smuggled liquor into the United States but defiantly denying he broke any Canadian laws. His mental toughness comes through clearly in one exchange with Calder which took place during his second day in the witness stand:

MR. CALDER: Q. With reference to what I was asking you yesterday, I put it to you that in the month of May, 1926 you went to Gooderham and Worts, and you placed an order for sixty-five cases of liquor, handing the order in to Mr. Ambrose who was then in the employ of the company, and that you paid for it and subsequently took delivery of it.
A. I never placed an order, I never paid for it, and I don't know Ambrose.
Q. Were you ever in the office of Gooderham and Worts?
A. Several times.
Q. In 1926?
A. I was in the office possibly two or three times in 1926.
Q. In the spring of 1926?
A. I could not say what date it was; it would be between the first of May and the first of November.
Q. As a matter of fact you went there in May, didn't you?
A. I could not say that; I do not remember that far back.
Q. Don't you remember what you did last year?
A. I remember a lot of things I did last year, but I could not write you a diary of the whole year.
Q. I am not asking you that.
A. You are almost asking me that.
Q. I am asking you about one isolated instance.

A. I answered, and I said I did not know.

The Commission lawyers had considerable evidence suggesting Kerr was a major buyer, but they could not shake his testimony that he was merely a carrier. After two days of intense questioning, he emerged unscathed.

At times, his self-confidence bordered on arrogance. He openly boasted that he could outwit the feds any time, and, when captured by the coast guard off Rochester, described the other rum-runners as, "too yellow to land over here very much."

After being released on bail in Buffalo, Kerr informed the press that he was returning to Canada to "rejoin the ale fleet." Statements such as these focused the attention of the coast guard on Kerr, and they made strenuous efforts to recapture him. But the Hamilton plumber had learned from his mistakes. He adopted a lower profile and disciplined his inclination to take unnecessary risks. His increasing wealth, his taciturn reserve, combined with his success at eluding the coast guard, contributed to a myth of invincibility.

Jack Morris Junior remembers Ben Kerr differently. He travelled with him on the *Pollywog* for three and a half years. Often living on Kerr's forty-foot speedboat for a week at a stretch, sharing meals and jokes, playing cards, picking up loads of whisky at Corby's or at Gooderham and Worts, and making secretive deliveries all along the south shore of Lake Ontario. In particular, he remembers a spot they called Lone Tree, after a giant pine that stood sentinel on the high bluff overlooking the beach. American bootleggers had mounted a wooden box in the tree, and the nights when Ben Kerr was to make a delivery, they placed a lighted lantern in the box to guide the *Pollywog* and her crew into the secluded cove.

Ben would not beach the *Pollywog* but would anchor with engine idling to allow a speedy escape. Jack would row the *Pollywog*'s tender to shore where he would be met by the Americans. They called him "the kid" and always shook hands and congratulated him on a safe trip. Then, they quickly set about transferring the load of whisky. A nearby boathouse contained a small flat-bottomed punt. By means of a rope running through a pulley on shore to a pulley on the *Pollywog*, the punt would be pulled to the boat, loaded, and hauled back to shore. The process was repeated until the entire load, usually seventy to a hundred burlap bags, had been hauled ashore.

Ben and his crew would make as many as four such deliveries a week, although not always to Lone Tree as Kerr supplied several bootlegging outfits. The Lone Tree deliveries all went to a group of bootleggers in Rome, New York.

Young Jack Morris first met Ben Kerr through his family's business. The Morris Boat Works had been established in 1874 by Jack's grandfather and great-uncle shortly after their arrival in Hamilton from England. Jack's father, known as Jack Senior, had carried on the family business from the original boat works at the corner of Wentworth and Land Street. In 1923, at the age of fifteen, Jack Junior had gone to work for his father, learning a craft that has changed little over the centuries. A year later, they began building the *Pollywog*. Using the techniques and skills passed on by generations of boat builders, augmented only slightly by electric power, it would take them slightly more than a year to construct Ben Kerr's beautiful, forty-foot speedboat.[1]

Building a wooden boat is an exacting and time-consuming process. Almost every joint must be notched and filled. Since hulls have few straight lines, almost every strip of wood must be individually shaped into its own unique curve, always following the natural grain of the wood for strength. For centuries, English ship-builders have preferred white oak for the ribs of the hull. Although incredibly strong and durable, when immersed in steam oak can be easily bent into any curve. For this reason it is also the preferred wood for the keel, stem, and stern. The basic strength of the hull depends on the keel and ribs; they constitute the heart of the boat's ability to withstand the constant pounding of the sea.

A variety of woods can be used for the planking. Pine and cedar are both used, but the latter is much preferred by Great Lakes fishermen. Thin planked pine is stronger than cedar but the fibres break with age and it rots quickly. Cedar withstands the elements particularly well and is almost totally free from rot. The *Pollywog* was planked in cedar with some fine mahogany trim for the rails and pilot house. Copper clout screws and nails were used to attach the planking to the ribs and other frame members. Although not as strong as steel, copper does not rust or react chemically to moisture. Each nail and screw had to be countersunk and covered with a wood plug. Finally, the hull was sheathed in Tonkin steel up to the gunwale. This feature of the *Pollywog* enabled it to travel Lake Ontario during the winter, a season when thin ice can slice through an ordinary wooden hull in a matter of minutes. The entire boat was then painted with several coats of black varnish. The addition of two six-cylinder Kermath engines completed the craft. Even when fully loaded with 100 cases of whisky and a crew of three, the *Pollywog* could still exceed forty knots, making her one of the fastest cruisers on the lake.

With the *Pollywog* ready for launching, Kerr decided he could use an extra crew member. He had taken a liking to the lanky teenager at the boat works whose exuberance might enliven the atmosphere aboard his boat. Alf Wheat, while reliable and courageous, was, like Kerr, somewhat taciturn; the two middle-aged men sometimes travelled for hours on the lake with not one word passed between them.

There were other considerations. Alf had been badly wounded in the hip and leg during the war, leaving him with a severe limp, which restricted his agility. His training was as an electrician and truck driver, not as a sailor.[2] Young Morris had demonstrated a talent for repairing marine engines and had clearly benefitted from his father's knowledge of boats. As well, an operation to correct crossed eyes had left him with the ability to see objects beyond the range of normal vision. These were all useful attributes for a rumrunner's assistant, but Ben Kerr's decision to take the teenager along was also affected by his own lack of a son. Although he wielded a sharp tongue on bunglers, Kerr never spoke harshly to young Morris, who remembers him as "a kind man, more like a father to me."

When Ben offered him the job, Jack Morris could barely restrain his enthusiasm. At $50 a trip, he could earn $150 to $200 a week, compared to $15 a week building boats. Even more intriguing were the risks and dangers involved. His mother, of course, was opposed, but Jack's father had known Ben Kerr for a long time and had confidence in him as a mariner. Moreover, in the fall of 1925, the coast guard had only just begun to equip with picket boats and cutters. Jack Morris Senior could have no idea of the dangers that lay ahead for his son.

They would be chased by the coast guard more times than "the kid" could remember. On one occasion they were pursued well into Canadian territory, the picket boat following them past Main Duck until it reached Timber Island, just a mile from the shore of Prince Edward County. The picket boats seldom got close enough to hit the *Pollywog* with their machine-gun but, on one occasion, succeeded in forcing Kerr to retreat all the way back to Hamilton without delivering his load. As they were low on gas, Kerr decided to put in at one of his boat-houses and deliver the load when coast guard activity had shifted to another part of the Lake. Rather than leaving the whisky in the boat-house and risk losing it to theives, Kerr opted to ferry it by automobile to the garage attached to his residence on Bay Street North. Alf Wheat stayed at the garage while Jack and Ben loaded bags of whisky from the boat-house into Kerr's powerful Willys-Knight sedan. Someone must have noticed the activity and tipped off the police because, on their third and final trip, Ben noticed two motorcycle policemen in hot pursuit. They raced west along Burlington Street, which was then unpaved. As it was the spring of the year, the road was full of potholes, which favoured the car over the motorcycles. Gradually, Jack, who was driving, out-distanced their pursuers. They tore onto Bay Street, rounded into Kerr's driveway, and screeched to a stop inside the garage. Fortunately, Alf had been ready and had the garage door up. The police went by without seeing them. Kerr had a secret storage room in the garage, which he used for just such occasions. Neither Alf nor Jack could ever figure out where it was.

Reflecting back on his three and a half years with Ben Kerr, Jack Morris realizes that "every minute was a risk." The risks came from the elements, the coast guard, the police, even fellow rum-runners. In 1925 and 1926, they frequently picked up their loads at Whitby where they ran into the Staud brothers. These tough ex-Nevada cowboys regarded other rum-runners as infringing on their turf and were not above "blowing away" the competition. Relations between the two groups were strained, but no violence ever occurred. Ben kept both a shotgun and a large-bore revolver on board and made it clear he would shoot anyone who attempted to hijack his load.

By 1928, the biggest danger lay with the coast guard. The previous year, only four picket boats and one six-bitter were on Lake Ontario, but in 1928 five six-bitters were assigned to Oswego alone. In all, there were twelve seventy-five-foot patrol boats and seven picket boats operating on Lake Ontario that year.[3] During the summer they were able to average a major capture every week.

To avoid capture, Kerr preferred to travel at night and only when the sky was overcast; he absolutely refused to make deliveries under a full moon. One dark night this worked to his disadvantage. A patrol boat heard the engines of the *Pollywog* and intercepted them on their way to the American shore. Like the rum-runners, the patrol boats ran with their lights off, so no one on the *Pollywog* detected the cutter until it was too late. The coastguardsmen must have recognized the *Pollywog* because they did not bother with the formalities of warning shots but simply opened fire with their machine-gun. Several bullets struck the *Pollywog* in the bows, but most missed and the rum-runners made good their escape. Jack Morris believes most of the bullets were fired too high as the *Pollywog* sat low in the water. Also, it takes expert marksmanship to hit a fast-moving target at night, and most coast guard crews received little training on the Lewis machine-gun.

In winter the coast guard took their boats out of the lakes and used their crews to assist the border patrol. Only a few hardy souls persisted at rum-running during this season. As the far eastern end of Lake Ontario freezes over, some rum-runners took to pulling sleigh-loads of booze across, using horses or old model cars. If the old car fell through the ice, it was no big loss. Others, more ingenious, mounted row boats on runners, which they would push and pull across the ice until they reached a stretch of open water. They would row across this and, when they reached solid ice, revert back to pushing their boat-sled. It was a laborious and time-consuming affair which sometimes ended in the rum-runners being arrested when they finally reached shore.[4] Ben Kerr avoided these methods, preferring to stick to the open lake where there was less risk of arrest.

Severe cold is hard on both men and machines. Mechanical breakdowns are not only more frequent in winter, they are harder to repair. On the return leg of a trip, one of the *Pollywog*'s Kermath engines burnt out a bearing. Kerr kept the boat going on just one engine, while Jack took the disabled engine apart and removed a piston. For the next three months they ran that motor with just five of its six pistons in place. Bent props were a common problem and could happen in any season, but were far more frequent in winter as a result of forcing the *Pollywog* through pack or shore ice. Changing an underwater prop in winter was a tough chore.

Kerr would not let either Jack or Alf attempt it, insisting on doing it himself.

He showed consideration for his crew in other ways as well. If the weather was bad, he would not insist on crossing the lake to make a delivery and would only attempt a crossing if both Alf and Jack agreed. When the coast guard was shooting at them, it was Ben who took the greatest risk by staying in the pilot house driving the boat. But he also took risks which endangered them all. On numerous occasions, the *Pollywog* would have to skirt around large areas of pack-ice that had drifted out into the lake. As a consequence of the extra miles covered and the extra gas consumed in beating through shore ice, the *Pollywog* would arrive back in port with most of her 150 gallons of fuel used up. Jack frequently complained to Kerr that they were taking unnecessary risks and should take more fuel. But the older man paid no attention; he was confident in his abilities as a seaman and told Jack, "Hell, I've been on this lake for years, I know what I'm doing."

On one trip, they returned with no more than a gallon of gas remaining in the tanks. Much of the lake had been covered in drifting pack-ice and, in the process of going around most of it and beating their way through some ten miles of it, they had severely damaged the wheel. As a result, the *Pollywog* had been able to go no faster than ten knots.[5] It had been a horrendous trip. Jack Morris decided he had had enough. He quit in early February, 1929.

Alf Wheat had quit the *Pollywog* sometime earlier to take a job as an electrician at Dominion Foundries. For some reason, perhaps a lay-off at the plant, he agreed to go back with Ben on a temporary basis until a replacement could be found for Jack Morris. The short, fair-haired Englishman was already forty-three years old, the father of five children, and step-father to two more.[6] He had tired of living on the *Pollywog*, which meant being away from home six days out of seven. His wife Rose, who had recently given birth to a son, was against the dangerous business he pursued with Kerr and urged him not to go. But Alf Wheat had a large family to support and certainly was not afraid of danger.

The Leicester native had enlisted in the Imperial Yeomanry before emigrating to Canada. When the war broke out, he was already married and a parent. Nevertheless, he enlisted in the Canadian Expeditionary Force and was sent overseas where he was posted to the 34th Battery as a linesman. Shortly after his arrival in France, he was promoted to bombadier and awarded the Military Medal. The officer who made the recommendation, wrote of his conduct:

> At St. Eloi, April 4th to May 1st, 1916, remarkable devotion to duty and courage in patrolling and maintaining telephone lines, showing great ingenuity and resource in establishing auxillery lines and loops through heavy hostile barrage.
>
> His cool-headedness and resourcefulness have a very great effect on the other linesmen of the Battery.

Two months after receiving his medal, Bombadier Wheat was reprimanded by his commanding officer and reduced in rank to gunner. In spite of this blemish, his conduct at the Battle of the Somme was so outstanding, he was recommended for the Bar to the Military Medal. The Citation read:

> For gallantry and conspicuous devotion to duty near Courcelette during the operations of Oct. 21, 1916. Gunner Wheat and Gunner Chivas were linesmen between the battery and the forward observing stations. Gunner Chivas was wounded early in the day and Gunner Wheat continued to mend the line which was continually cut, under

most heavy hostile fire. During a lull in the operation, Gunner Wheat carried Gunner Chivas to a place of safety, and carried on his work unaided through the day. Though the line was continually being cut, at no time was F.O.O. out of communication more than ten minutes and valuable information was sent through Gunner Wheat's untiring efforts.

Promoted back to bombadier, Alfred Wheat received his latest medal four days before Christmas in 1916. Four months later he joined 100,000 Canadians in Canada's greatest military achievement, the Battle of Vimy Ridge. Here, Canada's citizen army accomplished what the professional armies of France and Britain could not. It was a moment of great national pride for all Canadians. For Bombadier Wheat, it was the end of the war. Severely wounded in the arm, hip, and leg, he was invalided back to the army hospital at Sharncliffe, England. Seven months later, he was sufficiently recovered to return to Canada, where he received an honourable discharge.[7]

About a month after Jack Morris had quit working for Ben Kerr, Louisa Kerr phoned and asked him if he would go to Brighton. Ben usually called her over the wireless every three or four days, but she hadn't heard from him in over two weeks. "You know all the places he goes Jack," she asked. "Will you check and see if you can find him?" She didn't tell Jack Morris that a number of his friends and business associates had been looking for him for several days.

Alf Wheat and Ben Kerr had left Presqu'ile Point on Sunday, February 24, with a load of whisky which they had successfully delivered to the American side.[8] The Kingston, Picton, and Belleville papers all reported them missing early in March and speculated they were holed up at Main Duck with a disabled boat. Jack Beebe of Chicago, Alan Crowley of Hamilton, James Corcoran of Utica, New York, and Frank Ferski of Rome, New York, all friends and business associates of Kerr, chartered a plane and flew along the shore from Kingston to Main Duck to Brighton, but fog impaired visibility. Corcoran and Ferski returned to the U.S. to hire a tug to search the American shore. Meanwhile, residents of Prince Edward County reported seeing a light flashing from Main Duck. Possibly the *Pollywog* had gone ashore at Main Duck and the caretakers had turned on the light as a signal. Beebe chartered a plane from Leavens Brothers in Belleville to fly around Prince Edward County and to check out reports that a boat had been seen overturned on the shore of Main Duck Island. Walter Leavens, pilot of the plane, reported no trace of the boat and advised that mountainous cakes of ice made it futile to try to search the island. Jack Beebe and Alan Crowley then chartered a seaplane at Cobourg and searched along the north shore of Lake Ontario, but again fog impeded these efforts.

Beebe determined to search Main Duck. At Hamilton, he hired a motorboat, which he took by trailer to Long Point at the tip of Prince Edward County where he heard further reports of lights flashing from Main Duck. Beebe and Bill Young of Brighton were stuck in a cottage at Long Point, unable to cross the twelve miles to Main Duck because of pack-ice. Finally on March 20, after a three-day wait, they were able to get through to the island. The caretakers at Main Duck had neither seen nor heard of the two missing rum-runners. The light reported by County residents was not emanating from the Main Duck lighthouse but from Galoo Island, some twelve miles to the southeast. Apparently, the owners of a fox farm on the island had been using the light to signal the American shore that an epidemic was threatening to decimate the animals. Jack Beebe continued his search, shifting its direction to the shoreline between Kingston and Picton. Any hope that Kerr and Wheat would be found alive was abandoned.

On the 27th March, some boys were gathering driftwood off McGlenmon's Point, west of Colborne, when they found a badly mutilated body near the shore under the roots of a tree. Although the whole front of the torso was missing and much of the head, the arms and legs were in good condition. A rose was tattooed on the right wrist of the body and beneath the flower, the inscription, "Rose." Mrs. Rose Wheat was contacted and confirmed that her husband had such a tattoo. Grant Quick from Brighton and Belleville was able to identify parts of the boat as that of the *Pollywog*. Three days later, another body was found some distance along the shore from where Wheat's body had washed up. Len Wheat, eldest son of Alfred Wheat, was summoned to identify the bodies. Although the head of the second body had been entirely crushed, he was able to identify it as Kerr from the cluster of maple leaves tattooed on the arm. He was forty-five at the time of his death.

The peculiar condition of the bodies, the fact that they were found so far west of Presqu'ile, the supposed sighting of an overturned boat at Main Duck, and the rumour that Kerr had $3,000 in cash on his person, all touched off a spate of speculation. To this day, Len Wheat believes his father and Ben Kerr were hijacked. This theory was supported by the finding of the fifty-foot rum-runner *Sea Hawk* frozen in the ice in Pleasant Bay off Prince Edward County. Its motor and hardware had been stolen, its name painted over, and two of the crew were found frozen in the ice. This happened in December, just two months prior to the disappearance of Kerr and Wheat. There was little doubt that hijackers were involved in this instance. There was also some suspicion that hijackers were involved in the disappearance of the *Wasp* and in the deaths of Jack Copping and his two companions in October 1928.

In April, an inquest was held at Brighton into the deaths of Ben Kerr and Alfred Wheat. A woman who lived near McGlennon's Point testified that, on the night of February

26, she had seen lights flashing off the shore. If the *Pollywog* was returning that night, it could have been sunk by the violent storm which was raging on that section of the lake. The inquest also brought out the fact that both bodies had been found naked, and that pieces of the *Pollywog* found along the shore had been burned as if in an explosion. These facts could be interpreted either as a hijacking or that the *Pollywog* had gone down in the storm. The coroner found that there was no evidence of foul play and that the cause of death was accidental.[9]

On that last fateful trip, Ben Kerr had crossed the lake in a partially disabled boat; he had not repaired the damage from the earlier trip. Able to make no more than ten knots, her wheel damaged, the *Pollywog* was ill equipped to cope with a raging winter storm.[10] Boats of that era were more subject to collecting gasoline in their bilges than are modern launches. It is highly probable that the storms buffeting shook some gasoline into *Pollywog*'s bilges and, inevitably, there was an explosion which blew the boat apart and sent Alf Wheat and Ben Kerr to a sudden, frigid death.

Whether this was accidental or the result of a hijacking, it was Kerr's audacity in venturing onto the lake in a disabled boat at this time of the year that caused his death. Ultimately he was the victim of his own hubris.

20

REQUIEM
FOR A RUM-RUNNER

Two alleged rum runners were fished from the waters of Lake Ontario today after they scuttled their cabin cruiser while Coast Guardsmen dove into the lake...and salvaged a case of gin for evidence. Sheldon [Wild Bill] and Simpson said their boat contained 150 cases of gin. This was their third trip from [Brighton] for these two men this week.

Daily Intelligencer
June 8, 1928

The year 1928 marked the apogee of the coast guard. The force effected as many captures on Lake Ontario in that year as in the three previous years combined. The next year saw a general decline of liquor exporting from Lake Ontario ports, except from Kingston where the activities of the rum-runners actually increased.

It took American authorities some time to realize what was happening at the eastern end of the lake. Their first recognition of the problem turns up in a memo from the American consul in Kingston. Writing to the coast guard commander in July 1930, he notes, "there is an unusual amount of smuggling activity in this district." His statistics disclosed that in 1929, exports of whisky and gin had increased by 300 per cent over the previous year, while exports of beer and ale had jumped a whopping 2,100 per cent.[1]

A small core of local smugglers had been operating out of Kingston since the earliest days of Prohibition. After 1927, the locals were augmented by Wild Bill Sheldon and Tony Kane, and about the same time, three Prince Edward County smugglers, Bruce Lowery, and Herb and Kenny "Coo" Peterson, shifted their activities to Kingston where they joined a loosely knit group, headed by Vic Sudds, an ex-fisherman from Simcoe Island. This group ran booze for Bill Fischer, a Syracuse bootlegger. Fischer put up the money to buy the booze, handled its sale to various American bootleggers, and supplied fast boats to the rum-runners, including the thirty-five-foot open speedboat *Blackjack*. It was the fastest boat on the eastern end of the lake, capable of reaching speeds in excess of fifty knots because its design enabled the forward section of the hull to plane across the top of the waves. Fischer entrusted just two men, Victor Sudds and Bruce Lowery, to use this expensive piece of machinery. The two smugglers soon became good friends.

Lowery was a frequent visitor at Vic and Eva Sudds's home at 44 John Street in Kingston. Here he came to know the large Sudds clan, several of whom were involved in rum-running, including Vic's brothers, Wallace, Jack, and Wesley, his cousins, Art and Resh Sudds, and his brothers-in-law, Norman and Ernie Wells. Some of these men were fishermen and as experienced as Vic Sudds was on the lake, but none matched his dash and daring. Tall and lantern jawed, the extroverted Sudds had a reputation for sheer nerve that is still talked about by old-timers. He found the perfect partner in Bruce Lowery.

Norm Conley is one old-timer who remembers both Sudds and Lowery. A former rum-runner himself, Conley maintains that as a team the two men were unbeatable. Not only were they nervy and skilled, they had that ingredient essential to surviving any dangerous activity – luck. This was never more evident than in a story told and retold by Kingston and Amherst Island fishermen. The two smugglers had completed a midnight visit to the Oswego area and were preparing to return to Kingston. Lowery decided they should eat their lunch in the relatively calm waters close to shore before heading out onto the rough waters of the open lake. In the dark, a coast guard picket boat had been creeping up on them, its crew alerted by the soft throb of the *Blackjack*'s powerful engines. At the moment the coast-guardsmen had their gun aimed and ready to fire, Sudds bent over to pass Bruce a sandwich. A burst of fire from the Lewis machine-gun tore over the crouching Sudds, blasting the *Blackjack*'s windshield to smithereens.

Lowery reacted instantly, giving full throttle to the boat and swerving sharply. The air was alive with tracer and machine-gun bullets, but Lady Luck had kissed their bows; the two smugglers escaped without a scratch.[2] Back in Kingston, the *Blackjack*'s shattered windshield became the subject of conversation amongst the habitués of the dock area. Sudds enjoyed spinning a good yarn and the story of their escape spread quickly, no doubt embellished and exaggerated with each retelling.

In contrast to his friend, Bruce Lowery was more laconic, less willing to discuss his rum-running activities. He had learned that survival required secrecy. But, for all his common sense and discipline, Lowery was still the ultimate risk-taker. There are many tales, but one best illustrates Lowery's icy nerve and calculated risk-taking. A young American had been recruited by Bill Fischer to train as a crew member under Lowery. He arrived at Sandy Pond, near Oswego, where Lowery was to drop his load of Canadian booze and pick up the young trainee. Lowery was nowhere in sight, and the American buyer told the trainee he might as well go home. "Lowery is probably in hell right now," he opined.

"He won't need you anyway." When asked why, the bootlegger replied, "Well, when he took off from here all I could see was a streak of fire, they were pumpin' it right to him. Even if he makes it back to Kingston, he won't be back here."[3] Less than two hours later, the bootlegger got a phone call. Lowery had come back, dropped the load at an alternate spot, and was wondering where the American kid was.

Living on the edge, as the rum-runners did, changed the former fisherman. He remained soft spoken, his humour understated, but the old frugality was gone; the decrepid Star jalopy was replaced by a large yellow Packard in 1929. In place of the plain worsted garments of the fishermen, Lowery now sported the best silk shirts and Adam fedoras. He even wore these fancy duds when piloting the *Blackjack*. He occasionally observed with a smile, "the captain should look as classy as his boat." The aura of danger and excitement that surrounded whisky smugglers attracted the more liberated of Kingston's young women and, for a time, Bruce Lowery revelled in the role of the debonair man-about-town.

For the Kingston rum-runners 1929 and 1930 were halcyon years. The risks had driven up the prices American bootleggers were willing to pay. By 1929, the going-rate was $5 a case for beer and $8 for whisky.[4] The rum-runners were making enough in a single night's work to buy a brand new Ford roadster. Their pockets full of money, wearing the best clothes, driving fancy cars, and spending freely, they naturally attracted a following of friends and admirers. A favourite hangout was the Prince George Hotel on King Street where the rum-runners and bootleggers threw lavish parties, renting the main ballroom and inviting friends from all walks of life. Their profession enabled them to supply the most expensive brands of Scotch and champagne. Stylish young women in low-belted dresses and with bobbed hair earnestly threw off the inhibitions of their mothers to the bouncy rhythm of the Charleston and the Black Bottom. The roaring twenties were at their frantic peak.

It was at the Prince George Hotel that Bruce Lowery and Vic Sudds got to know Wild Bill Sheldon and Tony Kane. Wild Bill had shifted his activities eastward, after being captured in June 1928 near Rochester.[5] It was his seventh arrest. Facing certain imprisonment, he skipped bail and, operating under the alias of John Woover, relocated to Kingston, where he worked for the highly successful bootlegger and liquor exporter Tony Kane.

Like Sheldon, Kane had served in the U.S. Army during the war. Unlike Wild Bill, who was single and without roots, Kane was a successful businessman, married with two children, the owner of two homes, one in Syracuse and one in Solvay, and a man with many connections: one brother-in-law owned the funeral home in Solvay, the other was Tony's partner in a thriving trucking business. Although he had been arrested many times for rum-running, Tony Kane was never jailed, which led to speculation that he was able to buy off U.S. marshalls, local police, and even judges.

Retired coastguardsman Harvey Richardson was one of the arresting officers who captured Kane and two others bringing whisky across the ice from Stoney Island to the mainland. Richardson later went to Albany, to testify against Kane, only to watch the defence lawyer produce a letter stating his client was in hospital and unable to appear. The next sitting was held in Schenectady, and, again, Kane's lawyer was successful in having the case held over to the following session, which was to be held in Binghamton. According to Harvey Richardson:

> The Marshall kept us around all day. Kane was around and very friendly. His five bodyguards were never out of sight. In the early afternoon, Kane came to me, took out a big roll of bills on the outside of which was a one thousand dollar bill. He began to finger it and told me that he had been convicted three times and if he was convicted this

time, it would mean a jail sentence. I was very much impressed. I had never seen a thousand dollar bill before. He said that he was not going to jail and that I might as well have the money because someone was going to get it. All I had to do was let his lawyer confuse me because it was dark and not be sure myself of his identity. A Model T Ford cost $700. I did not have a car. For a minute, I thought a lot. Then I recited the definition of conspiracy. He turned away quickly, saying that I had had my chance.

His case came up very late in the afternoon. Kane's lawyer pleaded for five minutes that Kane was close by, and would be easily found. At the end of five minutes, Kane had not been found. The judge seemed disgusted and dismissed the jury. The U.S. Marshall dismissed us.

As the skipper [Chief Bo'sun Tifft] and I were leaving the courthouse, we met Kane and his lawyers, as well as the bodyguards, coming up the courthouse steps. We peeked through the little round windows in the courtroom door. The people present were Kane, Kane's guards, Kane's lawyers, the U.S Marshall, the judge, and the District Attorney. Kane's lawyer was talking fast and gesturing. Someone started towards the swinging doors. We left promptly for the hotel.

Next morning, we reported to the Marshall on time. Chief Tifft asked the Marshall how the court could have tried Kane without a jury and witnesses. The Marshall answered, "We have ways." Then the Chief waxed very angry. In this mood he accused the Marshall of many unpleasant things. The Marshall became angry too and accused the skipper of being over-zealous. He also threatened to have the Chief broken back to surfman.

A complete report of the "Kane Affair" was sent to Commander M.W. Rassmussen of Ninth District. The Commander replied that it would be useless to pursue the affair any further as similar situations had always been disregarded. However, if Chief Tifft wanted to try, that he would back him in such an effort.[6]

Tony Kane had several boats over the years, only two of which were ever seized by the coast guard. Of the two, the second seizure cost Kane the most. Vic Sudds was piloting the *Rene B*, a long, narrow speedboat owned by Kane, when he was spotted by the coast guard cutter, *Skip*. During the ensuing chase, Sudds and his crew managed to throw the cargo of beer overboard before being captured. Without the beer, the officers were forced to release Sudds, but they seized Kane's boat pending an investigation as revisions to the law now enabled the coast guard to confiscate rum ships. The *Rene B* ended its days chasing rum-runners under its new designation as *CG-916*.[7]

Kane had more success with the speedboat *Firefly*, which he had fitted with a 100-horsepower Kermath engine from a boat he had wrecked at Main Duck. The *Firefly* was seized only once, when he tried to land it in the United States without paying the lawful duty on its hull, which he had bought in Toronto. Kane paid a small fine, plus the duty on the hull, and entered the *Firefly* into active service in September 1927. The graceful thirty-two-foot mahogany speedboat was never again captured by the coast guard and continued to carry booze for Kane until 1931.[8] Victor Sudds was its captain in the early years until he switched to the *Blackjack*. Wild Bill Sheldon piloted the *Firefly* in its final years.

These two boats, the *Firefly* and the *Blackjack*, were the cream of the twenty boats that constituted the rum fleet operating out of Kingston. Writing in July 1930, the American consul noted that during the months of April and May there had been 103 shipments of alcohol to the United States. In addition to these "legal" exports, there were many illegal and unrecorded shipments. Of the recorded shipments, three boats alone accounted for forty-five of the consignments. The names of these three boats tell us nothing because all, or almost all, of the names given to Canada customs were false. For example, neither the *Blackjack* nor the *Firefly* were ever listed as export boats. The rum-runners preferred to submit names like *Mary*, *Betsy*, and *Mary Anne*. As the consul noted in his memo, "similar names are chosen so that the name can be altered readily after the boat clears." This was one of the tactics employed to confuse the coast guard. Canada customs phoned the Americans with the misleading names of those vessels clearing with cargoes of alcohol. The Kingston customs officers did not demonstrate any curiosity as to the real names of the departing boats. In part, their attitude arose from the rum-runners' penchant for generously tipping the outside customs inspector whenever they cleared port with a load.

Another factor contributing to this indifference on the part of Canadian customs officials was resentment at American attempts to coherce Canadians into enforcing American laws. The Americans were lobbying the Canadian government to stop the practice of granting clearances to liquor-laden boats bound for the U.S.A. Canadian writers and politicians responded that it was not Canada's job to enforce American laws. For several years, Mackenzie King had resisted this pressure. In earlier years he had made a few concessions, agreeing that Canadian customs officers would inform their American counterparts whenever a liquor boat cleared for a U.S. destination. He had also stopped the practice of allowing rum-runners to clear for Cuba and other distant destinations when their boats were clearly too small for the trip. But, in practice, the same boats and men carried on with their smuggling activities. The only change was that they now openly gave their destination as the United States.

Unfortunately for Mackenzie King, an increasing proportion of the public began to see the Liberal government as protecting rum-runners and bootleggers. In the House of Commons, King was accused of "shielding a bunch of outlaws."

King was in a difficult position. He had been steadily weaning Canada away from its traditional ties to Britain and could not afford to be seen to be too friendly to the United States government as English-speaking Canadians maintained strong loyalties to England and were generally suspicious of the U.S.A. King had lived in New York for many years, where he had been an employee of the Rockefeller Foundation, making his loyalty to the British Crown highly suspect in the eyes of many voters.

King was therefore subjected to conflicting pressures on the issue of liquor exports. If he gave in to the Americans, he would be confirming the suspicion that he was anti-British. Yet, when he did nothing, he was seen as an immoral supporter of the liquor interests. By 1929 King had become increasingly uncomfortable with his own do-nothing policy and was moving toward accommodating the Americans. He was tilted in this direction by a desire to appease the American government and to convince it not to impose a tariff against Canadian agricultural products. Such a tariff would wreak havoc on the Canadian economy, particularly on the Prairie provinces. This region was crucial to the Liberal Party if it was to win a majority in the upcoming election.

As the economic depression worsened, American protectionist sentiments increased. King decided that the time had come to get off the fence. Stressing the morality of his new position, he introduced legislation in March 1930 that ended the clearance of boats carrying liquor to American ports. The House of Commons quickly passed the bill, which was to take effect on June 1, 1930.

At first glance, it appeared that the Prime Minister was going to end what had become one of Canada's largest export industries. In fact, he was doing no such thing. It was well known that Canadian distilleries were shipping a large part of their production to companies in the French islands of St-Pierre-Miquelon. These companies, which were set up by the distilleries, then sold the liquor to rum-runners operating large ocean-going ships. They, in turn, delivered their cargoes to the United States. It was all perfectly legal and had the advantage of reducing the liquor's cost by the $9 a gallon excise tax previously levied on all Canadian liquor exported to the States. As the liquor was exported to St-Pierre-Miquelon, which did not have prohibition, the officials there were quite happy to certify that the goods had been legally delivered to their islands.

A building boom resulted, involving dozens of new warehouses and improvements to the islands' docks. The French Government let out contracts to a value of 20 million francs to make St-Pierre's harbour bigger and better for rum-running ships. There was such a shortage of warehouse space, the liquor companies even rented rooms and basements in private homes to house their stock. St-Pierre, with a population of 3,500, was, at any given moment during the early 1930s, storing within its confines some 4 million bottles of champagne and whisky.

In the interval between March, when the Liberal government in Ottawa announced its new legislation, and June, when the law banning liquor exports to the U.S.A. came into effect, the breweries and distilleries had time to attempt some large-scale smuggling on the lakes.

Canadian Industrial Alcohol was already shipping two-thirds of its production to St-Pierre-Miquelon when Mackenzie King announced his new policy on liquor clearances. The Hatch organization did not have this advantage.[9] Gooderham and Worts, with its own docks conveniently located on the Toronto waterfront, had relied on the rum fleet plying Lakes Ontario and Erie. Hiram Walker, which owned 1,400 feet of land fronting the Detroit River, had depended heavily on that waterway to move its product. To stay in business after June 1, 1930, the Hatch organization had to develop an organization on the French islands. In the interval, they continued to export massive quantities of liquor via their traditional waterways.

Canadian breweries were at a more serious disadvantage, as the ten export docks along the lakes would be shut down by government order on June 1, 1930, effectively barring the breweries from the American market. To get their product into the American market via St-Pierre-Miquelon was simply too expensive. Moreover, there was an acute shortage of storage space on the tiny French islands. Liquor, a more valuable commodity than beer, was able to bear a higher rent for this space.

The period between the introduction and the implementation of the legislation prohibiting liquor clearances was a particularly black time for Canada's beer and ale industry. The *Financial Post* noted that Carling's Brewery was exporting 18,000 cases a week to the United States and advised its readers not to invest in the company's stock as, "in future [it] will have to rely on [the] domestic market."[10]

The knowledge that the huge and immensely profitable American market would soon be closed to them sparked a rush by the export companies and by the breweries to export as much product as possible before June 1, 1930. American prohibition forces made an all-out effort to stop the traffic and were partially successful. At Amherstburg, the coast guard was able to keep the dozen rum boats bottled up for several days.[11] Despite this success, A.J. Woods, who owned the export dock at Amherstburg, claimed to have sent more than 1,000 cases of whisky across the lake during the last week of May. He also claimed that, during the same period, over 5,000 cases of whisky crossed the Detroit River, and that an even larger quantity of beer and ale made it to the American side.[12]

Inevitably, some of the smugglers' efforts came to grief. Their most spectacular failure involved the shipment of 4,000 cases of beer on the old steamer the *Amherstburg 18*. The capture of this vessel, in May 1930, raises some interesting questions about J. Earle McQueen, who had ostensibly quit the rum-running trade when he moved from Belleville to Amherstburg. McQueen had started up a salvage business and had obtained a federal government contract to service the channel buoys from Pelee Island to Windsor. It would have embarassed government politicians for this recipient of their largesse to be implicated in large-scale smuggling. But the seizure of the *Amherstburg 18* provides some evidence that McQueen had simply shifted his rum-running activities from Belleville to Amherstburg.

As befitted a black ship, the *Amherstburg 18* had several names. Formerly the Canadian Government light ship *Geronimo*, it was sold to Captain John S. McQueen of Amherstburg. This was the same old sea dog who lost the *City of Dresden* in a violent storm off Long Point in Lake Erie, an event that hit the headlines when its cargo of 500 barrels and 4,000 cases of Corby's whisky came floating into shore. John McQueen's son, J. Earle McQueen was the seaman recruited by Herb Hatch and Larry McGuiness to organize the rum fleet out of Belleville. Captain John McQueen subsequently sold the *Geronimo* to the Carling Brewery.

If there was any doubt as to what the old tug was being used for, these were put to rest by the U.S. coast guard. In May 1928, the patrol boat *Cook* chased the *Geronimo* in the Straits of Mackinac. In an effort to escape, the black ship laid out a dense smoke-screen. Captain Skeen ordered a few rounds fired from the *Cook*'s one-pound cannon, and the chase ended. The *Geronimo* was carrying 3,000 cases of beer and 700 cases of liquor, worth an estimated $100,000. Captain Skeen noted that *Geronimo*'s name boards were reversible; its other name was *Arbutus*. The eighty-six-foot tug was then towed by armed escort to Detroit, where it remained under seizure until the night of December 5, 1928, when her hawser lines mysteriously parted and she "drifted" to the Canadian side of the Detroit River.

Attempts by the Coast Guard to reclaim the *Geronimo* were frustrated by a Canadian Admiralty lien, conveniently placed on the vessel by the Parent Machine Company of Windsor. The Windsor *Star* called the *Geronimo* the "Mystery Ship," as no one would admit ownership. Someone hired Lloyd Pilon to tow her from the river bank to Queen's Dock in Windsor. Pilon claimed not to know the man, but was confident he would be paid. A Canadian sheriff placed watchmen on board to ensure that the controversial tug did not "drift" across the river to the American side. Later, when press attention shifted elsewhere, the *Geronimo* resumed its services to the liquor exporters under the name of the *Amherstburg 18* and cruised the Detroit River, acting as an ice-breaker for the smaller booze-carrying speedboats.[13]

On the 14th May, 1930, the old tug took on 4,000 cases of beer and ale at the port of Goderich on Lake Huron and, with a crew of six, steamed out of harbour bound for Green Bay, Wisconsin, on Lake Michigan. Aware of her departure, the coast guard laid a trap, which led to the seizure of the *Amherstburg 18* as it was entering Green Bay. The boat was kept closely guarded by coastguardsmen, state patrol officers, Milwaukee detectives and motorcycle police, all armed with revolvers and submachine-guns. The arresting officers could find no papers identifying who had shipped the cargo, or who was to receive it. They did discover that the tug's name-boards were reversible and that its alternate name was *Espanola*. The only clue to its ownership was a steamship inspection certificate dated December 31, 1929, made out to John S. McQueen of Amherstburg, Ontario.[14]

The *Amherstburg 18* represented the last major seizure on the Great Lakes prior to the new law, after which smuggling on the lakes began to dry up. Those smugglers who contin-

ued generally fell into two categories; the larger-scale operators, who trucked beer in from Quebec and shipped it across
at Kingston or the St. Lawrence River (taking advantage of
the many islands as hiding or caching spots), and the independents, who bought small quantities of beer from several
government stores and, when they had accumulated enough
to make it worthwhile, ran their load across the lakes. Both
groups worked under a new handicap. They were now breaking Ontario law and faced arrest by the OPP, the local police
force, and the Customs Preventative Service. This last organization had risen in just four years from 127 to over 600
officers and men.[15]

The Kingston smugglers resented the increased costs and
risks associated with trucking the beer in from Quebec.
Bruce Lowery began talking of giving up the business. But,
as Norm Conley puts it, "there was less profit but, after eight
or ten years of easy money, you weren't going to go to
work." Conley kept a sharp eye out for Leo Walsh, the customs officer at Kingston, and a man whom Conley could not
buy off. Coast guard intelligence noted that smuggling from
Kingston, while down, was still active. During the summer of
1930, two truckloads of beer arrived nightly at Portsmouth
harbour, where they were loaded onto waiting boats.[16] Despite this activity, the Kingston smuggling fraternity was
coming to an end.

On December 23, 1930, Tony Kane and Wild Bill Sheldon
left Bath in the *Firefly*, bound for Oswego with a load of
Frontenac ale. Three days later, word reached Kingston that
the *Firefly* had not arrived. The smuggling fraternity rushed
to the rescue. Bruce Lowery, Vic Sudds, Cecil Phillips, and
Chuck McMahon hired Captain Harry Free to fly them out
to Main Duck, where they hoped to find the missing
smugglers. But the attempt failed when a snow storm drasti-
cally lowered visibility, forcing the searchers to return to
Kingston. The four men then set out in a motorboat for the
fifty-mile run to Main Duck Island, where they found Shel-

don and Kane in the home of Claude Cole. The *Firefly* had developed engine trouble, which Wild Bill was repairing. Cecil Phillips elected to stay on the island while Lowery and Sudds returned to Kingston with the news that their friends were safe. That news was premature.

New Year's day found the three rum-runners contemplating a return to Kingston. Cecil Phillips, who was something of a braggart, stated he would rather not die by drowning and would stay on the island, an indication of the severity of the weather. Convinced he could make it, the audacious Sheldon persuaded Kane to accompany him, and the two men headed back to Kingston. They became lost and, after five hours on the lake, wound up back at Main Duck.

The next day brought more snow flurries and blinding winds. Nevertheless, at 8 a.m., the *Firefly* started out once again. This time, all three rum-runners were on-board. As there was no telephone at Main Duck, there was no way of communicating their departure to Kingston. Two days later, Bruce Lowery was returning from a delivery to Sandy Pond when his windshield was taken out by a particularly vicious wave. He stopped in at Main Duck to dry out and was informed that the *Firefly* had left for Kingston on Friday morning. When Lowery returned, he initiated the second search for the ill-fated boat.

The search involved many men and, for the times, a great deal of equipment. Clarence Phillips, sales agent for Labatt's brewery and a brother of Cecil, hired the *Privateer*, an amphibious airplane, which was putting on demonstrations at Kingston airport. Unfortunately, an engine failed on take-off, and the *Privateer* made an unscheduled crash landing. No one was injured, but the aircraft was out of commission.

At Bath, the winter headquarters of the beer smugglers, Stanley Fairbanks, Walter Rikley, and Russel Wemp set out that Sunday night in a motorboat to scour the area. Dense fog forced them back, but the next day they made it to False

Duck Island, where they were pinned by bad weather until late Wednesday night.

In Kingston, Major Wright and members of the civic finance committee voted to order out the tugboat *Salvage Prince* under the captaincy of Grant Pike. Captain Pike's log book indicates something of the conditions faced by the beer smugglers and their would-be rescuers:

> 9.40 a.m. Left Cape Vincent...went to Horne's Point, Wolf Island.
>
> 10.23 a.m. Abreast Bear Point, 200 fathoms off. Encountered fresh south-west wind.
>
> 11.16 a.m. Slowed down at Pigeon Island. Blew whistle several times. Looked carefully with glasses. No sign of life or wreckage.
>
> 12.19 p.m. Arrived at Main Duck. Water flying over the Bow and rigging was forming into ice, and causing a list to Starboard.
>
> 1.38 p.m. Slowed down at False Duck...Everything was covered with ice, and ice banks along the shore were 10 and 12 feet high...Strong wind from south-west still blowing.

Captain Pike and crew arrived in Kingston harbour Wednesday evening, without having seen any sign of the missing men.

On Thursday, a week after the *Firefly* left Main Duck, two groups again scoured the area. One party, led by Captain Harry Free, flew over Amherst Island, the Ducks, and along the eastern shores of Prince Edward County. Bruce Lowery who headed the second party in the *Blackjack*, searched the shores of Amherst Island. Neither group uncovered any trace of the *Firefly* or of its occupants.

Meanwhile, parts of a boat had blown on shore at Pleasant Point, about five miles west of Kingston. Bruce Lowery was called to the police station where he identified a piece of wood as part of the *Firefly*. Other pieces were found in the same area. Hope that the men would be found alive died, and the search parties began the grim task of looking for bodies.[17]

On January 13, 1931, the body of a man washed ashore at Cape Vincent, New York. He was approximately five feet, five inches tall, with jet black hair, two gold teeth in the upper left jaw, and a scar on the right side of his throat. Claude Cole identified the body as Anthony Kane. His body was found on what would have been Kane's thirty-sixth birthday.[18]

Sergeant Armstrong of the Kingston Police force, a man with vast experience in finding drowned men, advised that the other bodies would not likely be found until spring, when the warming water would bring them to the surface. He was right. On April 18, 1931, the body of Cecil Phillips washed up at Connolly's Bay on Wolfe Island. Phillips, who was thirty-seven when he died, left a widow but no children.[19]

The location of Phillips's body helped to confirm the theory that the *Firefly* and her occupants had come to grief near the Brothers' Islands, which are located just north of Amherst Island. Some fishermen had seen a boat that day, travelling at top speed towards Kingston.[20] One old-timer who knew Phillips claims the rum-runner wouldn't have had the sense to drive slowly enough to avoid the floating chunks of ice.

Wild Bill Sheldon, alias Wild Bill Sheridan, alias John Woover, was the last man to be found. His body was discovered in May 1931 by school children on Grenadier Island near Watertown, New York. The body was badly decomposed and papers on the body illegible. A belt buckle bore the letter "W." This, plus a watch bearing the inscription "Sheldon," provided the identification. The bodies of the other two men had been encased in life jackets, but Wild Bill, true to form, wore only a heavy blue Mackinaw jacket.[21]

The Rochester *Democrat and Chronicle* gave Sheldon an appropriate epitaph:

> DARING SMUGGLER'S BODY FOUND AT LAST
> Known here as William Sheldon, Sheridan was one of the most daring and skilful lake pilots in this vicinity. He was considered an old time smuggler rather than a rum-runner, for he was willing to carry out any sort of contraband, police say. He never carried arms or attempted to resist arrest, but confined his efforts to making trips across the lake in any season and under any weather conditions. Sheldon did not maintain a residence in this city and no relatives could be found last night.

For two days no one appeared to claim the body and preparations were begun to bury the old smuggler in a pauper's grave. He had never used his real name, William Assman, and, consequently, it took his relatives some time to realize his identity.[22] Wild Bill Assman was buried in Rochester's Holy Sepulchure Cemetery.

At the service, only a handful of relatives and a few old friends were in attendance. A clutch of farded ladies, uncomfortably prim in black dresses, cast anxious glances at a knot of men who stood apart from the rest. These men were all deeply tanned, their faces scoured and bronzed by exposure to the elements. Occasionally, a reminiscent chuckle broke their grim reflections. They were bearing witness both to the loss of a friend and to the end their way of life.

Jim Hutchison and Goff Williams were there, both now working at the Port Milford canning factory. Hutchison was preparing to leave for the gold mines of Timmins. The Great

Depression was in its trough, and the canning factory would soon close its doors permanently. Claude Cole and his son, Cecil, bridged the awkward gap between the smugglers and the more respectable citizens attending the funeral. The laird of Main Duck was still a commanding presence, but business reverses had drained his exuberance. With fish prices and catches down, and beer smuggling coming to an end, the King faced an uncertain economic future.

Bruce Lowery was there, chatting amiably with Claude Cole. Lowery had already quit the smuggling game and had moved to the Oswego area to run a still for a local syndicate. Nearby, Vic Sudds stood uncharacteristically subdued, the right side of his neck and face beginning to wattle from the cancer that would shortly take his life. Eva Sudds would always maintain that the cancer was caused by the frostbite he suffered while on the lake with Bruce Lowery, searching for the lost men.

The funeral of Wild Bill Sheldon was a final reunion for these men. When it was over, they adjourned to a local speakeasy, to reminisce and to spin tales about the halcyon days, about Wild Bill and all the others who were not present. Then they dispersed, each on his own peregrination.

EPILOGUE

The smuggling of liquor into the United States was too large and too profitable an industry to end suddenly. When the Canadian government put an end to liquor clearances, it succeeded in ending large-scale smuggling on the Great Lakes and along the Detroit River, but small-scale rum-running continued. The smugglers quickly found that Quebec outlets were less restrictive. Large quantities of beer were trucked in from Montreal and then shipped into northern New York State along the St. Lawrence River. But the volume of beer smuggled in this manner, while considerable, was a mere trickle compared to the former traffic on the Detroit River.

Large-scale smuggling took place out of St-Pierre-Miquelon. In response to the shift of activity to these islands the coast guard transferred much of its Great Lakes fleet to the Atlantic. One result was a dramatic increase in smuggling vessels seized on the seaboard. In 1929, the coast guard seized 2,571 vessels, and in 1930, 2,441 vessels, but in 1931 the number climbed to 2,929, a 20 per cent increase.[1] This was the peak year for the coast guard. After that, the value of liquor and the number of vessels seized declined dramatically. This decline parallelled the collapse in demand for liquor, which was a direct result of the deepening economic depression. When Franklin Delano Roosevelt took office as president on March 4, 1933, he began the political process to end Prohibition and large-scale smuggling, as well. A consumate politician, Roosevelt had accurately judged the mood of the nation: Americans were disillusioned with Prohibition. The Twenty-first Amendment, which ended the "great experiment," passed quickly through Congress and, on December 5, 1933, the amendment came into law. Because the long-dormant American liquor industry would not be able to supply the demand for some time, the American government made provision to permit legal access of Canadian liquor into the American market. Fifty years later, Canadian distillers remain among the largest in the world, with more than 60 per cent of their total production going to export markets.[2]

After Prohibition, the smugglers and rum-runners of this story shifted to other pursuits. A few followed illegal and violent paths, but most returned to society's mainstream, playing out the remainder of their lives in honest, if more prosaic, endeavours:

BESSIE PERRI. On the night of August 13, 1930, the "Queen of the Bootleggers" was gunned down in the garage at the back of her home on 166 Bay Street North in Hamilton. The identity of her killers was never determined. The police believe she may have been shot by mobsters from Rochester.

In true gangland style, Rocco gave Bessie the grandest funeral ever held in the city of Hamilton. Bessie's solid copper coffin was trimmed in silver and her hearse followed by fifteen open automobiles, each one carrying the most elaborate and beautiful floral arrangements. Thousands of onlookers attended the funeral, all craning to get a glimpse of the Bootleg King. The pushing and shoving threatening to get out of control and force those nearest it into the open grave. Police later reported that pick-pockets made a killing, working through the mob outside the Perri home and at the gravesite.[3]

ROCCO PERRI. Without the direction of his consort, Rocco's fortunes declined. Three years after her death, Perri had to spend ten days in jail for failing to pay a $20 car repair bill. He was briefly in the news five years later when unknown mobsters dynamited the veranda of his home. Another attempt was made on his life in the same year, but Perri's luck miraculously held. As he turned the ignition key, an enormous explosion blew his car into a twisted mass of wreckage, gouged a three-foot deep crater in the concrete, and injured two men standing nearby. Rocco emerged with only minor abrasions.

In 1940, he was incarcerated by the government as an enemy alien. Not long after his release from this imprisonment, he went to visit a cousin in Hamilton. On Sunday morning, April 23, 1944, Rocco stepped out for some air. He took his car keys with him, but left the vehicle parked outside his cousin's house. He was never seen again. The police believe he never left Hamilton, and that his remains lie encased in cement at the bottom of Hamilton Bay.

J. EARL MCQUEEN returned to Amherstburg, where he founded a highly successful marine salvage business. When World War II broke out, McQueen was already a wealthy man. At the age of forty-seven, he joined the RCNVR, rising to the rank of full commander in charge of boom defence for all of Canada. One of the officers serving under him was Captain Harold Bould. Bould had spent a decade chasing rum-runners, first with the Customs Preventative Service and then as a member of the RCMP. At the war's conclusion, Commander McQueen returned to his home and business in Amherstburg, where he remained until his death in 1957. John Marsh, editor of the Amherstburg *Echo*, wrote

McQueen's obituary, which said, in part:

> Captain McQueen loved Amherstburg and
> through his efforts the town got a lot of interna-
> tional publicity...In spite of his busy marine life
> [he] took time to take part in community service.
> He served as a member of town council...He was
> known and worshipped by every youngster in
> town.[4]

GENTLEMAN CHARLIE MILLS. After quitting rum-running in
1928, Mills and Jennie Batley and her two boys moved to
Erie, Pennsylvania, were they were married. Later, they returned to his father's farm at Sanborn, near Niagara Falls,
where Charlie worked until his death on August 30, 1943.

AMOS "NICK" VANDEVEER. Like so many rum-runners did,
the Port Colborne native spent his money almost as fast as he
made it. After his first wife died of diabetes in 1926, Amos
met and married Thelma, a registered nurse from Buffalo.
Ironically, Thelma became an alcoholic and the marriage
broke up. Some years later, Amos remarried for a third time.
During these years, he owned and operated the Belmont
Hotel in Port Colborne. Later, he moved to the Huntsville
area, where he ran a small sawmill. He died in 1964 in his
early seventies.

DOCTOR HEDLEY WELBANKS. The hard-working horse doctor
carried on a thriving practice for many years, accumulating a
comfortable estate in the process. Although he was well into
his seventies when he died, Doc Welbanks never retired. His
obituary noted that:

> He enjoyed a wide circle of friends, and his one
> great delight was to meet with friends around the
> tack room after the day's work was done and swap

tales about racing and the breeding of horses.[5]

CLAUDE "KING" COLE. The laird of Main Duck Island suffered a number of setbacks in the later years of his life. When their son's marriage broke up, Claude and his wife, Annie, took over the raising of their grandaughter. After some years, their ex-daughter-in-law launched a suit for custody of the child. Claude and Annie waged an expensive court battle for custody, but eventually lost. He continued his fish-hauling business but fell steadily into debt to Booth Fisheries. At the time of his death in 1938, he was in serious financial difficulties. In spite of these problems and setbacks, Claude Cole managed somehow to hang on to Main Duck Island. At the time of his death he was still "King of Main Duck."

THE MCCUNE BROTHERS. Merle, Mason, and Maurice all remained in the coast guard until they reached retirement. Merle and Mason lived into their eighties, and Maurice, the captor of Ben Kerr, died in January 1979, just two months short of his ninetieth birthday.

BRUCE LOWERY. The friendly ex-fisherman was forced to abandon his job of running a still when federal agents closed in on the operation. Lowery escaped and fled to Norfolk, Virginia, where he found work in the shipyards. The job didn't last, and in the winter of 1931 he returned to Canada with his pregnant girlfriend, Bea. It was the depths of the Depression and, as the saying went, "you couldn't buy a job." Lowery contacted Mac Howell, the man who had first put him in touch with Gooderham and Worts. The ex-rumrunner told Howell he was looking for work and could he help? Howell picked up the phone and called his old friend Harry Hatch. He asked if he had a job for Bruce Lowery. "Hell, yes," replied Hatch. "If there's anyone we owe a job to, it's Bruce Lowery."[6]

Lowery worked in the warehouse at Gooderham and

Worts until his retirement. On his annual two-week vacation, he usually made fishing trips to Prince Edward County or to Sandy Pond, New York. He retained close friends at Sandy Pond, the result of the countless loads of whisky he had delivered to the bootleggers of that area during Prohibition.

HARRY HATCH became one of Canada's most successful and wealthiest citizens. In 1926, when Harry Hatch acquired Hiram Walker, he hired Bill Hume, the plant manager at Corby's, to Windsor as general manager. A few years later, Hatch relinquished control over the day-to-day operations of the company, and Hume assumed the presidency of Hiram Walker-Gooderham and Worts Limited. Harry Hatch remained as chairman of the board, involved only with major policy decisions. This gave Hatch time to pursue his new hobby, thoroughbred horse-racing.

Hatch quickly moved to the forefront in the sport of kings. He purchased prime breeding stock, and provided his thoroughbreds with the most up-to-date facilities. In horse-racing circles, he was the E.P. Taylor of his time. During a nine-year stretch, his Argonaut double-blue racing silks won the King's Plate on five occasions, beginning in 1936 and repeating in 1937, 1941, 1944, and 1945.

The profits of Hiram Walker-Gooderham and Worts did not follow the straight upward path of Harry Hatch's racing stable. Profits peaked at just over four million in 1929 but began to decline in 1930, partly as a result of the new law banning direct exports to the United States, and partly because of the economic depression. By 1932, the corporation's profits had almost disappeared, forcing preferred shareholders to settle for just half the dividends due them. In that year, the Hatch racehorses netted more profits than the distilleries.[7] Hatch made a daring move. Even as President Franklin D. Roosevelt was moving to amend the Constitution and end Prohibition, Harry Hatch had already begun construction of a giant distillery in Peoria, Illonois. When

Epilogue

completed in early 1934, it would be capable of producing fifty million gallons of whisky a year, making it the world's largest distillery. Its construction enabled Hiram Walker-Gooderham and Worts to beat the competition in the race to supply the huge and now legal American market.

By 1945, it was clear that Hatch's health was in decline. For ten years since Hume's death in 1935, he had shouldered the dual responsibilities of chairman of the board, as well as being president and chief executive officer in charge of the day-to-day running of the business. In the winter of 1945-46, he laid plans for a new racing stable to be built in New York State. Death intervened.

Hatch's burial was a reflection of the contradictions in the man. A private railroad car took his friends, relatives, and business associates from Toronto to Belleville where they were met by a fleet of twenty-five automobiles and an OPP escort.[8] This impressive cortege then proceeded to the little town of Deseronto where, many years before, Herb and Harry had attended school and worked in their father's hotel. Harry Hatch was buried in the town's cemetery. For a man of such wealth and prominence, his resting place is surprisingly modest and simple. There is no private crypt, no large headstone. The whisky baron had left instructions that he was to be buried beside his father and grandfather using the same headstone already in place. It is inscribed simply:

HARRY CLIFFORD HATCH
APRIL 12, 1884 - MAY 08, 1946

NOTES

Abbreviations:

NA: United States National Archives
PAC: Public Archives of Canada
PAO: Public Archives of Ontario

Chapter 1: Goodbye John Barleycorn

1. Rochester *Times Union*, 18 January 1920.
2. Syracuse *Post Standard*, 16 January 1920.
3. W.J. McNulty, "Canada Reaping a Harvest from Liquor Business," *Current History*, June 1925, p. 377.
4. Vernon McKenzie, "Customs House-Cleaning Imperative," *Maclean's*, 1 March 1926.
5. "Estimate of the Smuggling Situation Subsequent to the Repeal of the 18th Amendment," Coast Guard Intelligence Report, NA.
6. Interview with Cecil Lobb.

Chapter 2: The Raid on Main Duck Island

1. Details of the raid are taken from the daily newspapers of the time, including: The *Daily Intelligencer*, 12, 13 May and 1 June 1921; the *Daily Ontario*, 12 May 1921; and the Picton *Gazette*, 2 June 1921. Information on Claude Cole was obtained from interviews with Cecil Lobb and Wes Thomas and from Willis Metcalfe, *Canvas and Steam on Quinte Waters*, (South Bay, Ont: The South Marysburgh Marine Society, 1979).

Chapter 3: Closing the Cellar Door

1. *Daily Intelligencer*, 14 January 1920.
2. Gerald A. Hallowell, *Prohibition in Ontario*, Publication No. 2, (Ottawa, Ontario Historical Society, 1972), 85.

3.   The *Globe*, 19 April 1920.

Chapter 4: Violence on the Waterfront

1.   *The Globe*, 14 October 1921
2.   *Daily Intelligencer*, 29 June 1920
3.   Estimates of the amount of beer and whisky crossing via the Detroit River vary. Some investigative writers of the time, Ken Campbell, for example, claimed that 70 per cent of the spirits entering the U.S.A. came via this route. New York *World*, 4 June 1929, PAC

Chapter 5: The Gogo Affair

1.   Details of the shooting, the inquest, and the police trial are from *The Toronto Star*, 6, 9, 12, 23, and 26 October 1923 and 10, 17, 21, 22, and 23 November 1923; *The Globe*, 18 October 1923; *Daily Intelligencer*, 6, 13, 26 October 1923 and 15, 22 and 26 November 1923. The autopsy report was obtained from the PAO.
2.   In its issue of 20 June 1929, the Kingston *Whig-Standard* noted that American rum-runners were leaving their "hardware" on the other side of the river.
3.   *The Toronto Star*, 18 October 1923.
4.   *Ibid.*, 19 November 1924.
5.   *Daily Intelligencer*, 24 January 1924.
6.   *Hamilton Review*, 25 March 1954.

Chapter 6: The Short Trip to Mexico

1.   *Daily Intelligencer*, 30 January 1920
2.   *Ibid.*, 12 June 1920
3.   Allan S. Everest, *Rum Across the Border*, (Syracuse: Syracuse University Press, 1978), 38.
4.   Details of Woodward's smuggling activities and subsequent trial are from the *Daily Intelligencer*, 15 and 16 May 1922 and 6 June 1922.
5.   The figure of 80 per cent is cited in a number of sources, including: Coast Guard Intelligence Report, 1930, RG26,

NA., and the *Business Year Book* (Toronto: *Financial Post*, 1932).
6. *Daily Intelligencer*, 16 May 1922.
7. *Ibid.*, 6 June 1922.
8. *Ibid.*, 22 May 1920.
9. Picton *Gazette*, 29 May 1929.
10. Willis Metcalfe, *Marine Memories*, (Picton: *Gazette*, 1976), p. 26.
11. Letter from Inspector E. Hammond of C.I.D. to Alfred Cuddy, Assistant Commissioner, Ontario Provincial Police, 11 December 1926, RG4, C-3, File 1829, PAO.
12. Information on the carrying capacity of the *Martimas* is from the Rochester *Democrat-Chronicle*, 27 May, 1925.
13. Interview with Jack Staud.
14. Information on Rocco's and Bessie's finances came from the Royal Commission on Customs and Excise, Hamilton, Vol. 15, PAC.
15. Peter C. Newman, *Bronfman Dynasty: The Rothschilds of the New World*, (Toronto: McClelland and Stewart, 1978), pp. 85–86.

Chapter 7: From Bar Room to Board Room

1. Interview with Gwen Braidwin, whose grandfather, Mr Lingham, owned the hotel at the time.
2. Peter Newman, *Bronfman Dynasty*, 31.
3. Interview with Herbert W. Hatch.
4. *The Toronto Star*, 5 December 1928.
5. Letter from Cliff Hatch.
6. Interview with William L. Hatch.
7. *Ibid.*
8. Interview with Herbert W. Hatch.
9. *The Toronto Star*, 5 December 1928.
10. Interview with William L. Hatch.
11. Interview with Herbert W. Hatch.
12. Interview with John A. Marsh.
13. Information on McQueen's military career from the

Amherstburg *Echo*, 10 October 1957; the Windsor *Star*, 8 October 1957; *Maclean's*, 1 September 1947; and the files of the National Personnel Records Centre, PAC.

14. The *Daily Intelligencer*, 25 August 1921.
15. *Ibid.*, 22 December 1925.
16. McQueen's drinking prowess was noted by Captain Harold Bould, who served under McQueen during World War II. *Maclean's*, 1 September 1947, and interview with Harold Bould.
17. The *Daily Intelligencer*, 17 November 1922; interview with John Marsh.
18. Interview with Vern Goyer.
19. Transcript of interview by Tom Winn with Lester B. Winn.
20. Interview with George Haggis.
21. Interview with Herbert W. Hatch.
22. *Who's Who in Canada, 1923*.
23. Information on the Gooderham and Worts purchase is from: Testimony of H.C. Hatch, Royal Commission on Customs and Excise, Vol. 2, Part 7, p. 13459, PAC; the *Financial Post*, 23 July 1926; *Fortune*, November 1933; *The Toronto Star*, 5 December 1928; *The Globe*, 5 December 1928; Interview with Herbert W. Hatch.
24. Testimony of Harry C. Hatch, Royal Commission on Customs and Excise, Vol. 2, Part 5, p. 13089, PAC.
25. Interview with Herbert W. Hatch.
26. Interview with Maxwell Henderson, former Auditor General of Canada. Henderson's information is supported by the Royal Commission on Customs and Excise. Clement King, a director of Hiram Walker, admitted to the commission that his company had paid out over $250,000 to politicians in a three-year period, and that it was constantly pestered by both parties to contribute funds, *The Toronto Star*, 5 May 1927.
27. Testimony of Harry C. Hatch, Royal Commission on Customs and Excise, Vol. 2, Part 7, pp. 13,440–41, PAC.

28. Royal Commission on Customs and Excise, Vol. 12, Parts 16 and 17, pp. 15186–87; Vol. 2, Part 7, p. 13467, Part 8, pp. 13796–97, and Part 9, pp. 13616–17, PAC.
29. Interview with Allan Shannon.
30. The *Daily Intelligencer*, 19 September 1924.
31. *Ibid.*, 8 February 1924.
32. The *Financial Post*, 13 November 1925.
33. *The Toronto Star*, 5 December 1928.
34. The *Financial Post*, 13 November and 11 December 1925.
35. *Ibid.*, 11 December 1925.
36. *Ibid.*, 15 October 1926.

Chapter 8: Easy Money Days

1. The Ninth District's stations and equipment are listed in Coast Guard Records, File 11100, NA.
2. R. Salerno and J.S. Tompkins, *The Crime Confederation*, (New York: Doubleday, 1969), p. 276.
3. Coast Guard Arrest Report, Fairport Station, 20 November 1928, NA.
4. Interview with Joe Large.
5. A number of Claude Cole's acquantances stated that he bribed officers. Interviews with: Garfield Thomas, Cecil Lobb, Les Thomas, Allan Shannon, Ken McConnell, and Ray Lancaster.
6. Details of the *Semaj* incident are from R.B. McBride, unpublished MA thesis, Oswego University, 1973, 54–55.
7. Information on the *Maple Leaf* incident comes from: Oswego *Paladium-Times*, 13 and 14 November 1923; R. Bruce McBride, M.A. thesis, 144–51; R. Bruce McBride, *Prohibition and the Corruption of Civil Authority in Oswego*, (Oswego: Oswego County Historical Society, 1973), 62–77.
8. Ferguson's arrest and the seizure of the *Pinta* are described in the Oswego *Paladium-Times*, 20 July 1926, and in the Coast Guard Seizure Report, 22 September 1926, by George Jackson, Commander, Oswego Station.

9. Letter from George Jackson, Commander, Oswego Station, to the Commander, Ninth District headquarters, Buffalo, 12 January 1925, NA.
10. Vernon McKenzie, "Customs House-Cleaning Imperative," *Maclean's*, 1 March 1926.

Chapter 9: Danger on the Lake

1. Interview with Ken McConnell.
2. Information on Jack Copping from: *Daily Intelligencer*, 6 October 1928, and interviews with John Carey, Gerald Mouck, and Ken McConnell.
3. Letter from Captain E.P. Bertholf, commander of Big Sandy Station, to Commandant, U.S. Coast Guard, Washington, D.C., 21, September 1916, NA.
4. Willis Metcalfe, *Canvas and Steam on Quinte Waters*, p. 29.
5. *Daily Intelligencer*, 17 November, 1923.
6. *Ibid.*, 6 September 1921.
7. Interviews with Ron Batley, Mills's stepson, and Ken Fillingham. An unidentified newspaper clipping supplied by Ron Batley describes Mills's crash into the Niagara River.
8. Interviews with Wesley Thomas, Cecil Lobb, and Francis Welbanks.
9. Interview with Freeman Cory.
10. Interviews with Wesley Thomas, Cecil Lobb, Jack Morris Jr., and Don Harrison.
11. Interview with Jack Morris Jr.
12. Kerr named these three boats in his testimony before the Royal Commission on Customs and Excise, 30 March 1927, Vol. 2, Part 7, p. 13592, RG33/80, PAC.
13. Rochester *Democrat-Chronicle*, 27 May 1925.
14. Coast Guard Records, Box 1755, NA.
15. Malcolm F. Willoughby, "Rum War at Sea," (Washington: Treasury Department, 1964), p. 90.
16. Information on Kerr's activities in the Rochester area is

from: the Rochester *Democrat-Chronicle*, 27 and 28 May 1925; *The Mail & Empire*, 31 July 1926; *The Toronto Star*, 27 May 1925; Coast Guard Arrest Report 27 May 1925, NA.

17. Hamilton *Spectator*, 28 May 1925; Rochester *Democrat-Chronicle*, 2 June 1925.

18. Rochester *Democrat-Chronicle*, 29 May 1925.

Chapter 10: End of the Easy Money

1. Rochester *Democrat-Chronicle*, 18 and 23 September 1925.

2. The coast guard's annual report for 1925 states on pages 12 and 13: "The notorious rum row, formerly lying off the entrance to New York, and off Long Island and New Jersey, has been effectively scattered." NA.

3. Rochester *Democrat-Chronicle*, 24 August 1924.

4. Coast Guard Records, Box 19, File 3451, NA.

5. Commander E.J. Clemons of the coast guard states that Friche got his ale from Main Duck Island in his Arrest Report, 22 August 1924, NA. Cole's role as a middle man was verified by interviews with Wes Thomas, Cecil Lobb and Ray Lancaster.

6. Coast Guard Records, Box 1755, File 1100, NA.

7. Interview with Mrs James Leete, daughter of Maurice McCune.

8. *Ibid*.

9. Details of Vandeveer's capture from the Arrest Report, 12 June 1925, Coast Guard Records, NA.

10. The policy change was noted in the *Daily Intelligencer*, 14 August 1924.

11. Coast Guard Records, 13 September 1924, Document 1583, NA.

12. Coast Guard Arrest Report and letter from Mason McCune to Superintendent, Ninth District, File 64, NA.

13. Memo from Mason McCune, 11 November 1925, Coast Guard Records, NA.

14. Letter to author from Captain Don McCune, son of Merle McCune, 15 July 1984.
15. Coast Guard Arrest Report, 5 September 1925, NA.
16. Interview with Paul K. Lobdell, former coastguardsman.
17. *Daily Intelligencer*, 20 September 1925, and interview with Ron Batley.
18. Information on Wild Bill Sheldon from interviews with: Gerald Mouck, Allan Shannon, Ken McConnell, and Ann Jones. Additional information from: the Watertown *Daily Times*, 11 and 13 May 1931; Kingston *Whig-Standard*, 11 May 1931; Rochester *Democrat-Chronicle*, 11 May 1931; Picton *Gazette*, 29 May 1929; Docket 8919, U.S. District Court Records, Utica, NY.
19. Rochester *Democrat-Chronicle*, 18 and 23 September 1925.
20. *The Globe*, 18 July 1925.
21. *Daily Intelligencer*, 16 December 1925.

Chapter 11: Girding for Battle

1. Information on Harry Hatch's activities from interviews with William L. Hatch, grandson of Big Maudie Hatch. Corroborating evidence on the armed rum-runners from: Report of Commander G.B. Lok, Coast Guard Records, 24 July 1929; and Report of William Kelly, special agent, Coast Guard Intelligence, 4 October 1929, NA. Bob Humphreys, Slim Humphreys's son, was able to corroborate his father's role, as was Don Fisher: interviews
2. Details on Kerr's mark-up on whisky from documents seized by the Ontario Provincial Police, Poison Liquor Investigation, 1926, File 1829, PAO.
3. Description of the *Pollywog* from the Picton *Gazette*, and from Jack Morris Jr., who helped to build it.
4. Details of Wild Bill Sheldon's many arrests and trials from: Oswego *Palladium-Times*, 18 May 1926; coast guard arrest reports of 18 May and 24 June 1925; Affi-

davits for Warrant of Arrest, Nos. 294 and 295, 17 February 1926; Certified Copy Sentence Nos. 8356 and 8507, 9 June 1926; Information No. 8356, 6 May 1926; Information 8507, 9 June 1926; Indictment No. 2044–13, 18 December 1929, Western District Court Records, NY.; also, Docket Sheet Nos. 8919 and 2044–B, Northern District Court Records, NY.

5. Poison Liquor Investigation, RG4, C–3, File 1829, PAO.
6. Description of Wild Bill Sheldon from the Kingston Whig-Standard, 11 May 1931, and from interviews with Gerald Mouck, Allan Shannon, and Don Harrison.
7. Coast Guard Seized Vessel Report, Charlotte Station, 26 March 1927, NA.
8. Coast Guard Arrest Report, Oswego Station, 5 September 1925, NA.
9. Receiver General of Ontario 1926, File 1560, PAO.

Chapter 12: The Battle of Point Abino

1. Royal Commission on Customs and Excise, Vol. 2, PAC.
2. Interview with Mel Thomson.
3. Letter to author from Ken J. Whatmough, Amos Vandeveer's grandson, 15 February 1985.
4. Details on the battle of Point Abino from the Port Colbourne *Citizen*, 28 October 1926; Coast Guard Records, Buffalo Station, letters to the Collector of Customs and to the Secretary of the Trasury, 12 and 22 June 1925, NA.; RG4, C–3, No. 1560, PAO.
5. This view of coast guard corruption was expressed in a letter from OPP District Inspector Chris Airey to the Commissioner, 13 July 1926, PAO.
6. Information on the battle between Yott and McCune from the Wellington *News*, 22 July 1926; the Rochester *Democrat-Herald*, 17 July 1926; Coast Guard Arrest Report, Oswego Station, 19 July 1926, NA.
7. Letter to author from Captain Donald McCune, 15 July 1984; interview with Mrs James Lette.

Chapter 13: Smuggling into Canada

1. The alcohol traffic was first noted in the 1923 annual report of the OPP Commissioner, Royal Commission on Customs and Excise, Niagara Falls, Vol. 3, pp. 18126–35, PAO.

2. Royal Commission on Customs and Excise, Vol. 3, pp. 18126–33, PAC.

3. Interview with William L. Hatch.

4. Rex *v.* Smith, 1926, RG4, C-3, File 2553, PAO.

5 Information on Joe Burke's smuggling from interviews with Nels Anderson and Dr. Lorne Joyce, and from the Royal Commission on Customs and Excise, RG35/88, pp. 15575, 75591, PAC.

6. Royal Commission on Customs and Excise, RG33/88, pp. 13588–89, PAC.

7. Hamilton *Spectator*, 19 July 1924.

8. *Ibid.*, 1 April 1927; Royal Commission on Customs and Excise, Vol. I, 17215–16, PAC.

9. Interview with Russell Pertell.

10. Kingston *Whig-Standard*, 16 October 1929.

11. Interview with Norm Conley.

12. Details of the McQueen and Boyle trails from the *Daily Intelligencer*, 27 October, 17 November 1922; 5 February, 24 and 27 October 1923.

13. *Daily Intelligencer*, 7 November 1925.

14. *Ibid.*, 16 May 1923; 24 June 1924; 14 and 22 May, 16 June, 17 and 22 October, 6, 7, and 13 November 1925; 14 August, 2 and 9 September 1926; 27 February 1927; 3 May 1929.

15. *Ibid.*, 7 November 1925.

16. *Ibid.*, 8 February 1924.

17. Annual Report, Department of National Revenue, 1922, 1923, 1924, 1925, 1926, 1927, PAC.

18. Land Registry Office, Prince Edward County, Ont.

19. The nineteen drinking establishments were located on

Front Street, between Bridge Street and Victoria Avenue. Editorial, *Daily Intelligencer*, 16 June 1925.

20. Information on Doc Welbanks from the *Daily Intelligencer*, 18 November 1961; interviews with Doug Welbanks, Jack Welbanks, Doc Younghusband, Elmer Young, and Dr. Paul Foster.

21. Interview with Joe Large.

22. Dr. D.H. Ackerill, veterinary surgeon, wrote a letter to the editor citing prices and profits garnered by other veterinarian-bootleggers and complaining that they were stealing all his business. *Daily Intelligencer*, 11 September 1924. Allan Shannon supplied the details of Doc Welbank's White Liniment.

23. *Daily Intelligencer*, 5 and 14 March 1924.

24. *Ibid.*, 14 and 26 May 1925; interviews with Reg Powers and Earl Hicks.

25. *Daily Intelligencer*, 11 May 1925.

26. *Ibid.*, 7 and 19 December 1925.

27. *Ibid.*, 20 November 1924.

28. *The Toronto Star*, 27 May 1925.

Chapter 14: Poison Liquor

1. Undated report of Inspector Stringer, Criminal Investigation Department, OPP, to Assistant Commissioner Alfred Cuddy, RG4, C–3, PAO.

2. Hamilton *Spectator*, 30 July 1926.

3. Inspector Stringer's report to Assistant Commissioner Alfred Cuddy, RG4, C–3, PAO.

4. Hamilton *Spectator*, 30 July 1930.

5. *Daily Intelligencer*, 7 August 1926.

6. RG4, C–3, PAO.

7. Hamilton *Review*, 25 March 1954.

8. RG4, C–3, PAO.

9. Enquiry into Organized Crime in Ontario, 1961, RG18, PAO.

10. *Daily Intelligencer*, 19 October 1926.

11. Hamilton *Review*, 25 March 1954.
12. *Daily Intelligencer*, 16 June 1927.
13. *The Toronto Star*, 15 May 1926.
14. *Daily Intelligencer*, 17 October 1926.
15. *Ibid.*, 12 November 1926.
16. Letter from Carrol Hele, the Premier's secretary, to the Almonte Gazette, 24 November 1926, quoted by Peter Oliver in G. *Howard Ferguson, Ontario Tory*, (Toronto: University of Toronto Press, 1977), p. 257.
17. *The Globe*, 7 December 1928.
18. *Daily Intelligencer*, 19 November 1928.
19. *Ibid.*, 12 July 1928.
20. Enquiry into Organized Crime in Ontario, 1961, RG18, PAO.

Chapter 15: Harry Hatch Builds an Empire

1. Royal Commission on Customs and Excise, PAC.
2. *Ibid*.
3. Gratton O'Leary, "More Revelations at Ottawa," *Maclean's*, 15 June 1926.
4. Royal Commission on Customs and Excise, Interim Report #4, p. 19, PAC.
5. Vernon McKenzie "Customs House-Cleaning Imperative – No Matter Whose Head Comes Off," *Maclean's*, 1 March 1926.
6. *Financial Post*, 18 June 1926.
7. *Canadian Annual Review*, 1925–1926.
8. *Fortune*, November 1933; letter to author from H. Clifford Hatch.
9. *Financial Post*, 3 June 1927.
10. Information on the negotiations leading to the purchase of Hiram Walker from: *The Toronto Star*, 23 December 1926; *Fortune*, November 1933; *Financial Post*, 3, 23, 24, and 31 December 1926.
11. *Financial Post*, 7 January 1927.
12. *Ibid.*, 24 December 1926.

13. *Daily Intelligencer*, 21 and 31 December 1926; 4 January 1927.
14. Royal Commission on Customs and Excise, Vol. 16, PAC.
15. *Financial Post*, 8 April 1927.
16. Testimony of Major Geen, Royal Commission on Customs and Excise, Vol. 8, PAC.
17. Letter to author from H. Clifford Hatch; interview with William L. Hatch.
18. Interview with William L. Hatch.
19. *Ibid*.

Chapter 16: Turning Point

1. Oswego *Daily Palladium*, 2 May 1927; *Daily Intelligencer*, 2 and 3 May 1927; Coast Guard Arrest Report, Oswego Station, 4 May 1927, NA.
2. Information on the Goyer brothers from interviews with Vern Goyer and Norma Pukancik.
3. *Daily Intelligencer*, 4 and 6 May 1927.
4. *Ibid.*, 9 May 1927; Coast Guard Arrest Report, Oswego Station, 10 May 1927, NA.
5. *Daily Intelligencer*, 20 October 1927.
6. *Ibid.*, 20, 21, and 25 October 1927.
7. *Ibid.*, 16 June 1927; Coast Guard Arrest Report, Oswego Station, 7 September 1927, NA.
8. *Daily Intelligencer*, 16 June 1927.
9. *Ibid.*, 16 and 17 June 1927; Oswego *Palladium-Times*, 15 June 1927.
10. *Daily Intelligencer*, 6 September 1927; Coast Guard Arrest Report, Oswego Station, 7 September 1927, NA.
11. *Daily Intelligencer*, 27 May 1927.
12. Royal Commission on Customs and Excise, Vol. 11, Part 8, PAC.
13. Hamilton *Spectator*, 5 April 1927; Royal Commission on Customs and Excise, Vol. 15, PAC.
14. Hamilton *Spectator*, 18 November 1927; *The Toronto*

Star, 18 November 1927.

15. Hamilton *Review*, 25 March 1954.
16. Rev *v.* Gooderham and Worts, *Canada Law Review 1928*, 233–247.
17. *The Toronto Daily Star*, 5 December 1928.
18. RG25 C–1, Vol 1511, File 895, PAC.
19. Annual Reports, Hiram Walker-Gooderham and Worts, 1928 and 1929.
20. *Daily Intelligencer*, 26 May 1927.
21. Annual Report 1932, RCMP, PAC.

Chapter 17: Doc Welbanks Hijacks a Boat

1. *Daily Intelligencer*, 26 October 1927.
2. Record of Convictions, Prince Edward County, 1919–58, RG22, PAO.
3. Picton *Gazette*, 1 April 1915; letter to author from Ethel Deshane, 8 March 1983.
4. National Personnel Records, PAC.
5. Interview with Francis Welbanks.
6. *Ibid.*
7. *Ibid.*; Interview with Ray Lancaster.
8. Interview with Wes Thomas; Picton *Gazette*, 26 March 1954.
9. Coast Guard Records, Box 1755, NA.
10. Oswego *Palladium-Times*, 27 July 1927.
11. *Daily Intelligencer*, 25 October 1927.
12. *Ibid.*, 19 October 1927.
13. *Ibid.*, 25 October 1927.
14. *Ibid.*, 26 October 1927.
15. *Ibid.*, 31 October and 5 November 1927.
16. *Ibid.*, 21 November 1927.
17. Information on the meeting of Kerr and Lowery and on the rescue of the rum-runners is from: Interview with Wesley Thomas; Picton *Gazette*, 26 March 1954.
18. Interview with Jim McConnell.
19. This story was related by several people, including Ray

Lancaster, Ken McConnell, Allan Shannon, and Francis Welbanks.

Chapter 18: War on the Lakes

1. Kingston *Whig-Standard*, 27 June 1929.
2. Letter from Charles S. Root, intelligence officer, to Mr Lowenthal, National Commission on Law Enforcement, 4 December 1929, Coast Guard Records, NA.
3. Statement by Seymour Lowman, Assistant Secretary of the Treasury in *The Globe*, 1 December 1928.
4. Kingston *Whig-Standard*, 25 June 1929.
5. *Ibid.*, 14 August 1928; 13 and 27 June 1929.
6. *Ibid.*, 27 June 1929.
7. Frederick Edwards, "Men Will Kill for Whiskey," *Maclean's*, 15 December 1928.
8. *Daily Intelligencer*, 11 July and 11 August 1928; 29 November 1929.
9. Kingston *Whig-Standard*, 1 and 20 June 1929.
10. *Ibid.*, 5 July 1929.
11. *Ibid.*, 12 October 1929.
12. Interview with Lester Winn.
13. Report of J.C. Rider, Pittsburgh, PA, 11 May 1928, Coast Guard Records, NA.
14. Hamilton *Spectator*, 23 March 1929.
15. Royal Commission on Customs and Excise, Niagara Falls, Part 2, pp. 18041–42, PAC.
16. Memorandum for the Commandant, 18 October 1928, Coast Guard Records, NA.
17. Details on Kelly's career from his file, Coast Guard Records, NA.
18. Report of Charles Root to Commandant, Rear-Admiral F.C. Billard, 18 October 1929, Coast Guard Records, NA.
19. *Ibid.*, 5 October 1929.
20. Interview with Norm Conley, alias Leo Gauger.
21. Rochester *Democrat-Chronicle*, 10 August 1928.

22. Kingston *Whig-Standard*, 13 June 1929.
23. *Ibid.*, 29 April 1931.
24. Letter to author from Dr Lorne Joyce, 5 December 1983.
25. *The Globe*, 1 December 1928; *The Toronto Star*, 5 December 1928; *Border City Star*, 6, 14, 15, and 18 December 1928.
26. *Chicago Daily Tribune*, 12 April 1929.
27. Letter from William Kelly to Charles Root, 13 August 1929, Document 11724, Coast Guard Records, NA.
28. Information on the coast guard's pay is from Memorandum between Charles Root and Lowenthal, Secretary of the Crime Commission, 6 November 1929, Coast Guard Records, NA.
29. Interviews with Francis Welbanks and Norman Sudds.
30. Arrest Report, Niagara Station, 31 August and 12 September 1928, Coast Guard Records, NA.
31. *The Globe*, 30 November and 3 December 1928.
32. *Border City Star*, 17 December 1928.
33. Letters to Rear-Admiral Billard and the Hon. Royal Copeland, Niagara Station, 29 December 1928, Coast Guard Records, NA.
34. Interviews with Richard Lowery, Don MacLean, and Len Duetta.
35. Interview with Jack Staud.
36. Intelligence Reports, Ninth District headquarters, Buffalo, 19 September; 1 and 4 October; 1 November 1929; interview with Jack Staud.
37. Report of G.B. Lok, Ninth Distrct, 24 July 1929, Coast Guard Records, File 11176, NA.
38. Activity Report by G.B. Lok, 10 October 1929, Coast Guard Records, File 10204, NA.
39. Interview with Ron Batley.
40. Correspondence of 20 November 1928 and 24 May 1929, Fairport Harbor Coast Guard Station, NA.
41. Letter from John Marsellus to Ogden Mills, 30 July

1928, Coast Guard Records, Box 53, File 9911, NA.

42. Rochester *Democrat-Chronicle*, 10 July 1928.

43. Kingston *Whig-Standard*, 21 June 1929.

44. Memorandum to Commander Charles Root, 17 August 1929, Coast Guard Records, Document 11455, NA.

45. John L. Field, "Rum Runners of Niagara," *Niagara Advance*, Historical Issue, Spring 1983, pp. 6–7.

46. M.W. Rassmussen, commander Ninth District, to Charles Root, 1 November 1929, Coast Guard Records, File 11705, NA.

47. Tom Winn, interview with Lester Winn.

48. Kingston *Whig-Standard*, 28 March 1929.

49. Interview with Cecil Lobb.

50. Press Release, 16 August 1929, Coast Guard Records, File 11455, NA.

51. *Ibid.*; Kingston *Whig-Standard*, 18 June 1929.

52. Interview with Bill Lynch.

Chapter 19: Travelling with Ben Kerr

1. Interview with Jack Morris; Picton *Gazette*, 16 March 1929.

2. Interview with Len Wheat.

3. R.B. McBride, unpublished MA Thesis, 1973, *op. cit.*, 172.

4. Arrest Report, 5 March 1929, Coast Guard Records, File 601, NA.

5. Picton *Gazette*, 20 October 1927.

6. Interview with Len Wheat.

7. National Personnel Centre, PAC.

8. Details on the search for Kerr and Wheat from: *Daily Ontario*, 6 March 1929; Picton *Gazette*, 6, 13, 16, 20, 23 and 27 March and 3 April 1929; Brighton *Ensign*, 15 and 29 March 1929; Kingston *Whig-Standard*, 5, 19, 21 and 22 March and 1 April 1929; *Trentonian*, 28 March 1929; Hamilton *Spectator*, 30 March and 2 April 1929.

9. Information on the proceedings and findings of the

coroner's jury from: *Daily Ontario*, 19 April 1929.

10. None of those interviewed recalled the damage to *Pollywog*'s wheel. However, it was mentioned in the Picton *Gazette*, 16 March 1929.

Chapter 20: Requiem for a Rum-runner

1. Memo from U.S. Consul at Kingston, George D. Miller, to Commandant, Ninth District, 31 July 1930, Coast Guard Records, NA.
2. Interviews with Norman Sudds, Edmund Bongard, Francis Welbanks, and Maida Peterson.
3. Interview with Edmund Bongard.
4. Picton *Gazette*, 29 May 1929.
5. Arrest Report, 11 June 1928, Coast Guard Records, File 9519, NA.
6. Letter to author from retired coastguardsman Harvey E. Richardson.
7. Arrest Report, 23 June 1929, and Seized Vessel Report, 29 September 1929, Coast Guard Records, Files 11101 and 11150, NA.
8. Reports, Oswego Station, 5 and 8 September 1927, Coast Guard Records, File 8129, NA.
9. *Financial Post*, 10 April 1930.
10. *Ibid.*, 13 May 1930.
11. *The Globe*, 2 June 1930.
12. *Ibid.*
13. Information on *Geronimo*'s career is from: *Border City Star*, 7, 8, and 12 December 1928; letter from F.H. Yount, Customs Agent to Captain Fischer, U.S. Coast Guard, 9 May 1928, Coast Guard Records, Box 5, File 1222, NA.
14. Milwaukee *Sunday Journal*, 17 May 1930; Coast Guard Records, Files 12201–50, NA.
15. Kingston *Whig-Standard*, 10 June 1929.
16. Memorandum from Assistant Commandant B.M. Chis-

well to Commander Ninth District, 7 June 1930, Coast Guard Records, NA.

17. Information on the *Firefly* is from: Kingston *Whig-Standard*, 5, 6, 7, 8, 9, and 10 January 1931; Watertown *Daily Times*, 10 and 12 January 1931.
18. Kingston *Whig-Standard*, 13 January 1931; Watertown *Daily Times*, 13 and 14 January 1931.
19. Kingston *Whig-Standard*, 19 and 21 April 1931.
20. *Ibid.*, 13 January 1931.
21. *Ibid.*, 11 May 1931; Watertown *Daily Times*, 11 May 1931.
22. Rochester *Democrat-Chronicle*, 11 May 1931.

Epilogue

1. U.S. Coast Guard Annual Reports, 1930, 1931, 1932, Coast Guard Records, NA.
2. Association of Canadian Distillers, "Presentation to the Royal Commission on Economic Union and Development Prospects for Canada," *Hospitality Magazine*, January 1984.
3. Details of the shooting are from: Hamilton *Spectator*, 14 August 1930; details of the funeral are from *The Globe and Mail*, 25 June 1983.
4. Amherstburg *Echo*, 10 October 1957.
5. *Daily Intelligencer*, 18 November 1961.
6. A number of Prince Edward County residents are familiar with this anecdote, including Richard Lowery, Bruce's son, and Allan Shannon, who provided this version.
7. *Fortune*, November 1933.

BIBLIOGRAPHY

Books

Boyer, Dwight, *True Tales of the Great Lakes*, (New York: Dodd, Mead & Co, 1971).

Brown, Ron, *Ghost Towns of Ontario, Vol. 1: Southern Ontario*, (Langley, BC: Stagecoach Publishing, 1978).

Cauz, Louis E., *The Plate: A Royal Tradition*, (Toronto: Deneau Publishing, 1984).

Cherrington, Ernest, *Anti-Saloon League Year Book, 1925*, (New York: Anti-Saloon League of America, 1926).

Cochran, Hugh, *Gateway to Oblivion: The Great Lakes Bermuda Triangle*, (New York: Avon, 1981).

Coffee, Thomas J., *The Long Thirst*, (Toronto: George J. McLeod, 1975).

Drury, E.C., *Farmer Premier: The Memoirs of E.C. Drury*, (Toronto: McClelland and Stewart, 1966).

Dulmage, Howard, *Memories of South Bay*, (Picton: Author, 1980).

Everest, Allan S., *Rum across the Border: The Prohibition Era in Northern New York*, (Syracuse, NY: Syracuse University Press, 1978).

Gervais, C.H., *The Rumrunners: A Prohibition Scrapbook*, (Thornhill: Firefly Books, 1980).

Gray, James H., *Booze: The Impact of Whiskey on the Prairie West*, (Toronto: Macmillan, 1972).

Greenway, Roy, *The News Game*, (Toronto: Clarke Irwin, 1966).

Hallowell, Gerald, *Prohibition in Ontario*, Research Publication No. 2, (Ottawa: Ontario Historical Society, 1972).

Henderson, Maxwell, *Plain Talk! Memoirs of an Auditor General*, (Toronto: McClelland and Stewart, 1984).

Kobler, John, *The Life and World of Al Capone*, (Greenwich, Conn: Fawcett, 1972).

Metcalfe, Willis, *Canvas and Steam on Quinte Waters*,

(South Bay, Ont: South Marysburg Marine Society, 1979).

_____ , *Marine Memories*, (Picton: *Gazette*, 1976).

Newman, Peter C., *Bronfman Dynasty: The Rothschilds of the New World*, (Toronto: McClelland and Stewart, 1978).

Oliver, Peter, *G. Howard Ferguson, Ontario Tory*, (Toronto: University of Toronto Press, 1977).

_____ , *Public and Private Persons*, (Toronto: Clarke Irwin, 1975).

Patton, Janice, *The Sinking of the I'm Alone*, (Toronto: McClelland and Stewart, 1973).

Rowe, Percy, *Native Wines of Canada*, (Toronto: McGraw Hill, 1970).

Salerno, R., and Tompkins, J.S., *The Crime Confederation* (New York: Doubleday, 1969).

Willoughby, Malcolm F., *Rum War at Sea*, (Washington, DC: Treasury Dept., United States Coast Guard, 1964).

Magazines, Periodicals, and Journal Articles

Bauer, Jack, *List of U.S. Warships on The Great Lakes, 1796–1941*, Ontario Historical Society, March, 1964.

Bowman, M.W., and Gray, Gratton, "Thar's Gold in Them Thar Hills," *Maclean's*, 1 September 1947.

Edwards, Frederick, "Men Will Kill For Whiskey." *Maclean's*, 15 December 1928.

Field, John L., "Rum Runners of Niagara," *The Niagara Advance*, 13th Annual Historical Issue, Niagara-on-the-Lake, Spring 1983.

"Hiram Walker," *Fortune* Magazine, New York, November 1933.

McBride, R. Bruce, *Prohibition and The Corruption of Civil Authority in Oswego*, Oswego County Historical Society, Oswego, New York, 1973.

McBridee, R. Bruce. *Prohibition in Oswego*, unpublished MA thesis, State University College, Oswego, N.Y., February 1973.

McKenzie, Veron, "Customs House Cleaning Imperative – No Matter Whose Head Comes Off," *Maclean's*, 1 March 1926.

McNulty, W.J. "Canada Reaping A Harvest From Liquor Business," *Current History*, June 1925.

McNulty, W.J., "Smuggling Whiskey From Canada," *Current History*, April 1923.

Morton, Guy E., "Balking the Bootlegger: How The Fight Against Liquor Selling Is Waged," Maclean's, 1 March 1920.

O'Leary, Gratton, "More Revelations at Ottawa," *Maclean's*, 15 June 1926.

Primary Sources
Canada Law Review, 1928

Hiram Walker-Gooderham and Worts, *Annual Reports*, 1928, 1929, and 1985.

District Court of the United states, Western District of New York, Buffalo, New York.

District Court of the United States, Northern District of New York, Utica, New York.

Newspapers

Amherstburg	–	*Echo*
Belleville	–	*Daily Intelligencer*
		Daily Ontario
		The Ontario
		Ontario Intelligencer
Brighton	–	*Ensign*
Chicago	–	*Daily Tribune*
Hamilton	–	*Review*
		Spectator
Kingston	–	*Whig-Standard*
Oswego	–	*Daily Palladium*
		Palladium-Times
Picton	–	*Gazette*
Port Colborne	–	*Citizen*

Rochester	–	*Democrat*
		Democrat-Chronicle
		Democrat and Herald
		Times-Union
Syracuse	–	*Post Standard*
Toronto	–	*Financial Post*
		Globe
		Globe and Mail
		Mail and Empire
		Star
Trenton	–	*Trentonian*
Watertown	–	*Daily Times*
Wellington	–	*News*
Windsor	–	*Border Cities Star*
		Star

Archives

Public Archives of Canada (PAC)
Marine Records
Ministery of Justice: Case Files
Ministry of National Revenue
National Personnel Records Centre
RCMP – Annual Reports
Royal Commission On Customs and Excise

Public Archives of Ontario (PAO)
Records of the Attorney General: Case Files
Inquiry into Organized Crime in Ontario, 1961

U.S. National Archives (NA)
Coast Guard – Arrest Reports, Intelligence Files,
    Seized Vessel Files.

INDEX

Fowler, George, 227
France, 279
Franks, Constable, 137
Fraser, George, 52
Free, Capt. Harry, 297, 299
Frenchman's Bay, 51
French Riviera, 215
Fricke, Fred, 130–31
Frontenac ale, 133, 134, 297
Front St., Belleville, 185

G

Galloo Island, N.Y., 236, 266, 281
Gauger, Leo, *see* Conley, Norm
Gazette (Picton), 244
Geen, Rev. A.L., 179
Geen, Maj. E. Albert, 179, 214, 237–38, 239
Genesee, Fred, 60
Genna brothers, 90–91
Geon, A.D., 55, 57
George V, 78, 212
Geronimo tug, 295–96
Gin, 91, 147, 155, 285
Globe (Toronto), 54, 73, 250
Goderich, Ont., 296
Gogo, Mrs., 53
Gogo, James, 50, 51, 53
Gogo, John, 50, 51, 53, 54, 56
Gogo, Sidney, 50, 51, 53–54, 57, 58
Gogo Affair, 49, 50–61, 171–72
Gogo family, 50–51, 53
Goldstein, Harry, 191
Gooderham, Sir Albert, 84
Gooderham, Eddie, 85, 86
Gooderham, William George, 84–85
Gooderham and Worts Bonded Stock, 86

Gooderham and Worts Distillery, Toronto, 24, 84–85, 86, 140, 141, 214
Gooderham and Worts Ltd., 85–87, 92–94, 154, 155, 166, 171, 172, 177, 197–98, 205, 207–8, 210, 211, 214–15, 222, 224, 245, 271, 272, 293–94, 307
Gooderham family, 84
Gordon, Frank, 150
Gorenflo, Lt., 163–64
Goyer, Archie, 82–83, 218–21
Goyer, Ethel, 218
Goyer, Lawrence "Gilly," 218, 219, 220
Goyer, Napoleon "Nap," 218, 219, 220
Goyer family, 218–19
Graham, Dr. George, 54, 56
Grand Trunk Railway, 64
Grant, J.A., 224
Grant Springs Brewery, 92
Great Britain, 225, 292
Great Lakes, 24, 111–12, 128, 138, 144, 165, 213, 227, 248–51, 268, 269, 303
Green Bay, Wis., 296
Grenadier Island, N.Y., 300
Grey, Miss, 174
Grey Goose, 267
Griffiths, Inspector, 171
Guelph, Ont., 54
Gull Bar, Ont., 111
Gungo, Harry, 108–9
Guy cabin cruiser, 219

H

Hageny, Constable, 105
Haig, Field Marshal, 206
Halifax, 210, 214

Imperial Yeomanry, 279
Indian Burial Ground, Amherst-
    burg, 48

J

Jackson, Comm. George E., 95,
    102, 106, 152, 161, 219, 220
James St., Belleville, 234
J.C.S. (undercover agent), 192–
    93
Jennings, Mr., 261
Jessup, Joseph, 106
Jim Lulu cabin cruiser, 149–50,
    151
Johnson, Mr., 267
Johnson, Mike, 174–75
John St., Kingston, 285
Jones, Edward "Peg Leg," 220
Jopp, Arthur, 190
Jopp Drug Co., 190–91
Justice, Dept. of, (U.S.), 133,
    203

K

Kaiser, Wes, 98, 100, 180
Kane, Anthony, 130, 245, 285,
    288–90, 297–98, 300, 301
Keegan, George, 115
Kelly, Moe, 188
Kelly, William J., 254–55, 258–
    59, 263
Kemptville, Ont., 194
Kenilworth Park race track,
    Windsor, 77
Kenny, Constable, 185
Kermath engine, 145, 274, 277
Kerr, A.H., 27
Kerr, Ben, 69, 72, 82, 98, 116–
    18, 119–20, 121–23, 125–28,
    132, 133, 137, 138, 145, 146–
    47, 162, 188, 191–92, 193,

214, 217, 228, 242–43, 244–
    45, 246–47, 269, 270–78, 280–
    83, 307
Kerr, Sergeant Bill, 52–53
Kerr, Louisa May, 117, 280
Kerr family, 191
Ketcheson, Harry, 175, 176–77
Key West steamer, 115
King, Mackenzie, 130, 203, 204,
    226, 268, 291–93
King's Plate, 72, 308
Kingston, 24, 35, 41, 82, 172–73,
    174, 182, 184, 196, 232, 236,
    245, 280, 281, 284–86, 287,
    288, 290–91, 297, 298, 299
Kingston Ale Co., 175
Kingston Police, 300
King St., Kingston, 287
King St., Oshawa, 75
Kioster, Fritz, 21
Kirkendall, Joe, 265–66
Kitchener, 170, 213
Kuntz, Herb, 211

L

Labatts, 298
Labrusca grape, 90
Lacona, N.Y., 220
Lady rum boat, 253
LaGuardia, Fiorello, 266
Lake Champlain, 164
Lake Erie, 83, 97, 112, 113, 118,
    121, 132, 143, 154–55, 164,
    210, 235, 248, 250, 251, 253,
    254, 256, 262, 265, 266, 267–
    68
Lake Huron, 296
Lake Michigan, 250, 296
Lake Ontario, 24–26, 27, 51, 69,
    80, 82, 98, 102, 108–9, 112,
    118–19, 121, 130, 131, 132,

309; Criminal Investigation Branch, 169; OTA division, 169
Oriental Hotel, Deseronto, 75
Orpen, Abe, 77
Oshawa, 75–76
Oshawa House, 75
Oswego, N.Y., 19–20, 21–22, 25, 30, 63, 65, 95, 101, 102–4, 105, 106, 126, 127, 132, 135, 137, 151, 152, 159, 160, 161, 174, 217, 219, 220, 235, 236, 238, 241, 276, 286, 297, 302
Oswego County Jail, 236
OTA, *see* Ontario Temperance Act
Ottawa, 41
Over the Top speedboat, 253

P

Packard car, 168, 287
Packard engine, 141, 142
Paeny, Bill, 160, 221
Paige car, 185
Pallace, John, 101–2
Palmer, Dwight, 237, 238, 240–41
Palmer Fish Co., 237, 239, 240
Parent Machine Co., 296
Parliament St., Toronto, 166
Paxton, Arthur, 59
Payne, C.A., 239–40
Peace Bridge, 255, 258
Peerless motor, 149
Penna, J., *see* Perri, Rocco
Pennsylvania, 164, 255
Peoria, Il., 308
Perri, Rocco, 49, 51, 52–53, 54, 57–61, 70, 72, 89, 143, 165, 166, 170–72, 186, 188, 191, 192, 193, 196, 200, 211, 214,

216, 221–23, 224, 258, 270, 304–5
Peterson, Herb, 231, 285
Peterson, Ken "Coo," 231, 285
Peterson family, 231
Phillips, Cecil, 245, 297–98, 300, 301
Phillips, Clarence, 298
Pickford, Mary, 254
Picton, 32, 33, 109, 116, 160, 181, 230, 233, 280
Pike, Capt. Grant, 299
Pilon, Lloyd, 296
Pinta schooner, 106
Pleasant Bay, Ont., 109, 282
Pleasant Point, Ont., 300
Plebesites, 56, 194–95, 197; *1898*, 38; *1921*, 34, 38, 40–42; *1924*, 187, 194, 232
Point Abino, 155, 157
Point Anne, Ont., 116, 178
Point Breeze, N.Y., 264
Pollywog cabin cruiser, 145–46, 147, 228, 242–43, 245, 246, 272–75, 276–78, 281, 282, 283
Pontiac Hotel, Oswego, 19
Port Arthur, Ont., 41
Port Credit, Ont., 165–66, 268
Port Colborne, Ont., 24, 82, 83, 115, 133, 154–55, 191, 192–93, 251, 253, 255, 268
Port Dalhousie, Ont., 82
Port Dover, Ont., 200
Port Hope, Ont., 263
Port Milford, Ont., 148, 230–31, 301
Port Rowan, Ont., 113
Port Whitby, Ont., 143, 264
Post Standard (Syracuse), 20
Prendergast, Walter, *see* Kelly, William J.

Presbyterian Church, 20
Prescott, 24, 79
Presqu'ile Point, Ont., 244–45, 280
Price, Mr., 199
Prince Edward County, 25, 27–28, 73, 98, 109, 110, 148, 177, 178, 179, 181, 184, 228, 230–31, 245, 275, 281, 282, 285, 299, 308
Prince George Hotel, Kingston, 287, 288
Prinyer Cove (Booze Bog), Ont., 116, 118, 181
Privateer airplane, 298
Progressive Party, 196, 198
Prohibition Amendment, 148
Protestant Church, 40
Powers, Stewart, 182, 183, 184
Pultneyville, N.Y., 122, 263
Purtell, Russell, 173

Q

Quebec, 23, 32, 37, 38, 174, 184, 185, 186, 195, 199, 203, 297, 303
Queen's Dock, Windsor, 296
Queen's University, 173
Quick, Grant, 213, 244, 282

R

Rae, Sergeant, 185
Raishie, Frank, 266
Raney, William E., 38–39, 45, 63, 64, 169, 196
Rassmussen, Cmdr. Norman W., 248, 265, 290
Raw alcohol, 31, 71, 91, 162, 163–64, 165, 170, 180
RCMP, 190, 222, 227, 305
RCNVR, 305

Redfern, Capt., 108
Regio Calabria, Italy, 191
Rene B speedboat, 290
Reo truck, 170
Richards, Mr., 92
Richardson, Harvey, 288–90
Rikley, Walter, 298
Robinson, Clarence, 220–21
Roblin Mills, Ont., 74
Rochester, N.Y., 20, 21, 69, 99, 101, 108, 109, 114, 117, 120–21, 122, 123, 125, 130–31, 145, 147, 148, 151, 159, 180, 191, 199, 219, 237, 238, 262, 264, 272, 288, 301
Rockefeller, Pearl, 113
Rockefeller Foundation, 292
Rogers, Dave, 58–61
Rogers, Joe, 169
Roman Catholic Church, 187, 197
Rome, N.Y., 273, 281
Rooney, Jim, 52
Roosevelt, Franklin Delano, 304, 308
Root, Charles, 254, 259, 267
Rosella rum boat, 229, 235–36, 237, 239–41
Ross, W.H., 206
Rothschild family, 70
Royal Commission on Customs and Excise (1927), 61, 70, 80, 101, 118, 172, 186, 200–1, 205, 210, 212, 214, 215, 216–17, 221, 222, 223–24, 227, 252, 270–72
Royal Grenadiers Band, 40
Royal Navy, 81
Rowdy rum boat, 130
Rum Row, 23, 128–29, 141, 145, 212

Sparkley motorboat, 134, 137
Spectator (Hamilton), 191–92
Spracklin, Mrs., 46
Spracklin, Rev. Les, 45–47
Spracklin family, 46
Sprague, C.A., 217
Straits of Mackinac, 295
Spray Z900 master cruiser, 142–43, 165, 264
Sprung, Fred *see* Lowery, Bruce
Standard Brewing Co., 121, 123
Star (Windsor), 296
Star sedan, 234, 287
Starkman, Bessie, 58–61, 70, 89, 143, 170–71, 172, 217, 222–23, 271, 304–5
Staud, Ed, 262
Staud, George, 69, 262
Staud, Karl "The Bishop," 69
Staud, Midge, 69, 262–63
Staud brothers, 69, 72, 263, 265, 276
Sterling, Mildred, 193
Sterling motor, 262
Stevens, Harry, 202
Stewart, Charlie, 242, 244
Stinson Detroiter airplane, 174
Stoney Island, N.Y., 288
Sturgeon Falls, Ont., 187
Sudbury, 41
Sudds, Art, 285
Sudds, Eva, 285, 302
Sudds, Jack, 285
Sudds, Resh, 285
Sudds, Vic., 245, 285–86, 288, 290, 297–98, 302
Sudds, Wallace, 285
Sudds, Wesley, 285
Sudds family, 285
Sullirano, Mr., 258
Sullivan, Mr., *see* Sullirano, Mr.

Sunnyside Hotel, Windsor, 46
Swamp-whisky, 89, 91
Sylvester, Louis, 191
Syracuse, 20, 21, 30, 102, 105, 145, 151, 159, 161, 163, 174, 285, 288

T

Tariff Act, 133, 137, 151; Section *593*, 133
Taylor, Mr., 88
Taylor, E.P., 308
Thesan, Mr., 265–66
Third Ward Political Club, 190–91
34th Battery, 279
Thomas, Eddie, 218–19
Thomas, Garfield, 233
Thomas, Wesley, 109, 118, 236, 242–44
Tifft, Bo'sun, 289–90
Timber Island, Ont., 275
Times Union (Rochester), 19
Timmins, Ont., 301
Toby (dog), 82
Toledo, Ohio, 154
Toronto, 24, 41, 44, 50, 53, 70, 76, 77, 84, 90, 142, 149, 166, 171, 184, 190, 191, 223, 251, 290, 293, 309
Toronto Conference of the United Church, 197
Toronto Star, 50, 53, 54, 58, 60, 61, 62, 78–79, 172, 188, 211, 223, 225–26
Treasury Dept. (U.S.), 96, 121, 225, 257–58, 266
Trenton, 65, 116
Trumble, Mrs., 47
Trumble, Babe, 46–47
Turnbull, William, 55